Employee Benefit Plans: A Glossary of Terms

Ninth Edition
1997

Employee Benefit Plans: A Glossary of Terms

Ninth Edition
1997

Edited by Judith A. Sankey

International Foundation
OF EMPLOYEE BENEFIT PLANS
18700 W. Bluemound Road
Post Office Box 69
Brookfield, WI 53008-0069

Copies of this book may be obtained from:

Publications Department
International Foundation of Employee Benefit Plans
18700 West Bluemound Road
P.O. Box 69
Brookfield, Wisconsin 53008-0069
(414)786-6710, ext. 8240

Payment must accompany order.

Call (888) 33-IFEBP for price information.

Published in 1997 by the International Foundation of Employee Benefit Plans, Inc.

Library of Congress Catalog Card Number: 97-071751
ISBN 0-89154-513-1
Printed in the United States of America

15M-597

Contents

Foreword

Employee Benefit Plans: A Glossary of Terms was compiled initially in 1975 to bring together, in one volume, terms applicable to the employee benefits field. The present edition has been expanded to include more than 2,500 definitions derived from current Canadian and U.S. sources covering the following:

Accounting
Actuarial science
Compensation
Employee benefits design and administration
Government regulations and legislation
Health care and health care cost-containment strategies
Human resources
Insurance
International benefits management
Investments
Labor and business law
Labor relations.

A special feature of the ninth edition is an updated list of almost 800 acronyms and abbreviations, covering a wide range of benefits-related topics.

This glossary is designed to provide a practical, easy-to-use guide to terminology presently used in the context of employee benefits. It is intended to provide assistance and should not be viewed as a definitive source. We have made every effort to present accurate and up-to-date information. The employee benefits area is complex and rapidly changing, and it would be impossible to include every applicable term and acronym. Therefore, use the glossary as a resource, not as an authority. Users should refer to standard texts and reference works for more detailed analyses of the definitions presented. Seek professional assistance in making decisions involving benefit planning and administration.

The International Foundation welcomes feedback for future updates of this glossary. Please contact the Publications Department directly with any suggestions.

Acknowledgments

The International Foundation extends its sincere appreciation to all the dedicated individuals who contributed to the numerous source materials used to compile this glossary.

A

A—The third highest rating assigned by Standard & Poor's for investment grade bonds. Strong capacity to pay interest and repay principal, although it is somewhat more susceptible to the adverse effects of changes in circumstances and economic conditions than debt in higher rated categories.

AA—The second highest rating assigned by Standard & Poor's for investment grade bonds. Differs from the highest rated issues only in small degree.

AAA—The highest rating assigned by Standard & Poor's. Capacity to pay interest and repay principal is extremely strong.

Aaa (Triple A) Tenant—A well-known tenant, usually with a net worth in excess of $1 million. Sometimes, if large and important, called an *anchor tenant.*

Access—The ability to obtain health care. Elements of access include affordability; approachability, such as clinic location; and availability of health services.

Accident Insurance—A form of health insurance against loss by accidental bodily injury.

Accidental Death and Dismemberment (AD&D)—One of the four components of health insurance coverage that employers provide their employees. (The others are life, disability and medical insurance.) AD&D provides coverage for death or dismemberment resulting directly from accidental causes. Provides benefits in the event of loss of life, limbs or eyesight as the result of an accident.

Accidental Death Benefit (ADB)—A provision added to an insurance policy for payment of an additional benefit in case of death by accidental means. It is often referred to as *double indemnity.*

Accommodation—Modifications or changes made by an employer to assist an individual with a disability in the performance of a job.

Account Balance Plan—See Cash Balance Plan.

Account Limit—The maximum addition to a qualified asset account of a welfare benefit fund that an employer is permitted to deduct. It equals the amount reasonably and actuarially necessary to fund benefit claims incurred but unpaid as of the end of the taxable year, plus administrative costs and certain contributions to an additional reserve for postretirement medical or life insurance benefits.

Accountable Health Plan (AHP)—A form of health care plan held accountable for the cost of health care, the effectiveness of medical services and patient satisfaction. It consists of a network of health care providers, managed care companies and private insurers that provides consumers with a comprehensive range of health services. AHPs can take several forms and are sometimes called integrated care systems. Synonyms(s): accountable health partnership (AHP), approved health plan (AHP).

Accounting Principles Board (APB)—Predecessor group to FASB. Opinions published as APB releases are applicable today unless superseded or revoked by FASB opinions.

Accreditation—Formal recognition by an agency or organization that evaluates and recognizes a program of study or an institution as meeting certain predetermined standards; may be either permanent or for a specified period of time. See also Certification; Licensure.

Accretion—A straight-line accumulation of capital gains on discount bonds in anticipation of being paid par at maturity.

Accrual of Benefits—In the case of a defined benefit pension plan, the process of accumulating pension credits for years of credited service, expressed in the form of an annual benefit to begin payment at normal retirement age. In the case of a defined contribution plan, the process of accumulating funds in the individual employee's pension account.

Accrue—When actuaries say that pension benefits, actuarial costs and actuarial liabilities have accrued, they ordinarily mean that the amounts are associated, either specifically or by a process of allocation, with years of employee service before the date of a particular valuation of a pension plan.

Accrued Benefit—For any retirement plan that is not a defined benefit pension plan, a participant's accrued benefit is the balance in his or her plan account, whether vested or not. In the case of a defined benefit pension plan, a participant's accrued benefit is his or her benefit as determined under the terms of the plan expressed in the form of an annual benefit commencing at normal retirement age. Under ERISA, three alternative methods of benefit accrual are allowed. (See Fractional Rule; 133⅓% Rule; 3% Rule.) See also Backloading.

Accrued Benefit Cost Method—See Unit Credit Actuarial Cost Method.

Accrued Future Service Benefit—That portion of a participant's retirement benefit that relates to his or her period of credited service after the effective date of the plan and before a specified current date.

Accrued Interest—
—Interest earned on a bond since the last interest payment was made. The buyer of the bond pays the market price plus accrued interest.
—Interest that has already been earned; accumulated interest that is due and payable.

Accrued Liability—See Actuarial Accrued Liability.

Accumulated Benefit Obligation (ABO)—The actuarial present value of benefits (whether vested or nonvested) attributed by the pension benefit formula to employee service rendered before a specified date and based on employee service and compensation (if applicable) prior to that date. The accumulated benefit obligation differs from the projected benefit obligation in that it includes no assumption about future compensation levels. For plans with flat benefit or nonpay-related pension benefit formulas, the accumulated benefit obligation and the projected benefit obligation are the same. See also Projected Benefit Obligation (PBO).

Accumulated Earnings—The accumulation of taxable earnings by a corporation. A separate tax is imposed on these accumulations when they cannot be justified, based on the assumption that the corporation is limiting dividend declarations to lower stockholders' declared income.

Accumulated Funding Deficiency—
—In connection with ERISA's minimum funding standards, the excess of the total charges to the funding standard account for all plan years (beginning with the first plan year to which the funding provisions apply) over the total credits to such account for such years or, if less, the excess of the total charges to the alternative minimum funding standard account for such plan years over the total credits to such account for such years.
—If the minimum contributions have not been made to a covered plan, the funding standard account will show a deficiency, called the *accumulated funding deficiency*. A plan will meet the minimum funding standard for a plan year if, at the end of that year, it does not have an accumulated funding deficiency.

Accumulated Plan Benefit Method—See Unit Credit Actuarial Cost Method.

Accumulation Period—
—The period during which premiums are payable on a deferred annuity.
—The period during which the insured person must incur eligible medical expenses at least equal to the deductible to establish a benefit period under a major medical expense or comprehensive medical expense policy.

Acid Test Ratio—A measure of financial liquidity (also known as the *quick assets ratio*): quick assets (current assets less inventories) divided by current liabilities.

Acknowledgment—A declaration by the party executing an instrument that it is his or her act and deed, generally formalized by signing before a notary and attaching a notary seal.

Acquired Immune Deficiency Syndrome (AIDS)—A fatal, incurable disease caused by a virus that can damage the brain and destroy the body's ability to fight off illness.

Acquired Rights (International Benefits)—The obligation on the part of the employer to continue to provide employee benefits or continue other practices that have been in effect for a period of time even if no promise has been made in writing or orally. This may be required by law or by local custom.

Active Account—A brokerage account with securities that are bought and sold frequently.

Active Management—A style of investment management that seeks to attain above-average risk-adjusted performance.

Active Market—A market where securities are heavily traded and the volume of sales is above normal.

Active Participant—An individual who is a participant and for whom at any time during the taxable year benefits are accrued under the plan on his or her behalf, or for whom the employer is obligated to contribute to or under the plan on his or her behalf, or for whom the employer would have been obligated to contribute to or under the plan on his or her behalf if any contributions were made to or under the plan. See also Plan Participant.

Activities of Daily Living (ADL)—Activities, such as bathing, dressing and toileting, that are needed for self-care. ADLs are measured to evaluate the continued feasibility of self-care.

Actual Contribution Percentage (ACP)—The average of the ratios of aggregate contributions (matching contributions and after-tax employee contributions) to compensation. It is figured for two groups: highly compensated employees and nonhighly compensated employees. The ratio for each employee is calculated, and then it is averaged for the group. See also Aggregate Limit; Alternative Limitation.

Actual Deferral Percentage (ADP)—The average of the ratios of elective contributions to compensation is figured for two groups: highly compensated employees and nonhighly compensated employees. The ratio first is figured for each employee, and then averaged for each group. See also Aggregate Limit; Alternative Limitation.

Actual Return on Plan Assets (Component of Net Periodic Pension Cost)—The difference between the fair value of plan assets at the end of the period and the fair value at the beginning of the period, adjusted for contributions and payments of benefits during the period.

Actuarial Accrued Liability—

—The actuarial accrued liability of a pension plan at any time is the excess of the present value, as of the date of valuation, of total prospective benefits of the plan (plus administrative expenses if included in the normal cost) over the present value of future normal cost accruals, determined by the actuarial cost method in use.

—That portion, as determined by a particular actuarial cost method, of the actuarial present value of pension plan benefits and expenses that is not provided for by future normal costs. The presentation of an actuarial accrued liability should be accompanied by reference to the actuarial cost method used.

Actuarial Adjustment—The result of offsetting the actuarial gains and losses in an annual actuarial valuation.

Actuarial Asset Value—See Actuarial Value of Assets.

Actuarial Assumptions—Factors used by the actuary in forecasting uncertain future events affecting pension cost. They involve such things as interest and investment earnings, mortality rates and turnover.

Actuarial Cost—A cost is characterized as actuarial if it is derived through the use of present values. An actuarial cost is often used to associate the costs of benefits under a retirement system with the approximate time the benefits are earned.

Actuarial Cost Method—

—A system for determining either the contributions to be made under a retirement plan or the level of benefits when the contributions are fixed. In addition to forecasts of mortality, interest and expenses, some of the methods involve estimates as to future labor turnover, salary scales and retirement rates. The methods of prime importance are those such as the entry age method, attained age method and unit credit method, which have been recognized by the Internal Revenue Service.

—A recognized technique for establishing the amount and incidence of the actuarial cost of pension plan benefits, or benefits and expenses, and the related actuarial liabilities.

—See also Actuarial Funding Method; Aggregate Actuarial Cost Method; Attained Age Actuarial Cost Method; Entry Age Actuarial Cost Method; Frozen Attained Age Actuarial Cost Method; Frozen Entry Age Actuarial Cost Method; Individual Level Actuarial Cost Method; Individual Spread Gain Actuarial Cost Method; Projection Actuarial Cost Method; Unit Credit Actuarial Cost Method.

Actuarial Cost Method, Open Group/Closed Group—Under an open group actuarial cost method, actuarial present values associated with expected future entrants are considered; under a closed group actuarial cost method, actuarial present values associated with future entrants are not considered.

Actuarial Equivalent—

—If the present value of two series of payments is equal, taking into account a given interest rate and mortality according to a given table, the two series are said to be actuarially equivalent. For example, under a given set of actuarial assumptions, a lifetime monthly benefit of $67.60 beginning at age 60 can be said to be the actuarial equivalent of $100 a month beginning at age 65. The actual benefit amounts are different but the

present value of the two benefits, considering mortality and interest, is the same.
—A benefit having the same present value as the benefit it replaces.
—Of equal actuarial present value.

Actuarial Funding Method—Any of several techniques that actuaries use in determining the amounts and incidence of employer contributions to provide for pension benefits.

Actuarial Gain or Loss—The effects on actuarial costs of deviations or differences between the past events predicted by actuarial assumptions, and the events that actually occurred. An *actuarial gain* results where the actual experience under the plan is more favorable than the actuary's estimate, while an *actuarial loss* reflects an unexpectedly adverse deviation.

Actuarial Liability—See Actuarial Accrued Liability; Projected Benefit Liability.

Actuarial Present Value (APV)—The value of an amount or series of amounts payable or receivable at various times, determined as of a given date by the application of a particular set of actuarial assumptions.

Actuarial Reduction—The reduction in the normal retirement benefit that offsets a cost increase to the plan when a participant retires ahead of schedule.

Actuarial Report—
—An actuary's report to the company recommending how much to contribute yearly to the pension fund to fund promised benefits.
—A report filed with the IRS by the administrator of a defined benefit pension plan that is subject to the minimum funding standards of ERISA.

Actuarial Reserve Deficiency—The excess of the actuarial accrued liabilities at the date of valuation of the retirement system over the available assets on hand to meet such liabilities; or the excess of accrued and prospective liabilities over the present and prospective assets.

Actuarial Reserve Plan—A method of financing a retirement plan where reserves are accumulated as the liabilities for benefit payments are incurred in order that sufficient funds will be available on the date of retirement of each member to pay future benefits for the term of the benefit payments.

Actuarial Revaluation Gains or Losses—The effects on actuarial costs of adopting different actuarial cost methods or making changes in actuarial assumptions as to future events.

Actuarial Soundness—
—An actuarial concept relating to the degree of assurance (existing under an employer's program for funding pension cost) that the funds set aside under a pension plan will be sufficient to meet the pension payments provided for in the plan. Actuaries have not defined objective standards for determining actuarial soundness.
—The statement that the money set aside under a pension plan will be sufficient to meet the pension payments as calculated.

Actuarial Table—A listing of assumed rates of decrement for death, disability, retirement and withdrawal from service according to age and sex. The table may consist of mathematical functions derived from the rates of probability combined with an interest discount factor.

Actuarial Valuation—
—An examination of a pension plan to determine whether contributions are being accumulated at a rate sufficient to provide the funds out of which the promised pensions can be paid when due. The valuation shows the actuarial liabilities of the plan and the applicable assets.
—The determination, as of a valuation date, of the normal cost, actuarial accrued liability, actuarial value of assets and related actuarial present values for a pension plan.

Actuarial Value of Assets—The value of cash, investments and other property belonging to a pension plan, as used by the actuary for the purpose of an actuarial valuation. The statement of actuarial assumptions should set forth the particular procedures used in determining this value.

Actuarially Reduced Annuity—See Actuarial Equivalent.

Actuary—
—(Pension) A person professionally trained in the technical and mathematical aspects of insurance, pensions and related fields. The actuary estimates how much money must be contributed to a pension fund each year in order to support the benefits that will become payable in the future.
—(Insurance) A person trained in the insurance

field who determines policy rates, reserves and dividends, as well as conducts various other statistical studies.

Acute Care—Treatment for a short-term or episodic illness or health problem.

Ad Hoc Postretirement Adjustment—Establishes a schedule of one-time increases in retirement allowances. Contrast with Automatic Postretirement Adjustment.

Additional Voluntary Contributions (International Benefits)—Voluntary employee contributions made to a pension plan to purchase extra benefits. They are in addition to required contributions. The employer assumes no additional cost.

Add-On Plans—A flexible benefits system whereby current benefit levels remain in effect and employees may purchase the benefits they desire, or extended coverage.

Adequate Consideration—In the case of a security for which there is a generally recognized market value, *adequate consideration* means either (1) the price of the security prevailing on a national securities exchange or (2) if the security is not traded on a national securities exchange, a price not less favorable to the plan than the offering price for the security as established by current bid and asked prices quoted by persons independent of the issuer and of any party in interest; in the case of an asset other than a security for which there is a generally recognized market, *adequate consideration* means the fair market value of the asset as determined in good faith by the trustee or named fiduciary.

Adjudication—The exercise of judicial power by hearing, trying and determining the claims of litigants before the court.

Adjustable Rate Mortgage (ARM)—See Variable Rate Mortgage.

Adjusted Community Rating—A form of community rating wherein group-specific demographics are considered.

Adjusted Plan Assets—The sum of the fair value of plan assets plus previously recognized unfunded accrued pension cost, or minus previously recognized prepaid pension on the employer's balance sheet.

Administrative Agent—See Third Party Administrator.

Administrative Manager (Employee Benefit Plans)—Firm or individual providing professional administrative services to an employee benefit plan. May be compensated under either a salaried or contract arrangement.

Administrative Services Only (ASO)—An arrangement in which a plan hires a third party to deliver administrative services to the plan such as claims processing and billing; the plan bears the risk for claims. Common in self-funded health care plans.

Administrator (Employee Benefit Plans)—Under ERISA, the person designated as such by the instrument under which the plan is operated. If the administrator is not so designated, *administrator* means the plan sponsor. If the administrator is not designated and the plan sponsor cannot be identified, the administrator may be such person as is prescribed by regulation of the secretary of labor. The administrator's responsibilities are as follows:

1. Act solely in the interest of plan participants and beneficiaries, and for the exclusive purpose of providing benefits and defraying reasonable administrative expenses.
2. Manage the plan's assets to minimize the risk of large losses.
3. Act in accordance with the documents governing the plan.

(Canada) The individual or company responsible for administering a group insurance contract including such services as accounting, issuance of certificates and settlement of claims.

Admission Certification—A form of utilization review in which assessment is made of the necessity—based on health status and treatment needs—of a patient's admission to a hospital or other inpatient institution; health status considerations include both physical and psychological conditions.

Admitted Carriers (International Benefits)—Insurance companies licensed to conduct specific types of business in a given country.

Adoption Assistance Program—Benefit programs created to reimburse employees who legally adopt a child, including such costs as adoption agency fees, legal fees, pregnancy and hospital expenses of the natural mother, and immigration and naturalization expenses.

Adult Day Care—Provision during the day, on a regular basis, of a range of services that may include health, medical, psychological, social, nutritional and educational services that allow a disabled person to function in the home.

Advance Funding—
- —An approach to funding retirement benefits whereby the employer sets aside monies for each employee or for the group of active employees as a whole on some systematic basis during their working years.
- —An employer sets aside funds on a systematic basis to provide pension benefits; involves periodic contributions on behalf of the active employee group.

Adverse Selection—The tendency of an individual to recognize his or her health status in selecting the option under a retirement system or insurance plan that tends to be most favorable to him or her (and more costly to the plan). In insurance usage, a person with an impaired health status or with expected medical care needs applies for insurance coverage financially favorable to himself or herself and detrimental to the insurance company. Also known as *antiselection.*

Advisory Opinion—A short written opinion by the Department of Labor regarding the legality of a given situation under ERISA.

Affidavit—A sworn statement in writing, made before an authorized official, generally a notary.

Affiliated Service Group—Two or more service or management organizations operating in separate units but providing common services to outsiders or for each other. Interlocking ownership is more concentrated than in a controlled group. Treated as a single employer for purposes of plan qualification.

Affiliation of Health Providers—The relationship between the organization operating a project and another health services delivery organization (a backup facility) created by a formal or informal agreement, under which the second organization provides certain health or other services to the project's patients. For example, a project often negotiates with a hospital for the provision of inpatient services to project patients. See also Backup Facility.

Affirmative Action—A positive program developed in response to civil rights laws and executive orders. Its purpose is to eliminate all forms of discrimination, both overt and subtle, within the employment processes and to provide minorities, women and members of other protected classes with the opportunity to compete for jobs on an equal basis. It is concerned with equality of results, not just equality of opportunity.

Affirmative Action Program (AAP)—A written, results-oriented program in which an employer or contractor details the steps it will take to ensure equal employment opportunity including, where appropriate, remedying discrimination against an affected class and so forth. Sometimes required by law or court order.

Aftercare—Continued contact that will support and increase the gains made to date in a health treatment process and prevent relapse.

After-Tax Contribution—A portion of a person's income that has already been taxed by the IRS that is contributed to a qualified plan. After-tax contributions are not as tax efficient as contributions with before-tax income.

Age and Service Vesting—See Vesting Schedules.

Age Discrimination—To discharge, refuse to hire or to otherwise discriminate against any individual with respect to the individual's compensation, terms, conditions or privileges of employment because the individual is age 40 or over.

Age Discrimination in Employment Act (ADEA)—Protects workers over 40 from compulsory retirement at any age as long as they are capable of performing their jobs adequately. It also protects them from adverse job actions based on age (e.g., refusal to hire; discriminatory layoff) and against benefits discrimination. Employers are subject to ADEA if they engage in an industry affecting interstate commerce and had 20 or more employees in each working day of 20 or more weeks in the current or preceding calendar year.

Age-Weighted Profit-Sharing Plan—Combines the flexibility of a profit-sharing plan with the ability of a pension plan to skew benefits in favor of older employees. This type of plan applies an age factor to the allocation formula of the profit-sharing plan. Each participant receives a contribution based on age as well as compensation.

Agency/Agent—A relationship in which one person acts for or represents another by the latter's authority.

Agency Bonds (Agencies)—The full faith and credit of the U.S. government is normally not pledged to payment of principal and interest on the majority of government agencies issuing these bonds, with maturities of up to ten years, so they are one step below Treasury issues on the marketing scale. Their yields, therefore, are normally higher and their marketability is good, thereby qualifying them as a low-risk/high-liquidity type of investment. They are eligible as security for advances to the member banks by the Federal Reserve, which attests to their standing.

Agent—See Agency/Agent.

Aggregate Actuarial Cost Method—

—A method under which the excess of the actuarial present value of projected benefits over the actuarial value of assets is allocated on a level basis over the earnings or service of the group between the valuation date and assumed exit. This allocation is performed for the group as a whole, not as a sum of individual allocations. That portion of the actuarial present value allocated to a valuation year is called the *normal cost.* The actuarial accrued liability is equal to the actuarial value of assets.

—An acceptable actuarial cost method under which the principles followed in the individual level cost method are applied on a collective basis to all participants.

Aggregate Contributions—The numerator of the ACP test, which is made up of employee after-tax contributions and employer matching contributions. For testing purposes, it can also include elective contributions and qualified nonelective contributions.

Aggregate Excess (of) Loss (Re)insurance—See Stop-Loss Insurance.

Aggregate Funding Method—A method of accumulating money for future payment of pensions whereby the actuary determines the present value of all future benefit payments, deducts from this value whatever funds may be on hand with the trustee or the insurance company, and distributes the cost of the balance over the future on a reasonable basis. No distinction is made between present and past service liability.

Aggregate Indemnity—The maximum dollar amount that may be collected for any disability, any period of disability or under the policy.

Aggregate Level of Cost Method—See Attained Age Actuarial Cost Method.

Aggregate Limit—In discrimination testing, this is used to determine inequities in the deferral or contribution rates of highly versus nonhighly compensated employees when at least one highly compensated employee is eligible to participate in a Section 401(k) plan. The aggregate limit is a combination of the ADP and ACP of the nonhighly compensated employees: 125% of the higher percentage and the lower percentage plus two points (the higher percentage can be up to 200% of the lower percentage). The sum of the ADP and ACP of the highly compensated cannot exceed the aggregate limit. See also Alternative Limitation.

Aggregate Projected Benefit Cost Method—See Aggregate Actuarial Cost Method.

Aggregation—Considering separate plans or companies as one plan or company to determine whether they satisfy certain requirements.

Aggressive Portfolio—A securities portfolio containing issues held primarily on the assumption that they will appreciate in value, as opposed to securities that provide greater yield or have good defensive qualities. Compare with Defensive Portfolio.

Alcoholism Program—Activities, services or functions connected with the planning, direction or coordination of treatment of the alcoholic or the prevention of alcoholism, including alcohol abuse education. Can be inpatient or outpatient.

Alienation of Benefits—ERISA provides that plan benefits cannot be assigned or alienated under a tax-qualified plan. Plan benefits cannot be paid to the employer or to a third party (except under a QDRO) when they would otherwise be paid to the participant. See also Assignment of Benefits.

All Causes Maximum—See Maximum Plan Limits.

All Clause Deductible—The application of a deductible under a health care plan to all covered expenses incurred by a person as a result of the same or related causes within a given time (accumulation period).

All Payers System—This subjects all third party payers

that are reimbursing hospitals for services, including both public and private payers, to the same rules. Especially used in reference to hospital rate-setting programs.

All Salaried Workforce—A pay policy that makes exempt/nonexempt status invisible to workers. All employees are paid on a salaried basis and all pay is defined in the same terms, such as a monthly or annual salary. Fair Labor Standards Act requirements for overtime and minimum wage must still be met, but exempt status is not made a basis for status differentials in the organization.

Allocated Contract—A contract with an insurance company under which payments to the insurance company are currently used to purchase immediate or deferred annuities for individual participants. See also Annuity Contract.

Allocated Funding Instrument—A funding instrument by which contributions are assigned to provide benefits for specific employees. Examples are individual insurance and annuity contracts, group permanent contracts and group deferred annuity contracts.

Allocation—The distribution of the employer's contribution to the account of each participant. In a profit-sharing plan, it also refers to the distribution of earnings and forfeitures for the various accounts.

Allowed Charges—Charges for services rendered or supplies furnished by a health provider that would qualify as covered expenses and for which the program will pay in whole or in part, subject to any deductible, coinsurance or table of allowance included in the program.

Alpha—The premium a fund would be expected to earn if the market rate of return were equal to the Treasury bill rate—that is, a premium of zero for the market rate of return. A positive alpha indicates that a fund has earned on the average a premium above that expected for the level of market variability. A negative alpha would indicate that a fund received on the average a premium lower than that expected for the level of market variability. Sometimes alpha is used as a performance indicator or as a surrogate for selectivity.

Alternate Payee—See Qualified Domestic Relations Order.

Alternate Treatment Benefit Provision—Health plan provision under which the amount of benefits payable gives consideration to professionally acceptable alternate procedures, services or courses of treatment that might have been performed to accomplish the desired result.

Alternate Ranking Method—A variation of the straight ranking method of performance appraisal in which the appraiser alternates the ranking by starting with the best employee and the worst employee.

Alternative Delivery System (ADS)—An organized, nontraditional system of financing and delivering health care services from participating providers on a prepaid basis to a voluntarily enrolled population. Examples include HMOs and PPOs.

Alternative Dispute Resolution (ADR) Procedure—A procedure designed to settle wrongful discharge claims and avoid costly litigation. It involves a written complaint, an automatic appeal to arbitration in termination cases, and a final and binding decision in all cases.

Alternative Limitation—An alternate discrimination test. The ACP and ADP percentage of highly compensated employees cannot be more than double the ACP and ADP of nonhighly compensated employees. In addition, the difference cannot exceed two percentage points. See also Aggregate Limit.

Alternative Minimum Tax—During the year certain incentive stock options are exercised, the paper gains must be included in a separate alternative minimum calculation. Either the regular or alternative minimum tax, whichever is higher, must be paid by the person exercising the option.

Amalgamation (Canada)—Merger; combining of two or more companies or corporations.

Ambulatory Care Benefits—Benefits for health care services received as an outpatient.

Ambulatory Care Facility—A freestanding or hospital-based facility providing preventive or diagnostic services, emergency or therapeutic services, surgery or other treatment not requiring overnight confinement.

Ambulatory Delivery System—A health care system in which care is provided on an outpatient basis, not during a hospital stay.

Ambulatory Surgical Center—Any public or private establishment with an organized medical staff of physicians; with permanent facilities that are equipped and operated for the purpose of performing surgical procedures; with continuous physician services and registered professional nursing services whenever a patient is in the facility; and which does not provide services for patients to stay overnight.

Amendment—
—(General) An addition, deletion or change in a legal document.
—(Employee Benefit Plans) A change in the terms of an existing plan or the initiation of a new plan. A plan amendment may increase benefits, including those attributed to years of service already rendered. See also Retroactive Benefits.
—(Insurance) A formal document changing the provisions of an insurance policy signed jointly by the insurance company officer and the policyholder or his or her authorized representative.

American Depository Receipts (ADRs)—American certificates of deposit issued by an approved New York bank or trust company against the deposit of the original (foreign) shares with a European branch of the New York institution. These receipts facilitate the financing of foreign companies in this country. As foreign shares are deposited abroad, the equivalent ADRs are issued to buyers in New York. When transactions are made, the ADRs change hands, not the certificates. This eliminates the actual shipment of stock certificates between the United States and foreign countries and expedites transactions in securities traded on foreign exchanges.

American Federation of Labor (AFL)—Formed in 1881 as a national federation of local unions organized originally on trade or craft lines, today it also grants charters to industrial unions. Each local retains the right to govern its own affairs. In 1955, the AFL and the CIO merged to form the AFL-CIO, with which most, although not all, major U.S. unions are affiliated. See also Congress of Industrial Organizations.

American Stock Exchange (AMEX)—A leading securities exchange located in New York City and the largest market for foreign securities in the United States.

American Stock Exchange (AMEX) Market Value Index—A capitalization-weighted index measuring the change in the aggregate market value of common shares, American depository receipts and warrants.

Americans with Disabilities Act (ADA)—A law enacted in 1990 that prohibits discrimination against persons with disabilities in such areas as public accommodations and terms and conditions of employment.

Amortization—Paying off an interest-bearing liability by gradual reduction through a series of installments as opposed to paying it off by one lump-sum payment. A technique for gradually extinguishing a liability, deferred charge or capital expenditure over a period of time. Includes such practices as depreciation, depletion, write-off of intangibles, prepaid expenses and deferred charges (e.g., mortgages are amortized by periodically retiring part of the face amount). The liquidation of a debt on an installment basis.

Amortized Value—The amount at a given point in time to which the purchase price of a bond purchased at a discount or premium has been increased or decreased.

Analyst—A trained person who investigates all the facts concerning a security or industry under study and reaches a dependable conclusion about its merits that may help an actual or potential investor decide what action he or she should take.

Anchor Tenant—See Aaa (Triple A) Tenant.

Ancillary Benefits—
—Dental, vision, hearing, prescription drug benefits, etc.
—(Canada) Benefits in addition to regular pension and survivor benefits, such as bridging and enriched early retirement benefits.
—See also Supplemental Benefits.

Ancillary Services—Supplemental services and procedures, diagnostic or therapeutic, offered in hospital or outpatient settings. Some examples are radiography, laboratory tests and physical therapy.

Annual Addition—Under a profit-sharing plan, and other plans that use individual account balances, it is the contributions made to a participant's account. An annual addition includes employer and employee (participant) contributions, and forfeitures under a formula provided by federal law.

Annual Benefits Statement—A statement of deferred vested benefits furnished to each employee who has been separated from service, showing whether the individual has vested pension rights, the amount of accrued vested benefits or the earliest date on which they will accrue, and the total accrued benefits.

Annual Registration—See Registration of Plans.

Annual Report—
—(Corporate) A formal financial statement issued annually by a corporation that depicts assets, liabilities, earnings—how the company stood at the close of the business year, how it fared profitwise during the year and other information of interest to shareholders.
—(Employee Benefit Plans) The employer or plan administrator is required to file an annual information return with the IRS regarding the qualification, financial condition and operations of any funded deferred compensation plan. This comprehensive information report is required for HR 10 plans and individual retirement accounts and annuities as well as for regular corporate plans.

Annual Statement (Canada)—The yearly report, provided by insurers to provincial and federal authorities, showing assets and liabilities, receipts and disbursements, and other financial data.

Annual Supplemental Cost—See Amortization.

Annual Yield—The money income or percentage of return in dividends or interest received annually from an investment.

Annualize—To express a rate of return for a period greater than one year or less than one year in terms of 12 months.

Annualized Linked-Median Return—Rates of return calculated by compounding the annual median returns and annualizing the result.

Annuitant—A person entitled to receive payments under an annuity; a person receiving such payments.

Annuity—
—A contract that provides an income for a specified period of time such as a number of years or for life.
—The periodic payments provided under an annuity contract.
—The specified monthly or annual payment to a pensioner. Often used synonymously with *pension.*

Annuity, Cash Refund—See Refund Annuity.

Annuity Certain—A contract that provides an income for a specified number of years, regardless of life or death. If an annuitant dies, his or her beneficiary will receive payments for the remaining number of specified years. Also referred to as *period certain, term certain* or *dollar temporary annuity.*

Annuity Consideration—The payment, or one of the regular periodic payments, an annuitant makes for an annuity.

Annuity, Contingent—See Contingent Annuity Option.

Annuity Contract—A contract in which an insurance company unconditionally undertakes a legal obligation to provide specified pension benefits to specific individuals in return for a fixed consideration or premium. An annuity contract is irrevocable and involves the transfer of significant risk from the employer to the insurance company. Annuity contracts are also called *allocated.contracts.* See also Allocated Contract.

Annuity Conversion Rate—A factor used to determine the amount of annuity payable for each dollar of a participant's contributions accumulated to the date of retirement. Annuity conversion rates generally vary by age and sex.

Annuity, Deferred—See Deferred Annuity.

Annuity Exclusion Rule—Rule under which a portion of each annuity payment received by an employee is treated as a recovery of his or her contributions if that employee was required to contribute toward the purchase of the annuity contract.

Annuity, Fixed—See Fixed Annuity.

Annuity, Joint and Survivor—See Joint and Survivor (J&S) Annuity.

Annuity, Modified Cash Refund—See Modified Refund Annuity.

Annuity Purchase Fund—The fund established to hold annuity purchase payments transferred from the unallocated active life fund under a deposit administration contract. Also known as the *retired life fund.*

Annuity Rate (Canada)—The price charged by an issuer of annuities to provide a dollar of annuity (usually per month) under specified conditions to an individual based on the person's age, interest rates, etc.

Annuity, Refund—See Refund Annuity.

Annuity Reserve Fund—A monetary sum equal to the actuarial present value of future payments to be made on account of annuities currently being paid, set aside in a reserve.

Annuity Starting Date—The first day of the first period for which an amount is received as an annuity.

Annuity Table—A listing of the present values of $1 per year or month payable for life, or for a term of years at specified ages for each sex, computed on the basis of assumed rates of mortality and interest.

Annuity, Tax-Deferred—See Tax-Deferred Annuity.

Annuity, Variable—See Variable Annuity.

Antialienation/Antiassignment Rule—This rule requires that a qualified retirement plan must provide that participants' benefits may not be assigned to someone other than the employee or otherwise pledged (e.g., to a creditor), either voluntarily or involuntarily, while they are held by the plan's trust. An exception to the general antialienation rule of ERISA exists for payments made under a qualified domestic relations order (QDRO). See Assignment of Benefits.

Anticipatory Action—Under COBRA, when an employer (and sometimes a covered employee) discontinues coverage for employees, spouses or dependents in anticipation of a qualifying event. Such an action will not be considered in determining whether those individuals lost coverage due to the qualifying event.

Anticutback Rule—A provision in the Internal Revenue Code that prohibits an employer from reducing accrued benefits under a qualified retirement plan by a plan amendment, other than an amendment that has been approved by the secretary of labor freezing benefit accruals only for the most recent plan year. Applies to benefits already accrued under the terms of the plan, early retirement benefits, early retirement type subsidies and optional forms of benefits.

Antidiscrimination Rules—A general requirement that a benefit be provided to lower level employees as beneficially as to highly compensated employees.

Antiselection—See Adverse Selection.

Antitrust Issues (Health Care Field)—Issues to be addressed in any joint efforts that may involve restraint of trade.

Any Willing Provider Law—A law that permits any medical provider holding required credentials and willing to conform to the terms and conditions of a network contract to be admitted to that network. Such legislation restricts payers' ability to contract selectively with a limited number of providers to save on health care premiums.

Appraisal—An estimation of quantity, quality or value. The process through which conclusions of property value are obtained; also refers to the report setting forth the estimate and conclusion of value reached by correlation, unless a single technique is used.

Appreciation—Synonymous with *price improvement,* one of the fundamental investment objectives. A stock advancing from 70 to 80 is said to have appreciated ten points.

Apprenticeship Plan—A training plan connected to a union as established under a trust format.

Approaches to Value (Real Estate)—The three generally accepted methods of determining fair market value are the cost, market and income approaches.

1. The *cost approach* considers the cost to reproduce or replace the property appraised. From this amount an allowance is deducted for any depreciation or obsolescence present, whether arising from physical, functional or economic causes.
2. The *market approach* considers prices recently paid for similar property, with adjustments made to the indicated market prices to reflect the condition and utility of the appraised property relative to the market comparative.
3. In the *income approach,* an estimate is made of the prospective economic benefits of ownership. These amounts are capitalized at appropriate rates of return into an indication of value.

Approved Plan—A pension, deferred profit-sharing or

stock bonus plan that meets the requirements of the Internal Revenue Code and the applicable regulations. Such approval qualifies the plan for favorable tax treatment. Approval of a pension plan does not indicate any judgment regarding the plan's actuarial soundness.

Approved Plan (Canada)—A pension, deferred profit-sharing or stock bonus plan that meets the requirements of the applicable Revenue Canada regulations. Such approval qualifies the plan for a favorable tax treatment. Approval of a pension plan does not indicate any judgment regarding the plan's actuarial soundness.

Appurtenance—Anything incident to or attached to the land; things that become a part of the land (easements, buildings).

Arbitrage—A technique employed to take advantage of price differences in separate markets. This is accomplished by purchasing in one market for immediate sale in another at a better price. Such transactions may be executed in the same type or similar types of securities.

Arbitrary and Capricious Standard—The standard employed by courts under which a plan trustee's decision to deny benefits must be upheld unless it is found to be arbitrary and capricious.

Arbitration/Arbitrator—The submitting of a matter in dispute to the judgment of a specified number of disinterested persons called *arbitrators,* whose decision, called an *award,* is binding upon the parties. See also Fact Finding.

As Is—Wording in a contract to indicate that no warranty or guarantee is intended, and that the purchaser should use caution in inspecting for possible defects in condition.

Asked (Asking) or Offering Price—The lowest quoted round lot price that any potential seller will accept for a security at any given time.

Assessed Valuation—Assessment of real estate by a unit of government for taxation purposes.

Asset Allocation—A process that determines the optimal distribution of funds among various types of assets that offer the highest probability of consistently achieving investment objectives within the confines of a predetermined level of risk. The process often includes the use of a computer model program to assist in the processing of a myriad of data.

Asset Allocation Models—The modern portfolio theory application area that addresses the problem of the amount of assets to be allocated among various investment alternatives.

Asset-Based Financing—Utilization of the value residing in current and fixed assets to provide collateral for loans for financing purposes.

Asset Depreciation Range (ADR) System—An elective system of composite accounting designed to be "audit proof" when examined by the IRS.

Asset Reversion—Following the termination of a pension plan, the recovery—by the sponsoring employer—of any pension fund assets in excess of those required to pay accrued benefits. The recovered assets are subject to regular corporate income tax as well as an excise tax of either 20% or 50%, depending on subsequent retirement arrangements made for employees.

Assets—The valuable resources, property rights and properties owned by a company, such as cash, investments, money due it, materials and inventories, which are called *current assets,* buildings and machinery, which are known as *fixed assets;* and patents and good will, called *intangible assets.*

Assigned Payment—In the Medicare program, the right to receive reimbursement for medical expenses may be *assigned* to the physician by the beneficiary. If the physician accepts assignment, he or she agrees to accept the amount allowed by Medicare for a given service as payment in full for that service, and agrees not to charge the beneficiary for any difference between what Medicare approves and what he or she charged.

Assignment of Benefits—

—(Health Care) The signed transfer of certain benefits by the insured person to a third party, e.g., to a health care provider such as a physician or a hospital.

—(Pension) Includes any arrangement that pays plan benefits to the employer when they would otherwise be paid to the participant. This is generally *prohibited* by ERISA so as to assure that the accrued benefits will be available to the employee when he or she retires. An exception permits assignments, not in excess of 10% of any benefit payment, which are voluntary and revocable. This provision is not intended to interfere with the practice of using vested benefits as collateral for reasonable loans from a plan. Under the Retirement Equity Act of 1984, the creation, assignment or recognition of a right to any benefit payable with respect to a participant pursuant to a qualified domestic relations order is not treated as an assignment or alienation prohibited by ERISA. See also Qualified Domestic Relations Order.

—(Canada) Assignment of group life insurance normally is not allowed under most plan provisions. Hospital and dental benefits, however, may be assigned to most providers.

Assisted Living Facilities—Shared and supervised housing for those who cannot function independently. Various types of homes serve those who need minimal support to those more severely impaired.

Associate of the Society of Actuaries (ASA)—Holders of this designation must pass five examinations covering such topics as general mathematics, probability and statistics, and numerical analysis.

Association Group—A group formed from members of a trade or a professional association for group insurance under one master health insurance contract.

Assumed Benefit Plan—See Target Benefit Plan.

Assuming Company—See Reinsurance.

Assumption of Mortgage—Taking title to property that has an existing mortgage and becoming personally liable for its payments.

Assumptions, Actuarial—See Actuarial Assumptions.

Assurance (International Benefits)—Commonly used in Canada and Great Britain, it is synonymous with *insurance.*

At a Discount—Below par value. A security is said to be selling at a discount when the market value is below the par value of the security. A bond selling at 85 (worth $850) with a par value of $1,000 is selling at 15% or $150, a discount from par value. A $25 par value stock selling at 23 is selling at an 8% or $2 discount.

At a Premium—(1) Above face value (par value). A security is said to be selling at a premium when its market price is above its par value. A $50 par value stock selling at 10% or $5 premium. See also Premium. (2) Refers to a condition that exists when an extra amount is charged to borrow in order to make delivery on a short sale. This "premium rate" is in addition to the regular rate, and is charged when a stock is particularly scarce and, therefore, difficult to borrow. (3) The redemption value of a security, if such price is higher than the market price or face value of the security.

At Par—The price that equals the face value (par value) of a security.

At the Close—An order calling for an execution at the best price obtainable at the close of the market on the day it is entered.

At the Market—An order that the broker will execute at the best price obtainable after he or she receives it on the trading floor. Synonymous with *market order.*

At the Money—An option in which the underlying stock is trading precisely at the exercise price of that option.

At the Opening—Designates an order to be executed at the best price obtainable as soon as the market opens; no actual price limit is set. Odd lot orders to be executed at the opening are contingent upon the opening price of the related round lot.

Attained Age—An individual's age at his or her last birthday.

Attained Age Actuarial Cost Method—A method under which the excess of the actuarial present value of projected benefits over the actuarial accrued liability in respect to each individual included in an actuarial valuation is allocated on a level basis over the earnings or service of the individual between the valuation date and assumed exit. The portion of this actuarial present value allocated to a valuation year is called the *normal cost.* The actuarial accrued liability is determined using the unit credit actuarial cost method.

Attained Age Level Premium Funding Method—See Actuarial Cost Method.

Attained Age Normal Cost Method—See Attained Age Actuarial Cost Method.

Attitude Survey—A device such as a questionnaire designed to elicit information about employee ideas, feelings, concerns, expectations and preferences on a broad range of managerial issues. The survey can uncover the causes of problems, probe feelings about situations or conditions, and draw out ideas for prevention.

Attribution—The process of assigning pension benefits or cost to periods of employee service.

Auction Market—The system of trading securities through brokers or agents on an exchange, such as the New York Stock Exchange. Buyers compete with other buyers while sellers compete with other sellers for the most advantageous price. Most transactions are executed with public customers on both sides since the specialist buys or sells for his or her own account primarily to offset imbalances in public supply and demand.

Audit—Any systematic investigation of procedures or operations for the purpose of determining conformity with prescribed criteria. The purpose of an audit by a CPA is to lend credibility to a company's financial statements.

Audit Finding—A weakness in internal controls or noncompliance with applicable laws presented in the audit report. Findings are ordinarily presented together with a response from management which states management's concurrence or disagreement with the finding and any plan for corrective action.

Audit of Provider Treatment or Charges—The qualitative or quantitative review of services rendered or proposed by a health provider, which may take the form of a comparison of patient records and claim form information, a patient questionnaire, a review of hospital and practitioner records, an examination of pre- or postoperative radiographs or a pre- or posttreatment clinical examination of a patient. Also may involve fee verification.

Audit Trail—The availability of a manual or machine readable means for tracing the status and contents of an individual transaction record backward or forward and between output, processing and source.

Automatic Enrollment—See Negative Election.

Automatic Postretirement Adjustment—A program providing for recurring adjustments in retirement allowances on a regular basis. Contrast with Ad Hoc Postretirement Adjustment.

Automatic Retirement—See Compulsory Retirement.

Automatic Survivor Coverage—Under the Retirement Equity Act of 1984, a defined benefit plan or a money purchase plan is required to provide automatic survivor benefits to the surviving spouse of a participant (1) in the case of a vested participant who retires under the plan, in the form of a qualified joint and survivor annuity and (2) in the case of a vested participant who dies before retirement, in the form of a qualified preretirement survivor annuity. The automatic survivor coverage rule also applies to a profit-sharing or stock bonus plan unless (1) the plan provides that the participant's full vested account balance will be paid to his or her surviving spouse (or to another beneficiary if the spouse consents or if there is no surviving spouse), (2) the participant does not elect payment of benefits in the form of a life annuity and (3) with respect to the participant, the plan is not a transferee of a plan required to provide automatic survivor benefits (for example, a defined benefit plan). A participant may, with his or her spouse's consent, elect out of joint and survivor annuity or preretirement survivor annuity coverage. See also Contingent Annuity Option; Joint and Survivor Annuity.

Auxiliary Fund—See Conversion Fund.

Average Age at Entry—The average age of members under a retirement plan at the time of entry. Frequently used for estimating cost.

Average Annual Compensation—An employee's average annual compensation is his or her annual compensation averaged over at least three consecutive years, under a uniform rule used for all employees. For this purpose, it is acceptable to use for each employee the period of consecutive years which will produce his or her highest average. See also Final Average Salary.

Average Daily Census—The average number of hospital or health institution inpatients (other than newborns) each day throughout a given period. The census is calculated by dividing the number of patient days during a period by the number of calendar days in the period.

Average Indexed Monthly Earnings (AIME)—A computation for determining a worker's Social Security benefits. Benefits are indexed ("updated") to reflect their relative values in comparison to earnings levels that prevail just prior to attaining age 62, disability or death. Indexed earnings are determined by multiplying the worker's actual earnings for that year by the ratio of average total wages of all workers in the indexing year to average total wages in the given year. The AIME is average monthly earnings adjusted for wage inflation over the employee's working career.

Average Length of Stay (ALOS)—The average number of patient days of service rendered to each inpatient (excluding newborns) during a given period. Varies for patients by diagnosis, age, hospital efficiency, etc. One measure of use of health facilities.

Average Life—Used in connection with the sale of mortgages or mortgage-backed securities. The prepayment expectations of a loan or a group of mortgages. An artificial number used primarily to allow comparison of one loan or pool of mortgages as opposed to another bearing a similar interest rate.

Average Price—The mean, or average, price obtained in the purchase, or sale, of a security by the process of averaging.

Average Wholesale Price (AWP)—The published suggested wholesale price of a drug. It is often used by pharmacies as a cost basis for pricing prescriptions. While a reliable pricing reference for brand-name drugs, it can be misleading in the case of generic drugs since each manufacturer establishes its own AWP for the generic drug. This can result in a broad range of prices for the identical product.

Averages—Various ways of measuring the trend of securities prices, one of the most popular of which is the Dow Jones Average of 30 industrial stocks listed on the New York Stock Exchange. Formulas—some very elaborate—have been devised to compensate for stock splits and stock dividends and thus give continuity to the average. In the case of the Dow Jones Industrial Average, the prices of the 30 stocks are totaled and then divided by a divisor that is intended to compensate for past stock splits and stock dividends and that is changed from time to time. As a result, point changes in the average have only the vaguest relationship to dollar price changes in stocks included in the average.

Averaging Up or Down—The practice of purchasing the same security at various price levels, thereby arriving at a higher or lower average cost.

B

Back Bond—Debt issued with a debt warrant.

Back End Load—A sales charge due upon the sale, transfer or disposition of securities, partnership interests, annuities, life insurances or mutual funds. Also called *exit* or *redemption fee.*

Backloading—The practice of providing a faster rate of benefit accrual after an employee has attained a specified age or has completed a specified number of years of service. For example, backloading occurs in a plan that provides a benefit of 1.5% of compensation for each year of service before age 50 and 2% per year thereafter. The practice is limited under ERISA. See also Accrued Benefit.

Backup Facility—An institution that, by formal or informal agreement with another health provider, has agreed to provide services to patients in another institution or program, e.g., hospital-provided inpatient services for patients receiving outpatient care in a neighborhood health center. See also Affiliation of Health Providers.

Bad Boy Clause—A provision requiring that an employee be disqualified from receiving his or her pension benefit if the employee has defrauded the employer or otherwise engaged in an act of dishonesty with respect to employer assets.

Balance Billing—The practice of charging full fees in excess of covered amounts and then billing the patient for that portion of the bill that the payer does not cover.

Balance of Payments—An itemized record of all financial transactions during a period of time, usually one year, between one nation and the rest of the world. Included are gold, trade, capital transactions, investments, services, tourist spending and military sales.

Balance Sheet—A condensed financial statement showing the nature and amount of a company's assets, liabilities and capital on a given date. In one column all the company's assets are listed with their values, and in the other all its liabilities and the equity of the stockholders.

Balance Sheet Reserve Plan—A plan that sets up a bookkeeping entry acknowledging some or all of the liability incurred for the payment of pensions, and thus taking this liability into account in determining profits and the stockholders' equity. Not necessarily accompanied by the earmarking of special funds for this purpose.

Balanced Funds—Investment companies that diversify their portfolio holdings over a wide list of common stocks, bonds and/or preferred issues.

Balanced Manager—An investment manager whose expertise includes the supervision of portfolios containing a variety of classes of investments (e.g., bonds, stocks and cash reserves).

Balloon Maturity—A type of maturity schedule for an issue of bonds that shows a relatively small number of bonds among the earlier maturities and a large number near the final maturity date. This kind of maturity schedule is sometimes called a *serial maturity.*

Balloon Mortgage—Though it starts off like a conventional mortgage, this mortgage requires the borrower to pay the balance or arrange new financing after a fixed period, usually three to five years. This allows borrowers to take advantage of lower rates, should they occur. If financing is difficult to get when the mortgage expires, however, the borrower may be forced to sell the house.

Bank Certificate of Deposit (CD)—See Certificate of Deposit.

Bank Draft—Similar to a bank check; however, it is not necessary for the drawer to cover the amount until the draft reaches the bank and the bank requests payment.

Bank Investment Contract (BIC)—A contract similar to a guaranteed investment contract (GIC), but it is issued by a bank. See Guaranteed Investment Contract.

Bank Master Notes—Variable rate notes of corporate issues held by commercial trust departments for participation by trust department customers.

Bank of Hours—See Hour Bank.

Bankers Acceptance (BA)—An irrevocable obligation of an issuing bank and the borrower whereby both are liable for payment. Used in domestic and/or international trade or commerce to finance the shipment and storage of goods or to facilitate dollar exchange transactions with foreign banks. A stronger instrument than a bank CD; there is no record of an investor sustaining a principal loss on an acceptance of a U.S. bank. Because of the varying dollar amounts involved in international and domestic trade transactions, acceptances are available in a wide variety of principal amounts. Maturities can range from any number of days (usually 30-60-90) up to a legal maximum of 180. Rates are posted and changed infrequently.

Bankruptcy—A condition characterized by the inability to repay debts in full because the liabilities (amounts owed) exceed the assets. Legally, a bankrupt is an individual or corporate debtor that is judged insolvent by a court.

Bargaining Contract—A contract under which both (or all) parties, as equals, set the terms and conditions of the contract.

Base Benefit Percentage—The percentage of compensation at which employer-derived benefits are accrued with respect to compensation of participants at or below the integration level.

Base Contribution Percentage—The percentage of compensation contributed by an employer with respect to compensation of participants at or below the integration level.

Base-Plus Plan—A health insurance plan that provides for basic medical coverage plus additional coverage for catastrophic health problems.

Base Rate; Base Wage Rate—The hourly money rate for a job performed at standard pace. Does not include bonuses or incentive premiums, shift differentials or overtime.

Basic Financial Statements—The financial statements necessary for a fair presentation of the entity's financial position and results of operations. Generally accepted accounting principles require the statement of financial position, operating statement, a budget comparison statement (if applicable) and the notes to the financial statement.

Basic Medical Benefits—Generally represent benefits for hospital, surgical, medical and other miscellaneous employee benefits, excluding major medical insurance.

Basic Value—The rate of interest on a bond or obligation that serves as the basis on which bond values are compared. Bonds are generally bought according to basis, as a "5% basis," or "to yield *x*%."

Basis—The yield to maturity at a given price when related to bonds as shown in bond tables.

Basis Point—A measurement of fluctuation in the current yield equal to 1/100 of 1% on bonds or bills.

Basket of Securities—A group of securities that have aggregate characteristics which cause the group to replicate the performance of a referenced index. Used in program trading strategies.

BB, B, CCC, CC—Ratings assigned by Standard & Poor's for speculative grade bonds. Regarded, on balance, as predominantly speculative with respect to capacity to pay interest and repay principal in accordance with the terms of the obligation. *BB* indicates the lowest degree of speculation and *CC* the highest degree of speculation. Although such debt likely will have some quality and protective characteristics, these are outweighed by large uncertainties or major risk exposures to adverse conditions.

BBB—Fourth highest rating assigned by Standard & Poor's for investment grade bonds. Regarded as having an adequate capacity to pay interest and repay principal. Whereas it normally exhibits adequate protection parameters, adverse economic conditions or changing circumstances are more likely to lead to a weakened capacity to pay interest and repay principal for debt in this category than in higher rated categories.

Bear—Someone who believes the stock market will decline.

Bear Market—A market where prices decline sharply against a background of widespread pessimism, growing unemployment and business recession. The opposite of bull market.

Bearer Bond—A bond made payable to its holder. The opposite of registered bond.

Bearer Form—A note or bond payable to the bearer of the instrument. Coupon bonds fall into this classification.

Bed Capacity—The total number of beds that are licensed or can be provided in an institution. Beds in the emergency, anesthesia and recovery rooms; beds for special diagnostic purposes; and newborn bassinets are generally excluded from bed capacity.

Bed Complement—The total number of beds normally available for inpatient use.

Bed Disability Days—The days an individual is confined to bed because of illness or injury. They include work-loss or school-loss days actually spent in bed.

Below the Par—A price below the face value (par value) of a security.

Benchmark—A standard job with characteristics so detailed that other jobs can be compared as being above, below or comparable to it.

Beneficiary—

—A person named by the participant in an insurance policy or pension plan to receive any benefits provided by the plan if the participant dies.

—A person designated by a participant, or by the terms of an employee benefit plan, who is or may become entitled to a benefit thereunder.

Beneficiary, Absolute or Irrevocable—An unalterable beneficiary. The owner relinquishes the right to change the beneficiary designation when such a beneficiary is named.

Beneficiary, Contingent—An alternate beneficiary. One whose rights under a contract are dependent upon the death of the original beneficiary or some other contingency.

Benefit—The rights of the participant or beneficiary to either cash or services after meeting the eligibility requirements of the pension or other benefit plans. Pension benefits usually refer to monthly payments payable on retirement or disability.

Benefit Accrual—See Accrued Benefit.

Benefit Approach—One of two groups of basic approaches to attributing pension benefits or costs to periods of employee service. Approaches in this group assign a distinct unit of benefit to each year of credited service. The actuarial present value of that unit of benefit is computed separately and determines the cost assigned to that year. The accumulated benefits approach, benefit/compensation approach and benefit/years-of-service approach are benefit approaches.

Benefit Booklet—A booklet for the employee that contains a general explanation of benefits and related provisions of the health plan. See also Summary Plan Description (SPD).

Benefit Formula—See Pension Benefit Formula.

Benefit Fund—The monies set aside by the plan sponsor with a trustee or insurance company for the payment of benefits.

Benefit Multiplier—A percentage that is multiplied by a participant's salary/pay (definitions of salary/pay vary from plan to plan) to determine a monthly benefit.

Benefit Package—A listing of specific benefits provided by an employee benefit plan.

Benefit Period—The period for application of deductibles, after which time deductibles must again be satisfied.

Benefit Plan Summary—See Summary Plan Description (SPD).

Benefits Specialist—An individual in an organization, typically in the human resource management function, whose responsibility it is to administer the employee benefits program.

Beta—Beta (market sensitivity) is a measure of the extent to which a fund's portfolio fluctuates with the market as represented by the S&P 500. To calculate beta, the sensitivity of the fund's portfolio to market patterns is measured. Beta is a statistical estimate of the average change in the fund's rate of return corresponding to a 1% change in the market. See also Systematic Risk.

Bid and Asked—Often referred to as a *quotation* or *quote.* The bid is the highest price anyone has indicated that he or she will pay for a security at a given time, and the asked is the lowest price anyone will accept at the same time.

Bid Price—The highest quoted price that any prospective buyer will pay for a security at a specific moment of time. The *bid price* is the real established market for a stock, regardless of the price of the last sale.

Big Board—A general name for the New York Stock Exchange.

Bill of Sale—An instrument used in a real estate transaction to transfer items other than real property. Furniture, fixtures, appliances, merchandise, motor vehicles and similar chattels are found in a bill of sale.

Binder—A written agreement (sometimes oral) whereby one party agrees to insure another party pending receipt of, and final action upon, the application.

Binding Receipt—A receipt for a premium payment accompanying the application for insurance. This binds the company, if the policy is approved, to make the policy effective from the date of the receipt.

Birth Rate—Generally, the number of live births per 1,000 population, calculated by dividing the total population into the number of live births and multiplying by 1,000.

Birthday Rule—Coordination-of-benefits rule whereby, if both spouses are working and carry dependent coverage, the responsibility for primary coverage falls to the parent having the earlier birthday in the calendar year, regardless of which parent is older. In the event that the birthdays occur on the same day, the employer-provided health insurance plan that has covered a parent the longest pays first. (Does not apply to self-funded programs.)

Biweekly Pay Systems—A pay system whereby employees receive their pay every two weeks. Under this system, there are normally 26 pay periods in a year.

Black Box—A projected working model of a wholly electronic stock exchange that some predict will eventually replace the traditional stock exchanges.

Blanket Contract—A contract of health insurance affording benefits, such as accidental death and dismemberment, for all of a class of persons not individually identified. Used for travel policy for employees.

Blanket Medical Expense—A provision in loss of income policies that entitles the insured person to collect up to a maximum established in the policy for all hospital and medical expenses incurred, without any limitations on individual types of medical expenses.

Block—A large holding or transaction of stock—often considered to be 10,000 shares or more.

Blocked Currency (International Benefits)—Local currency of a country that by law cannot be exported.

Blue Book—The generic name for a widely used pricing guide, actually entitled the *American Druggist First Databank Annual Directory of Pharmaceuticals.* Both brand-name and generic drugs are listed by product, manufacturer, national drug code or universal price code, direct price and average wholesale price. Other pricing guides include the *RedBook* and *Medispan's Pricing Guide.*

Blue Chip—The stock of a leading company that is known for excellent management and a conservative financial structure.

Blue Cross/Blue Shield Associations—Blue Cross and Blue Shield associations are independent, nonprofit, voluntary membership organizations formed for the purpose of prepaying medical care expenses for their subscribers (insured persons). Blue Shield plans provide payments mainly for physician services, while Blue Cross plans provide coverage primarily for hospital services.

Blue Sky Laws—State statutes that attempt to ensure that the terms of securities offerings are fair, just and equitable and meet minimum standards of investment quality. Blue sky laws impose requirements that are unique to securities offerings in a particular state.

Board Certified—A physician or other health professional who has passed an examination given by a medical specialty board and has been certified by that board as a specialist in the subject in question.

Board Eligible—A physician who is eligible to take a specialty board examination as a result of completion of medical school and a relevant residency. Some HMOs and other health facilities accept board-eligible physicians.

Bona Fide Occupational Qualification (BFOQ)—A legal term referring to permissible discriminatory job requirements as exceptions to Title VII of the Civil Rights Act of 1964. A BFOQ is a legitimate reason why an employer can exclude persons on otherwise illegal bases of consideration.

Bona Fide Purchaser—A person who buys real property, in good faith, for a fair value and without notice of any adverse claims or rights of third parties.

Bond—

—An obligation of an insurer to protect the insured against financial loss caused by the acts of another.

—A three-party contract guaranteeing that if one person (principal) fails to perform as specified or proves dishonest, the person to whom the duty is owed (obligee) will be financially protected by the issuer of the bond (surety).

—A certificate of debt (i.e., an IOU or promissory note) issued by such entities as corporations, municipalities and the government and its agencies, in multiples of 1,000 to 5,000 that represents a part of a loan to the issuer, bears a stated interest rate and matures on a stated future date. A bondholder is a creditor of the issuer and not part owner as is a stockholder. Short-term bonds, issued for five years or less, are often called *notes.*

Bond Anticipation Notes—Short-term notes sold in anticipation of a bond issue and retired by proceeds from the sale of the bonds.

Bond Discount—The discount is the amount by which the face value of a bond exceeds the issue price. A discount occurs when the coupon rate on the bonds is less than the market interest rate at the time the bonds are issued.

Bond Fund—An investment company that holds corporate, municipal or U.S. Treasury bonds. Such companies concentrate variously on high-grade bonds, medium grade bonds, convertible bonds, or a combination of bonds and preferred stocks. Their main objective is securing the principal with as much income as possible.

Bond Immunization—See Immunization (Bonds).

Bond Interest Coverage—A measure of bond safety: total income divided by annual interest on bonds (or earnings before interest and taxes divided by annual interest on bonds).

Bond Power—A power of attorney used in connection with the sale and transfer of registered bonds. It is necessary to obtain bond powers whenever registered bonds are pledged as collateral.

Bond Premium—The premium is the amount by which the issue price of a bond exceeds the face value. A premium occurs when the coupon rate of interest on a bond is higher than the market interest rate at the time the bonds are issued.

Bond Quality Ratings—A grading system for measuring the relative investment qualities of bonds by the use of rating symbols, which range from the highest investment quality (at least investment risk) to the lowest investment quality (greatest investment risk). These ratings according to Standard & Poor's are A1+, highest grade; A1, high grade; A, upper medium grade; B1+, medium grade; B1, lower medium grade; B, speculative; C1+ and C1, outright speculations; C, income bonds paying no interest and the best defaulted bonds; and D1 and D, in default, with the D symbol assigned to issues that appear to have little recoverable value.

Bond Swap—A technique used by investors in bonds that involves the sale of a bond or bonds and the simultaneous purchase of entirely different bonds in a like amount with comparable coupons and maturities.

Bond Tables—Mathematical tables that facilitate the conversion of bond yields into dollar values. They are employed for the pricing of municipal bonds, which frequently are quoted on a "yield basis"; for example, they are sold at a certain price which, taking into consideration both interest rate and maturity, will result in definite return on the amount paid.

Bond Yield—The rate of return on bonds.

Bonding—ERISA-required protection for fiduciaries and any plan officials handling plan assets to safeguard the plan against loss through acts of fraud or dishonesty, directly or indirectly.

Book Reserve (International Benefits)—A system of recognizing pension liabilities through the creation of a reserve on the employer's balance sheet. The corresponding reserves may or may not be segregated from the assets of the employer. In some countries, it is possible for the employer to take a deduction for income or other taxes, even when assets are not segregated.

Book Value—An accounting term determined by adding all of the company's assets, then deducting all debts and other liabilities, plus the liquidation price of any preferred issues. The sum arrived at is divided by the number of common shares outstanding and the result is book value per common share. Book value of the assets of a company or a security may have little or no significant relationship to market value.

Bottom-Up Manager—Common stock manager who places his or her selection emphasis on recognizing favorable characteristics of individual companies, as opposed to developing the portfolio with an emphasis on the economy and industries.

Brand-Name Drug—A drug protected by a patent issued to the original innovator or marketer. The patent prohibits the manufacture of the drug by other companies as long as the patent remains in effect. See also Generic Equivalent Drugs.

Breach of Fiduciary Duty—A fiduciary's violation of a duty owed to an employee benefit plan or a participant or beneficiary in such a plan.

Breach of Trust—Violation of a duty of a trustee to a beneficiary.

Breadth of Market Theory—A technical theory that forecasts the strength of the market based upon the number of issues that advance or decline in a particular trading day.

Break in Service—Under ERISA, a calendar year, plan year or other 12 consecutive month period designated by the plan during which a plan participant does not complete more than 500 hours of service. (This general rule has been modified for certain industries, particularly those characterized by seasonal employment patterns.) When a break in service occurs, the participant must again meet the plan's eligibility requirements to participate.

Breakout—Used in technical analysis to describe a stock that is either declining through a support level or rising through a resistance level.

Breakpoint—The dollar level of an investment in a mutual fund at which a purchaser qualifies for a reduction in sales charges on a quantity purchase.

Bridge Benefit (Canada)—A supplemental pension benefit payable from the date of early retirement until the age of entitlement for government pensions.

Broadbanding—A strategy for salary structures that consolidates a large number of pay grades into a few broad bands.

Broker—

—An insurance solicitor, licensed by the state, who places business with a variety of insurance com-

panies and who represents the buyers of insurance rather than the companies even though he or she is paid commissions by the companies.
—An agent who handles the public's orders to buy and sell securities, commodities or other property. For this service, a commission is charged that, depending upon the firm dealt with and the amount of the transaction may or may not be negotiated.

Broker-Dealer—A person or firm that buys and sells securities for others and also for its own account. With some exceptions, broker-dealers must register with the Securities and Exchange Commission and with the securities commissioner in the state where they transact business.

Brokerage—A fee charged by a broker for execution of a transaction; an amount per transaction or a percentage of a total value of the transaction; usually referred to as a *commission fee.*

Brokerage Accounts—See Self-Directed Brokerage Accounts.

Brokers' Fidelity Bonds—Bonds required by NYSE Rule 319 for all employees, officers and partners of member firms to protect clients against acts of misplacement, fraudulent trading and check forgery.

Brokers' Loans—Money loans made to brokerage firms by commercial banks and other lending institutions for financing margin account debit balances, financing inventories of stock, underwriting new issues and financing a firm's own investments.

Building Lien—A builder's charge or encumbrance upon property. See also Mechanic's Lien.

Building Loan—A loan for the duration of the construction of a building, usually providing for periodic payments for specified phases. Also called *construction loan* or *interim loan.*

Bull—One who believes the stock market will rise.

Bull Market—An advancing stock market. The opposite of bear market.

Bundling—Benefits offered by employers in packages. For instance, the grouping of vision or dental benefits with medical coverage (noncore and core coverage vs. core-only coverage).

Business Continuation Insurance—When a partner dies or is disabled, the remaining partners are provided with the funds to purchase that partner's interest in the firm. See also Key Employee Insurance.

Business Cycle—A regularly recurring period of undetermined scope and origin embracing prosperity, recession, depression and recovery.

Business Judgment Rule—A judicial doctrine offering protection to corporate officers and directors from personal liability for their actions, as long as they were taken in good faith and with reasonable care.

Business Life Insurance—See Key Employee Insurance.

Business Travel Accident Insurance—Coverage for an accident while traveling on company business. Generally applies to all accidents occurring while away from home, not just those during actual travel.

Buy-Back Provision—When terminating employees who are no more than 50% vested withdraw their own contributions and the employer cancels the remainder of their benefits, this arrangement allows the employees to buy back the forfeited employer contributions by repaying the withdrawn amounts.

Buy Order—An order given to a broker or a bank authorizing the purchase of a specified amount of securities or commodities. Unless otherwise stipulated as to time, all orders are treated as day orders, good only on the day they are given. However, orders may also be placed with a time limit.

Buy/Write Option Writing—A type of options management whereby one manager manages both stocks and options.

Buying Hedge (Long Hedge)—Buying futures contracts to protect against possible increased cost of commodities that will be needed in the future.

Bylaws—The rules adopted by the members or by the board of directors of a corporation or other organization for its government. Bylaws must not be contrary to the laws of the land, and affect only the members of the given corporation or organization; they do not apply to third parties.

C

C—Quality rating assigned by Standard & Poor's for speculative grade bonds. Reserved for income bonds on which no interest is being paid.

C Corporation—A regular corporation that elects to be taxed at the corporate, rather than individual level. See S Corporation.

Cafeteria Plan—Defined by the Internal Revenue Code as a plan that permits the participant to choose between two or more benefits consisting of cash and qualified benefits. See also Flexible Benefit Plan/ Flexible Compensation.

Calendar Year Deductible—A deductible that applies to any eligible medical expenses incurred by the insured during any one calendar year.

Call Date—The earliest date on which a bond may be redeemed before maturity at the option of the issuer.

Call Option—An option to buy a specified number of shares at a definite price within a specified period of time. See also Puts and Calls—Options.

Call Price—The price a which a corporation or other obligor is permitted to redeem securities containing call provisions. To compensate for this privilege, a price above par is usually paid.

Call Provisions—A description of the terms under which a bond may be redeemed by the issuer in whole or in part prior to maturity. The provisions give call protection to the bondholder until the call date.

Callable—A bond issue all or part of which may be redeemed by the issuing corporation under specific terms before maturity. The term also applies to preferred shares that may be redeemed by the issuing company.

Called Bond—A bond drawn for redemption before maturity.

Canada Pension Plan/Quebec Pension Plan (CPP/ QPP) (Canada)—The two major social security programs in Canada. The provisions of these two government-administered plans are virtually identical. Both are funded by employee and employer contributions on a partial pay-as-you-go basis. The Quebec Pension Plan operates in the province of Quebec; the Canada Pension Plan operates in the rest of Canada.

Canadian Association of Pension Supervisory Authorities (CAPSA)—Consists of senior government officials (provincial and federal) responsible for the administration of pension legislation in each jurisdiction.

Canon—A rule or law. Under civil law, the rules by which the title to real property is traced are known as *canons of inheritance;* under common law, such rules are known as *canons of descent.*

Capital—Money and other assets needed by a company to operate a business and provide facilities for production and distribution of a product or service.

Capital Accumulation Plan—An employer-sponsored plan in which contributions are made to participants' individual accounts (a defined contribution plan). In U.S. Bureau of Labor Statistics data, it refers to a plan in which employer contributions may be withdrawn at the participants' discretion prior to retirement, death, disability, separation from service, age 59½ or hardship (a defined contribution style arrangement that is not a qualified retirement plan).

Capital Appreciation—A rise in the market prices of shares owned.

Capital Asset Pricing Model (CAPM)—Describes the way prices of individual assets are determined in markets where information is freely available and reflected instantaneously in asset prices—that is, efficient markets. According to this model, prices are determined in such a way that risk premiums are proportional to systematic risk, which is measured by the beta coefficient. As such, the CAPM provides an explicit expression of the expected returns for all assets. Basically, the CAPM holds that, if investors are risk averse, high-risk stocks must have higher expected returns than low-risk stocks.

Capital Assets; Fixed Assets—Relatively permanent assets held for use or income rather than for sale or direct conversion into salable goods or cash. Examples would be plant, equipment and property—also such intangible assets as good will and patents.

Capital Consumption Adjustment—An adjustment in the estimates of the capital consumption allowance, or book depreciation, to reconcile these figures with actual economic depreciation.

Capital Expenditures—Monies appropriated to increase or improve capital assets.

Capital Gain or Capital Loss—Profit or loss from the sale of a capital asset.

Capital Gains Distributions—Payments to mutual fund shareholders that consist of the realized gains on the assets sold by the fund. These gains are usually paid once a year and are usually long term in nature.

Capital Market—That segment of the securities market that deals in instruments with more than one year to maturity, that is, long-term debt and equity securities.

Capital Market Line—A graphic portrayal of the average rate of return provided by the marketplace for various levels of risk.

Capital Stock—All shares representing ownership of a business, including preferred and common.

Capital Structure—The division of the capitalization among bonds, preferred stock and common stock. A high common stock ratio to the total is considered conservative, and a low one is considered speculative.

Capital Sum—See Principal Sum.

Capitalization—The aggregate or total amount of the various securities, in all forms, issued by a corporation. Includes bonds, debentures, preferred and common stock, and surplus. Bonds and debentures are usually carried on the books of the issuing company in terms of their par or face value. Preferred and common shares may be carried in terms of par or stated value. Stated value may be an arbitrary figure decided upon by the directors or may represent the amount received by the company from the sale of securities at the time of issuance. Determining a present value of income property by taking either the known or estimated annual net income and discounting by using a rate of return commonly accepted at the time by buyers of similar properties.

Capitalization Method—A means of appraising real property by subtracting expenses from income on an annual basis and multiplying the result by an accepted factor (the cap rate) to determine value. Also called *income approach.*

Capitalizing Fixed Charges—Computing the principal amount of a debt that would carry the fixed charges in question (i.e., divide the fixed charges contemplated by the assumed interest rate).

Capitation—A capitation benefit program is one in which a provider contracts with the program's sponsor or administrator to provide all or most of the services covered under the program to subscribers in return for payment on a per capita basis. This payment is known as a *capitation fee,* and it is fixed without regard to the actual number or nature of services provided to each person in a set period of time. Capitation is the characteristic payment method in health maintenance organizations.

Captive Insurance Company (International Benefits)—An insurance company that is a subsidiary of a noninsurance corporation. The insurer primarily writes insurance on its parent and the parent's other subsidiaries, although nonrelated business may be solicited.

Card Program—Use of a drug benefit identification card which, when presented to a participating pharmacy by employees or their dependents, usually entitles them to receive the medication for a minimal copay.

Cardiopulmonary Resuscitation (CPR)—Emergency medical procedure to deal with respiratory arrest or insufficiency, obstructed airway and cardiac arrest. Involves removing airway obstruction, rescue breathing and external chest compressions.

Career Average Pay Formula/Career Average Plan—A career average pay formula is a benefit formula that bases benefits on the employee's compensation over the entire period of service with the employer. A career average pay plan is a plan with such a formula.

Carrier—A commercial insurer, a government agency or a Blue Cross or Blue Shield plan that underwrites or administers programs that pay for health, life or other insurance services.

Carry Forward (Canada)—The portion of an RRSP deduction entitlement unused in a particular year may be carried forward for the following seven years. The amount carried forward is in addition to the regular RRSP contribution for that current year.

Carryover Deductible—The deductible payable under continuation coverage includes the portion of the deductible satisfied before the qualifying event.

Carryover Provisions—

—Since it is unlikely in a profit-sharing plan that the annual contribution will always equal 15%, carryover provisions help to secure maximum deduction. There are two types: (1) The credit carryover is created when the contribution formula calls for an annual contribution less than the maximum allowable deduction. Unused credit is carried forward and may be applied in a future year in which contributions exceed 15% of the then-current annual compensation of participants. (2) Contribution carryover is created whenever annual contributions exceed the maximum allowable deductions. This carryover can be deducted in future years in which contribution payments are less than the maximum allowable deduction.

—Provision in major medical plans to avoid two deductibles applied to covered medical expenses when expenses are incurred toward the end of one calendar year, and sickness or injury continues into next year.

Carve-Out—

—A program separate from the primary group health plan designed to provide a specialized type of care, such as a mental health carve-out. Also, a method of integrating Medicare with an employer's retiree health plan (making the employer plan excess or secondary) which tends to produce the lowest employer cost.

—(Canada) Used in reference to an integrated plan.

Case Management—A utilization management technique that focuses on coordinating a number of services needed by clients. It includes a standardized, objective assessment of client needs and the development of an individualized service or care plan that is based on the needs assessment and is goal oriented. See also Medical Case Management.

Case Mix—The classifications or categories of patients treated by a hospital.

Cash Balance Plan—A defined benefit plan that simulates a defined contribution plan. Benefits are definitely determinable, but account balances are credited with a fixed rate of return and converted to a monthly pension benefit at retirement. See also Target Benefit Plan.

Cash Equivalents—Short-term investments held in lieu of cash and readily converted into cash within a short time span (e.g., CDs, commercial paper, Treasury bills).

Cash Flow—The reported net income of a corporation plus amounts charged off for depreciation, depletion, amortization and extraordinary charges to reserves, which are a bookkeeping deduction and not paid out in actual dollars and cents.

Cash or Deferred Arrangement (CODA)—Section 401(k) of the Internal Revenue Code allows employers to offer employees a choice between receiving compensation and having a contribution made on their behalf to a qualified plan. See also 401(k) Plan.

Cash Out—A pension plan may provide for the forfeiture of an accrued benefit where the plan provides for a *cash out* of an employee's benefits by making a lump-sum distribution to the employee. The cash out applies only to the employee's nonforfeitable interest upon termination of service prior to retirement.

Cash Plan—See Deferred Compensation Plan.

Cash Refund Annuity—See Refund Annuity.

Cash Surrender Value—See Surrender Value.

Cash Withdrawal (Canada)—A return of personal pension contributions to a member whose employment is terminated.

Catastrophic Health Care—Health care for life-threatening conditions whose cost can drain an individual's family income.

Catch-Up Options—A recognition that special exceptions to the exclusion allowance provisions for tax-deferred annuity contributions are needed to make up for the effects of inflation because past service and contributions based on compensation frequently are inadequate in this regard.

Catch-Up Provision—A provision that allows employees covered by a 403(b) plan to make larger than typically permitted contributions to the plan.

Catchment Area—The geographic area from which a particular program or facility for health care draws the bulk of its users. See Service Area.

CD—See Certificate of Deposit.

Cede—To transfer to a reinsurer all or part of the insurance (or reinsurance) written by a given insurer (the ceding or direct writing company). See also Reinsurance.

Centers of Excellence—Specific providers selected to perform certain procedures because of their expertise and willingness to provide discounts.

CERES Principles—A ten-point environmental reporting and accountability code previously called the Valdez Principles and now named after the Coalition for Environmentally Responsible Economies (CERES). The ten principles are intended to expand the concept of socially responsible action with an emphasis on environmental issues.

Certificate—The actual piece of paper that is evidence of ownership of stock in a corporation. Watermarked paper is finely engraved with delicate etchings to discourage forgery. Loss of a certificate may at the least cause a great deal of inconvenience—at the worst, financial loss.

Certificate of Deposit (CD)—A written certification by a bank or a savings and loan association that a fixed dollar amount has been deposited with it for a fixed period of time at a predetermined rate of interest. Certificates are registered in the name of the depositor (fund) and are issued in negotiable and nonnegotiable form. If the fund needs the money before the expressed maturity, a negotiable certificate frequently can be sold to certain money brokers at the then-existing money rate.

Certificate of Insurance—A document that is given to insured members of a group insurance plan and that outlines the plan's coverage and the member's rights.

Certificate of Need (CON)—A certificate issued by a governmental body to an individual or organization proposing to construct or modify a health facility, acquire new medical equipment or offer a new health service. CON is intended to control expansion of facilities and services by preventing their excessive or duplicative development.

Certificate of Title—A certification of the ownership of land, based upon an examination of the record title.

Certification—The process by which a governmental or nongovernmental agency or association evaluates and recognizes a person who meets predetermined standards; sometimes used with reference to materials or services. *Certification* is usually applied to individuals and *accreditation* to institutions. See also Accreditation; Licensure.

Certified Employee Benefit Specialist (CEBS)—A designation granted jointly by the International Foundation of Employee Benefit Plans and the Wharton School of the University of Pennsylvania to individuals who complete ten college level courses and examinations in the areas of design and operation of employee benefit plans and who pledge to a code of ethical standards and continuing education. In Canada, the program is presented jointly by the International Foundation of Employee Benefit Plans and Dalhousie University of Halifax.

Certified Financial Planner (CFP)—A designation granted by the College for Financial Planning to individuals who complete a series of educational requirements, courses and examinations in the areas of personal financial and retirement planning and who pledge to a code of ethical standards and continuing education.

Certified Length of Stay—The period of time approved as necessary and appropriate for a patient to receive inpatient care in a hospital.

Certified Pension Consultant (CPC)—A designation awarded by the American Society of Pension Actuaries. Holders must combine required experience with passing three examinations covering employee benefits fundamentals.

Certified Public Accountant (CPA)—A professional license granted by the various states to persons meeting certain educational, experience and examination requirements. These requirements vary from state to state, but typically they include a college degree with accounting and auditing course work and qualifying experience. The examinations include passing the Uniform CPA Examination, covering accounting theory and practice, auditing and business law.

Change-in-Classification Card (Canada)—From time to time an employee will change his or her insurance classification and in that case a change-in-classification card is filled out in order that the coverage can be changed and the appropriate charge made thereafter. This may happen because of a change in salary, position, etc.

Change-of-Dependents Card (Canada)—When a single employee marries or when a married employee becomes single because of the death or divorce of a spouse without children, a change-of-dependents card is filled out to advise the insurance company of this change in status.

Channeling—A term used in long-term care in which efforts are made to avoid institutionalization of patients by having them directed ("channeled") to community-based long-term care services.

Chapter 218 Agreement—See Federal-State Agreement.

Charitable Corporations—Such employers are exempt from tax, and their employees enjoy a unique deferment of tax liability in connection with employer-purchased annuities.

Charter—A certificate of incorporation, issued by a state, legally authorizing a corporation to conduct business as stipulated in this charter.

Chartered Financial Analyst (CFA)—Awarded by the Institute of Chartered Financial Analysts. Holders must combine required experience and education with passing three examinations covering ethical and professional standards, securities laws and regulations, financial accounting and so on.

Chartered Financial Consultant (ChFC)—A designation granted by the American College to individuals who complete a ten-course program in the areas of personal financial and retirement planning and who pledge to a code of ethical standards and continuing education.

Chartered Life Underwriter (CLU)—A designation granted by the American College to individuals who complete a ten-course program in the areas of insurance and estate planning and who pledge to a code of ethical standards and continuing education.

Chartered Property and Casualty Underwriter (CPCU)—A designation awarded by the American Institute for Property and Liability Underwriters. Formal application and acceptance is required. Holders must combine required experience with passing ten examinations on various insurance topics.

Chattel Mortgage—A mortgage that encumbers personal property.

Chemotherapy—Treatment of internal disease by chemical reagents (including drugs), primarily involved in the treatment of cancer.

Child-Rearing Drop-Out (Canada)—Provision in the Canada and Quebec Pension Plans that allows parents to disregard, for pension purposes, years of low earnings or no earnings while their children are under the age of seven. Because of the drop-out, parents do not lose future pension benefits if they stay at home while their children are young.

Chiropractic—A system of medicine based on the theory that disease is caused by malfunction of the nerve system, and that normal function of the nerve system can be achieved by manipulation and other treatment of the structures of the body, primarily the spinal column and pelvis. A practitioner is a chiropractor, Doctor of Chiropractic (DC).

Church Plan—

—A plan established and maintained by a church or convention or association of churches that is tax exempt under Internal Revenue Code Section 501. The following, however, are not church plans: (1) a plan that is primarily for the benefit of employees of an unrelated business (as described in IRC Section 513) and (2) a multiemployer plan that includes one or more employers that are not tax-exempt churches or conventions of churches. For plan years beginning before January 1, 1983, employees covered by a plan (in existence on January 1, 1974) for employees of a tax-exempt agency of a church (or convention or association of churches) are considered employees of the church.

—Although exempt, a church (or convention or association of churches) can make an irrevocable election to be covered by the participation, vesting and funding requirements of ERISA.

Churning—

—A form of code gaming where the same medical procedure is billed more than once, or a provider sees a patient more often than medically necessary.

—Excessive trading in a customer's account. The term suggests that the registered representative ignores the objectives and interests of clients, and seeks only to increase commissions.

Civil Action—A proceeding in a law court or a suit in equity by one person against another for the enforcement or protection of a private right, or the prevention of a wrong. Civil action is in contrast to criminal action, in which the state prosecutes a person for commission of an illegal act or breach of a duty.

Civil Rights Act of 1964—This act, as well as its amendments and other similar legislation, prohibits discrimination on the basis of race, color, sex, national origin, age, religion, handicap status and Vietnam War veteran status.

Civilian Health and Medical Program of the Uniformed Services (CHAMPUS)—Provides coverage for armed forces personnel dependents and retirees receiving care outside a military treatment facility.

Claim—
—An itemized statement of services rendered by a health care provider for a given patient. The claim is submitted to a health benefits plan for payment.
—A demand to an employee benefit plan (pension or health and welfare) or insurer by a plan participant or beneficiary for the payment of certain benefits.
—The right to any debts, privileges or other things in possession of another; also, the titles to anything which another should concede to, or confer on the claimant.

Claim Administrator—Any entity that reviews and determines whether to pay claims to enrollees or physicians on behalf of the health benefit plan. Claim administrators may be insurance companies or their designated claims review organizations, self-insured employers, management firms, third party administrators or other private contractors.

Claim Form—The form used to file for benefits under a health plan.

Claimant—Plan participant who files a claim for benefits. See also Beneficiary.

Claims Experience—The frequency with which insured employees file claims to receive benefits. One of the primary factors used in calculating insurance premiums.

Claims Procedure—Under ERISA, each plan is required to provide a claims procedure, which must be explained to plan participants and beneficiaries. The denial of a claim made under the claims procedure must be in writing, with an explanation of the reasons for the denial.

Claims Reserve—See Reserve.

Claims Review—
—In health care prepayment, the routine examination by a carrier or intermediary of the claim submitted to it for payment or for predetermination of benefits; may include determination of eligibility, coverage of service and plan liability.
—In quality assurance, examination by organizations of claims as part of a quality review or utilization review process.

Claims Services Only (CSO)—A contract designed for fully self-insured employers that need very little administrative assistance. Under a CSO arrangement, the insurer administers only the claims portion of the plan.

Class Rating—An approach to rate making in which a price per unit of insurance is computed for all applicants with a given set of characteristics. For example, the rate may apply to all persons of a given age and sex, to all buildings of a certain type of construction or to all businesses of a certain type.

Clearing Title—The process of checking the recorded and unrecorded instruments affecting a property and taking whatever action is required to clear any defects so that it may become good, marketable or insurable.

Cliff Vesting—Full 100% vesting after *x* years of service, with no gradation of vesting before that time. Benefits must be 100% vested after five years. If participants leave the company or are terminated prior to the vesting date, no partial benefits are received. See also Vesting Schedules.

Clinic—A facility for the provision of preventive, diagnostic and treatment services to ambulatory patients.

Clinical Outcomes—Health status changes or effects that individual patients experience resulting from the delivery of health care, usually measured in terms of morbidity, mortality, functional ability and satisfaction with care.

Clinical Outliers—Cases that cannot adequately be assigned to an appropriate diagnostic related group (DRG) because of unique combinations of diagnoses and surgeries, very rare conditions or for other unique clinical reasons. Such cases will be grouped together into clinical outlier DRGs. See also Outliers.

Closed-End Fund—An investment company whose shares are traded on a securities exchange or the over-the-counter market. The number of shares outstanding is limited by the company's charter, and their value is determined in the open market.

Closed-End Mortgage—A mortgage that has no provisions for increasing the balance. This differs from an open-ended mortgage, which permits the mortgagor to continue borrowing from it in amounts up to the original sum.

Closed Group—See Open Group/Closed Group.

Closed Mortgage—A mortgage that cannot be paid off until maturity.

Closed Panel—
—A closed panel practice is established if patients eligible for health services in a public or private program can receive these services only at specified facilities through a limited number of providers. If the services are provided in a group practice facility and are prepaid by some agency, the practice may be termed *prepaid group practice.* Usually not applicable to emergency care.
—(Canada) The provision of legal services to plan members by a limited group of lawyers, whose fees are based on a predetermined schedule. The term also applies to a limited number of physicians who provide medical services to plan members.

Closely Held Corporation—A nonpublic corporation that is owned by a small number of shareholders.

Closing Costs—The numerous expenses buyers and sellers normally incur in the transfer of ownership of real estate.

Closing Price—The price at which the final transaction in a security took place on a particular business day. Stock prices are quoted daily in the financial pages of leading newspapers, where number of shares traded and the opening, high, low and last sale (closing) prices, plus net change from the previous day, are printed from left to right in that order.

Closing Transaction—A transaction in which the seller (writer) of an option terminates his or her obligation. In the case of a listed option, a seller effects a closing transaction by purchasing a listed option having the same terms as the option previously sold.

Cloud on the Title—An outstanding claim or encumbrance that, if valid, would affect or impair the owner's title: a mortgage or judgment.

Coalition—A joint program involving health care providers, purchasers of care, industry, consumers, labor or insurers in an attempt to deal with health care costs, issues and problems.

COBRA—See Consolidated Omnibus Budget Reconciliation Act of 1985.

Code—
—A collection or compilation of the statutes passed by a legislative body.
—A system of characters and syntax rules that can translate human language into computer language.
—Coefficient of Determination (R^2).
—Measures the percentage of total risk that is market related (i.e., systematic).

Code Gaming—The use of incorrect billing codes to increase provider income, or to enable a patient to receive reimbursement for a treatment that would otherwise be nonreimbursable.

Coding—A mechanism for identifying and defining physician services.

Coinsurance—A policy provision, frequently found in major medical insurance, by which the insured person and the insurer share the hospital and medical expenses resulting from an illness or injury in a specified ratio (e.g., 80%:20%), after the deductible is met. Also called *percentage participation clause.*

Collateral—Usually securities or other property pledged by a borrower to secure payment of a loan. However, collateral can also be intangible, such as an interest in future payments. Basically, it is anything considered to have value.

Collateral Dependents (Canada)—Those persons eligible for dependent coverage under a group contract by a broadening of the contract's definition of *eligible dependents.* May include parents, grandparents, siblings or grandchildren of the employee or employee's spouse who live with the employee and largely rely on him or her for their support. Also called *sponsored dependents.*

Collateral Trust Bonds—Bonds secured by other securities (stocks and bonds) often controlled by the issuer and deposited with a trustee. In the last analysis, they are as secure as the credit worthiness of the issuer and the real market value of the deposited securities.

Collateralized Mortgage Obligation (CMO)—A debt instrument that is collateralized by mortgage loans. The CMO is regarded as the debt of the issuer.

Collective Bargaining—The process of good faith negotiation between employer and employee representatives concerning issues of mutual interest.

Collective Bargaining Agreement or Contract—Formal agreement over wages, hours and conditions of employment entered into between an employer or group of employers and one or more unions representing employees of the employers.

Collective Investment Fund—A pool of investments managed by a bank according to a written plan on behalf of several individual fiduciary accounts whose assets are lawfully contributed to the fund. Participation in these funds is available only to fiduciary assets held in trust by a bank or other lawful trustee.

Collective Trust Fund—See Common Trust Fund.

Collectively Bargained Plan—A plan maintained pursuant to an agreement that the secretary of labor finds to be a collective bargaining agreement between employee representatives and one or more employers.

Combination Plan—An agreement under which two funding media are used, with a portion of the contributions placed in a trust fund and the balance paid to an insurance company as contributions under a group annuity contract or as premium on individual life insurance or annuity contracts. The entire pension for each participant is generally paid by the insurance company, with transfers from the trust fund being made as required.

Combination Profit-Sharing Plan—A profit-sharing plan where part of the contribution is paid in cash annually and part is deferred.

Combined Plan—A combined plan is most often a Blue Cross-major medical combination. Some companies—because of an unusually strong Blue Cross plan and an unusually weak Blue Shield plan—keep only the basic hospital and medical services plan (Blue Cross) and have the major medical plan pay physician charges from the onset of illness. With this type of arrangement, the major medical plan may begin paying for hospital room and board after the 365th day, for example, but pay the physician charges from the first day of confinement.

Commerce, Interstate—Trade, traffic, commerce, transportation or communication between a state and a place outside that state.

Commercial Health Insurance—Plans by private insurance firms as compared with plans offered by nonprofit firms.

Commercial Paper—Negotiable, short-term, unsecured promissory notes, issued in bearer form on a discount or coupon basis by a corporation to raise working capital for any term up to 270 days. A direct obligation of the issuer, they are sold in multiples of 25,000 and are rated by Standard & Poor's A-1, A-2 and A-3, and by Moody's Prime 1, Prime 2 and Prime 3. The three principal types are prime finance paper, issued by sales finance companies and certain large bank holding companies; prime industrial paper, issued by leading industrial corporations; and finance paper of less than prime quality. In the case of prime finance paper, the investor may specify both the issue and maturity date, whereas in the case of industrial paper, only those maturities listed on the market are available. Interest is paid at maturity, payment is required in federal funds on the settlement date (usually at buyer's option) and payment is received by federal funds on the maturity date at the issuing corporation's bank.

Commingled Funds—The collective investment of the assets of a number of small pension funds, usually through a bank-administered plan allowing for broader and more efficient investing.

Commission—The broker's basic fee for purchasing or selling securities or property as an agent. This fee may or may not be negotiated.

Commitment—A pledge or promise to do something in the future. Lending institutions generally give written commitment letters containing specific terms of mortgage loans they will give. Commitments can be either firm or conditional. Conditional commitments may be contingent upon such factors as the borrower's credit, completion of construction or that a certain percentage of occupancy be obtained. Often a charge, the standby fee, is made by the lender.

Commodity Exchange—An organization of traders who buy and sell contracts for future delivery of such things as grain, cotton, hogs, sugar, coffee, gold and mortgages.

Common Control—Unincorporated businesses whose ownership of interests in the businesses are intertwined in such a way that the businesses, if they were incorporated, would be members of a controlled group. See also Controlled Group.

Common Law—That body of law deriving from judicial decisions, as opposed to legislatively enacted statutes and administrative regulations.

Common Law Employee—A person who performs services for an employer, if the employer has the right to direct both the objective of the services and the manner in which they are performed.

Common Stock—Securities that represent an ownership interest in a corporation. If the company has also issued preferred stock, both common and preferred have ownership rights. The preferred normally is limited to a fixed dividend but has prior claim on dividends and, in the event of liquidation, assets. Claims of both common and preferred stockholders are junior to claims of bondholders and other creditors of the company. Common stockholders assume the greater risk, but generally exercise the greater control and may gain the greater reward in the form of dividends and capital appreciation. The terms *common stock* and *capital stock* are often used interchangeably when the company has no preferred stock.

Common Stock Fund—A mutual fund that primarily invests its assets in common stocks.

Common Trust Fund—A trust fund in which the assets of a number of trusts are commingled. Also referred to as a *collective trust.*

Commonly Controlled Businesses—All employees of corporations that are members of a *controlled group of corporations* are treated as employed by a single employer for purposes of plan qualification. A comparable requirement applies to partnerships, sole proprietorships and other businesses under common control.

Community Care Networks—In the American Hospital Association plan, community care networks are responsible for providing all patient services, from preventive care to long-term care. Hospitals, physicians, insurers and other participants may choose from a variety of roles in the network.

Community Health Center—An entity that provides, either through its staff or in conjunction with other resources, primary health services, prevention, appropriate supplemental and environmental health services, and information on the availability of health services.

Community Health Purchasing Alliance (CHPA)—Small employer purchasing cooperatives designed to help small employers gain increased access to health care and lower costs by their combined economic clout.

Community Health Resource—Voluntary health or other health-related agency or organization in a community that has programs to promote healthier lifestyles, counseling and treatment.

Community Hospitals—As defined by HCFA, those nonfederal acute care hospitals whose average length of stay is less than 30 days and whose facilities and services are open to the general public.

Community Mental Health Center—A facility or facilities licensed by the state and funded by the federal government to provide mental health services in a designated catchment area.

Community Rating—The process of determining the premium for a group risk on the basis of the average claims experience for the general population instead of a particular employer. This is especially helpful for small groups, whose claims experience over two or three years may not be typical. Community rating is used by most HMOs, which use the plan's entire client population to set premiums. See also Experience Rating.

Commuted Value—The single sum that represents the present worth (the discounted value) of a stipulated number of installments of proceeds payable at future dates.

Comorbidity—A preexisting condition that will, because of its presence with a specific principal diagnosis, cause an increase in length of hospital stay by at least one day in approximately 75% of the cases. (Synonym: substantial comorbidity)

Comparability Pension Plans—Defined contribution pension plans that allow allocations based on age, job classification or any other grouping. Nondiscrimination rules are satisfied by using the "cross-testing" provision in the 401(a)(4) regulations.

Comparable Worth—The doctrine that men and women who perform work of the same inherent value should receive comparable compensation.

Compensation—The amount of wages, salary or other earned income an individual receives from services rendered as a result of employment or self-employment.

Complication—A condition that arises during a hospital stay that requires special clinical management and prolongs the length of stay by at least one day in approximately 75% of the cases. (Synonym: substantial complication)

Composite Rate—A group premium rate that does not differentiate between single and family coverage.

Compound Interest—The interest upon principal that is being increased, or augmented, periodically by interest paid on the previous amount of principal. Interest may be compounded daily, monthly, quarterly, semiannually or annually.

Compounding—The arithmetic process of finding the final value of an investment or series of investments when compound interest is applied. That is, interest is earned on the accrued interest as well as on the initial principal.

Comprehensive Major Medical Coverage—This coverage provides protection similar to a combined basic and major medical plan and is often characterized by a low deductible, less than 100% reimbursement and a high maximum benefit. A typical type of comprehensive plan provides that most types of medical expenses are covered, usually after the satisfaction of a relatively low initial deductible (such as $100). After covered expenses exceed this initial deductible, the plan typically pays:

1. 100% of certain kinds of expenses up to a certain limit (such as 100% of the first $2,000 of covered hospital expenses after the deductible)
2. A percentage, such as 80%, of all other covered medical expenses, including the expenses that exceed the limit mentioned in item 1.

Comprehensive Medical Care—A complete package of health care services and benefits, including prevention, early detection and early treatment of conditions.

Comprehensive Medical Plan—A plan that combines basic and major medical coverages in a single plan.

Compulsory Retirement—When the employee must retire when he or she reaches a given age. Now prohibited under ADEA if based solely on age, except for certain executives or where public safety outweighs individual protection (e.g., airline pilots). Also known as *automatic* or *mandatory retirement.*

Computer Language—A group of symbols, numbers, letters, words or a combination of these that can be used to communicate with the computer and cause it to perform desired operations for processing data.

Computerized Axial Tomography (CAT) Scanner—Uses a minicomputer and highly sensitive X-ray detectors to produce extremely accurate three-dimensional pictures of body and brain tissues.

Concierge Benefits—Any kind of convenience service offered by an employer to employees, such as errand service (drycleaning pickup, shopping, waiting for the cable repair person) or onsite services (banking, medical services, mail room services). The benefits help employees balance work and personal needs and improve morale and productivity.

Concurrent Review—The process by which hospital admissions for elective and emergency treatment are certified for appropriateness at the time of service and by which continued stays are verified for medical necessity and level of care.

Condemnation—Taking private property for public use, with compensation to the owner, under the right of eminent domain, a power granted the government by the Constitution.

Conditional Vesting—That form of vesting under which entitlement to a vested benefit is conditional upon the nonwithdrawal of the participant's contributions.

Conduit IRA—While retirement funds are being rolled over from one qualified pension plan to another, a conduit IRA is used to temporarily hold the transferring funds.

Conflict of Interest—A situation that provides potential for self-dealing. For example, a trustee has a conflict of interest if he or she has an interest in a construction project to be financed by the plan the trustee represents.

Conglomerate—A corporation that has diversified its operations, usually by acquiring enterprises in widely varied industries.

Congress of Industrial Organizations (CIO)—A federation primarily made up of industrial unions originally established in 1935 as a committee within the AFL (the Committee for Industrial Organization) and later becoming an independent body. In 1955, the Congress of Industrial Organizations merged with the AFL to form the AFL-CIO, with which most, although not all, major U.S. unions are affiliated. See also American Federation of Labor.

Consideration—One of the elements of a binding contract. Consideration is acceptance by the insurance company of the payment of the premium and the statements made by the prospective insured in the application. Also means that each party to a contract has received or been promised something of value from the other party.

Consolidated Omnibus Budget Reconciliation Act of 1985 (COBRA)—Among the provisions of this legislation that deal with health care coverage are the following:

1. Employer-provided medical plans can no longer require Medicare to be the primary payer for participants age 70 and over.
2. Medicare coverage is extended to state and local government employees.
3. Almost every group health plan must provide each participant and qualified beneficiary under the plan the option to pay for continued coverage for a specified period of time under the plan in the event coverage would otherwise have ceased as a result of one of a number of "qualifying events."

Construction Loan—See Building Loan.

Constructive Receipt—Federal tax law doctrine that maintains compensation becomes taxable when it is made available to the taxpayer, even though it has not actually been received. If an employee can choose between immediate taxable income or a deferred income or benefit, the employee is in constructive receipt of the income. See also Economic Benefit.

Consultant—A person or firm specializing in the design, sale and service of employee benefit plans.

Consumer Price Index (CPI)—The name given in the United States and Canada to the series of numbers whose ratios measure the relative prices at various times of a fixed market basket of goods and services that typify those bought by urban families. The CPI is a measure of inflation.

Contingency Reserve—That portion of contributions or premiums set aside in a special account to cover possible loss resulting from adverse experience with respect to investments, interest earnings, mortality, withdrawals and so on.

Contingent Annuitant—A person named to receive annuity benefits if the primary annuitant is deceased.

Contingent Annuity Option—An option under which an employee may elect to receive, under certain conditions, a reduced amount of annuity with the same income, or a specified fraction, to be paid after his or her death to another person designated as his or her contingent annuitant, for that person's lifetime. The contingent annuitant is usually the husband or wife. See also Automatic Survivor Coverage; Joint and Survivor Annuity.

Contingent Beneficiary—Person(s) named to receive policy benefits if the primary beneficiary is deceased.

Contingent Employee—Any worker employed on less than a permanent full-time basis and who has no explicit or implicit expectation for continued employment.

Contingent Liabilities—

—Indeterminate liabilities as to either their amount or their occurrence (e.g., lawsuits, warranties or product guarantees).

—(1) The liability imposed because of accidents caused by persons other than employees for whose acts an individual, partnership or corporation may be responsible. (2) A liability that has not yet materialized at the time of financial statement but that might become definite at a future date.

—A liability that may be incurred by an insured as a result of negligence on the part of independent persons hired by the employer to perform work. The most common example is the contingent liability of a principal contractor, which may result from construction operations undertaken by the subcontractors.

Continuation Coverage—Coverage under a health

insurance plan paid for by a qualified beneficiary following the occurrence of a qualifying event under COBRA.

Continuation of Benefits (COB)—Under COBRA, employers have the obligation to make available to employees and their dependents some continued benefit coverage, even after the employment relationship ceases. Employees or dependents must pay for this coverage.

Continued Protection—See Waiver.

Continued Stay Review (CSR)—A review and an initial determination by a utilization review committee, during a patient's hospitalization, of the necessity and appropriateness of continuation of the patient's stay at a hospital level of care; sometimes called *recertification.*

Continuing Care Retirement Community (CCRC)—A residential community which, in exchange for an entrance fee and a monthly charge, guarantees lifetime housing and nursing care as required.

Continuity of Care—The result of a planned treatment program designed to provide the individual patient with the total range of needed services under continuing responsible direction.

Continuous Quality Improvement (CQI)—An approach to quality management that builds on traditional quality assurance methods by emphasizing the organization and systems, the need for objective data with which to analyze and improve processes, and the ideal that systems and performance can always improve even when high standards appear to have been met; similar to total quality management (TQM).

Continuous Service—All creditable service rendered by a member without a break in service including periods of absence for which salary is paid or for military service.

Continuous Service (Canada)—Period during which an employee is continuously employed by the same employer; may be defined in a pension plan (or by law) so as to include certain periods of absence and service with an associated or predecessor employer. To be distinguished from *credited service.*

Contract—A promissory agreement between two or more persons that creates, modifies or destroys a legal relation. In general, it must have the following elements: creates an obligation, competent parties, subject matter, legal consideration, mutuality of agreement, mutuality of obligation, must not be so vague or uncertain that terms are not ascertainable, and generally is in writing signed by both parties.

Contract Administrator—See Third Party Administrator.

Contract Group—See Enrolled Group.

Contract In/Out (International Benefits)—*Contracted out* refers to an employer providing benefits in lieu of the state earnings-related social security pension. If an employer is contracted in, the employee participates in the state earnings-related scheme.

Contract Term—The period of time, usually 12 months, for which a contract is written.

Contractholder—The group, entity or person to whom a group annuity contract is issued—in jointly administered plans, the trustees.

Contrarian—A common stock manager whose style of management places emphasis on stocks currently out of favor.

Contribution—The transfer of funds or property by either an employer or an employee to an employee benefit plan.

Contribution Carryover—This is created whenever annual contributions exceed the maximum allowable deductions. This carryover can be deducted in future years in which contribution payments are less than the maximum deduction.

Contribution Formula—As used under a qualified profit-sharing trust or money purchase pension plan, it is the formula that spells out when and in what amounts the employer will make contributions to the trust.

Contribution Limit—The maximum dollar limit on annual additions (employer contributions, certain employee contributions and forfeitures) for an employee under defined contribution plans of an employer.

Contribution Rate—

—As to an employee—a factor, such as a percentage of compensation, used in determining the amounts of payments to be made by the employee under a contributory pension plan.

—As to an employer—a factor, calculated in an actuarial valuation, to be used in determining the employer's annual normal cost contribution under a pension plan. An employer's contribution rate may be either a percentage to be applied to the total compensation paid to covered employees for a particular year, or an amount in dollars to be applied to the total number of covered employees at a particular date.

Contribution Requirement—In profit-sharing plans, a definite predetermined contribution formula is not required, but "substantially recurring" contributions must be made out of profits if the requirements of plan permanency are to be met. Nevertheless, liability must be established within the fiscal year.

Contributory Plan—

—A pension or welfare program that provides for employee contributions.

—A benefit plan under which employees bear part of the cost. In some contributory plans, employees wishing to be covered must contribute; in other contributory plans, employee contributions are voluntary and result in increased benefits.

Controlled Company—A company whose policies are controlled by another company through minimum ownership of 51% or more of its voting stock.

Controlled Group—Two or more companies with a defined level of common ownership that are treated as a single company for coverage and nondiscrimination purposes. See also Affiliated Service Group.

Controller—The officer responsible for the accounting function of the business.

Conventional Loan—A mortgage or deed of trust not obtained under a government-insured program, such as FHA or VA. The most prevalent type of mortgage loan made. These may or may not be insured by a private mortgage insurer.

Conversion—

—(Insurance) Privilege given to participant to convert to individual policies on termination of group coverage without evidence of insurability.

—(Investment) A type of options management that involves the purchase of a put option and the sale of a call option. An almost riskless transaction, this is an alternative to money market instruments.

—(Pension Plans) Refers to employers changing from one type of plan to another. For example, from a defined benefit plan to a defined contribution plan, or from a traditional pension plan to a cash balance plan.

Conversion Fund—An unallocated fund held either by a corporate trustee or by an insurance company and used for the purpose of buying annuities to supplement the annuities purchased through individual insurance contracts.

Conversion Option—An instrument that gives the investor the right to switch from fixed rate bonds into common stock.

Conversion Parity—A price of a convertible issue that is equivalent to a given number of common shares or vice versa (e.g., a convertible bond, convertible into four shares of common stock and selling at 100 would have a stock conversion parity of 25).

Conversion Premium (Convertible Securities)—The percentage difference between the conversion value and the market price of a bond or preferred stock.

Conversion Price—The price for which a convertible bond of a corporation may be exchanged for stock of the same corporation.

Conversion Privilege—The right of an individual to convert a group health or life insurance policy to an individual policy should the individual cease to be a member of the group. Under such a provision, a physical examination is usually not required.

Conversion Ratio (Convertible Securities)—The number of shares of common stock received when one bond or one share of preferred stock is converted.

Conversion Value (Convertible Securities)—Current market value of the total number of common shares into which a bond or preferred stock may be converted.

Convertible Bonds or Debentures—Bonds that are convertible into the common stock of a corporation at a prescribed price or ratio at the option of the holder, who is a creditor of the issuer, and who may share in additional profits over and above the coupon's rate of the bond, if the company prospers.

Convertible Mortgage—A mortgage where the pension fund gains interest and appreciation, based on the increase in rent. In addition, the fund has the option (usually between the seventh and tenth year of the loan) to convert into equity ownership, ranging from 50-80%. Primarily made on commercial properties.

Convertible Preferred Stock—Preferred stock that, in addition to having preference as to dividends and/or assets in the event of liquidation, is convertible into the common stock of the company, thereby enabling the holder to share in additional profits via appreciation and/or dividends. See also Cumulative Preferred Stock; Noncumulative Preferred Stock; Participating Preferred Stock; Preferred Stock.

Convertible Term Insurance—Term insurance under which the policy owner has the right (within the limitations stated in the policy) to exchange for insurance on a permanent plan without evidence of insurability.

Coordination of Benefits (COB)—A group health insurance policy provision designed to eliminate duplicate payments and provide the sequence in which coverage will apply (primary and secondary) when a person is insured under two contracts.

Copayments—Payments made by consumers, in addition to deductibles and coinsurance, to discourage inappropriate utilization and to help finance health benefit plans. See also Coinsurance; Deductible.

Core Alternative—Under a 404(c) plan, a participant's choice from at least three diversified investment options.

Core Benefits—The central components of a health care plan, generally comprehensive major medical and hospitalization benefits. These may be supplemented by additional noncore benefits such as dental and vision benefits.

Core Management—A method of supervising a portfolio of securities that is relatively passive in nature. Although fundamental analysis is applied to achieve performance in excess of the market indexes over the long pull, turnover ratios are limited in the interest of reducing transactions costs.

Core-Only Coverage—See Bundling; Unbundling.

Core-Plus Plan—A type of flexible benefits plan that provides a minimum level of benefits to all employees. Individuals then have the option of increasing the levels of some or all of these benefits above the minimums.

Coronary Care Unit (CCU)—A specified unit in a hospital designed to treat patients with serious cardiac diseases through the use of specialized equipment to provide continual monitoring.

Corporate Bond—An instrument written under seal whereby a corporation acknowledges a stated sum is owed, which it will repay at a specified date. It also obligates itself to pay a stipulated amount of interest to the bondholders for the privilege of using their money.

Corporate Governance—The legal and practical system for the exercise and control of power in the conduct of the business of a corporation. Includes relationships among the shareholders, board of directors and committees, and the executive officers.

Corporate Owned Life Insurance (COLI)—A policy covering an executive who is essential to an organization. The organization is the beneficiary; if the executive dies while covered, the organization pays an equivalent noninsured amount to designated survivors. Policy loans on the insurance are available to the organization; the interest is partially deductible. See also Split Dollar Insurance.

Corporation—An artificial being composed of one or more individuals and established by law for some specific purpose or purposes whose existence, power and scope of action are determined by its charter. The owners are not personally liable for any debts of the corporation.

Correspondent—A securities firm, bank or organization that regularly performs services for another in a place or market to which the other does not have direct access. Securities firms may have correspondents in foreign countries or on exchanges of which they are not members. Correspondents are frequently linked by private wires. Member organizations of the New York Stock Exchange with offices in New York City may also act as correspondents for out-of-town member organizations that do not maintain New York offices.

Corridor Deductible—A deductible provision separating an underlying basic medical expense plan from a supplementary major medical plan, which represents a margin of covered expenses to be borne by covered persons before the major medical plan provides benefits.

Cosmetic Treatment—
—Services provided by surgeons or dentists that are not deemed medically necessary.
—An operation aimed at improving appearance, except when required for prompt repair of accidental injury or for the improvement of the functioning of a malformed body part.

Cost Accounting—An accounting process that provides for accumulating all costs incurred to accomplish a purpose or to complete a unit of work on a specific job.

Cost Accounting Standards Board (CASB)—The managerial accounting equivalent of FASB.

Cost Approach—One of the two groups of basic approaches to attributing pension benefits or costs to periods of service. Approaches in this group assign net pension costs to periods as level amounts or constant percentages of compensation. See also Aggregate Actuarial Cost Method; Attained Age Actuarial Cost Method; Entry Age Actuarial Cost Method; Individual Level Actuarial Cost Method.

Cost/Benefit Analysis—A comparison of the cost of an action with the economic benefits it produces through elimination of other direct and indirect costs.

Cost/Compensation Approach—One of two cost approaches. Net pension costs under this approach are attributed to periods so that they are a constant percentage of compensation for each period.

Cost Containment—Activities aimed at holding down the cost of medical care or reducing its rate of increase.

Cost of Living—The average cost of the goods and services required by a person or family. Compare with Standard of Living.

Cost-of-Living Adjustment (COLA)—
—An across-the-board increase (or decrease) in wages or pension benefits according to the rise (or fall) in the cost of living as measured by some index, often the Consumer Price Index (CPI).
—In expatriate compensation, the amount by which base pay is increased or decreased to adjust for a geographic area's cost of living.

Cost Plus—A reimbursement formula whereby a medical provider or supplier is paid its costs, plus a percentage above the costs.

Cost Reimbursement—Method of provider reimbursement based on actual costs incurred.

Cost Sharing—Arrangements whereby consumers pay a portion of the cost of health services, sharing costs with employers. Deductibles, copayments, coinsurance and payroll deductions are forms of cost sharing.

Cost Shifting—
—(Employer) Policies designed to shift the relative burden of health care costs borne by one party or market segment to another. For example, many employers are shifting a portion of the costs of care to employees by copayments and increased contributions.
—(Provider) The practice by some providers of redistributing the difference between normal charges and amounts received from certain payers by increasing charges made to other payers.

Costing Benefits—The process of calculating how much each employee benefit costs the organization and also how much the entire benefits package costs.

Coupon—A certificate attached to a bond, which represents an obligation for interest on the bond. The coupons are in ticket form so they can be clipped off as they become due, and sold or deposited in a bank the same way as cash or a check.

Coupon Billing System—Employers provide qualified beneficiaries with payment coupon books so they can keep track of their premium payments, which are needed for their continuation coverage to remain in effect.

Coupon Bond—A negotiable bond, the regular interest of which is payable to the person who clips the coupon and deposits it at his or her bank for collection. Upon maturity, the bearer is paid the face value of the security.

Coupon Rate—The contract interest rate on the face of a note.

Coupon Stripping—The process of separating the interest payments of a bond from the principal amount that is due at maturity. Once separated, each coupon, as well as the principal amount (the corpus), represents a different single payment claim due from the issuer of the security. Each single payment claim, then, becomes tantamount to a zero-coupon bond. By "stripping" a bond, a yield curve of zero-coupon bonds can be created; the maturity of each may be used independently. For example, if $1 million par amount of a 14% bond due in ten years was stripped, the result would be a series of 20 semiannual zero-coupon bonds, each with a par value of $70,000, and one ten-year zero coupon bond, with a par value of $1 million.

Covariance—A measure of the degree to which two variables move together. A positive value means that, on average, they move in the same direction.

Coverage—
- —Describes the employees eligible for participation under an employee benefit plan.
- —Benefits available to eligible individuals under an employee benefit program.
- —With reference to revenue and corporate bonds, it indicates margin of safety for payment of debt service, reflecting the number of times by which earnings for a period of time exceed debt service payable in such period.

Covered Call—A call whose seller (writer) owns the underlying security (or a call thereon with an exercise price equal to or less than the exercise price of the call sold) or a security convertible into the underlying security; or a call whose holder has sold the underlying security short.

Covered Call Writer—An investor who sells a call against a stock that he or she owns (or is simultaneously buying).

Covered Compensation—The amount of compensation for which old age and survivors insurance benefits would be provided under the Social Security Act computed as though, for each year until the employee reaches age 65, his or her annual compensation is at least equal to the taxable wage base.

Covered Employee—A person covered by a pension plan is one who has fulfilled the eligibility requirements in the plan; for whom benefits have accrued, or are accruing; or who is receiving benefits under the plan.

Covered Expenses—Hospital, medical and related costs incurred by those covered under the insurance policy that qualify for reimbursement according to the terms of the contract. Most commonly used in regard to major medical plans.

Covered Option—A situation in which the writer (seller) of the option owns the underlying stock.

Covered Put—A put whose seller (writer) owns a put on the same underlying security with an exercise price equal to or greater than the exercise price of the put written, or who has sold the underlying security short; or a put whose holder owns the underlying security or a security convertible into the underlying security.

Covered Put Writer—An investor who writes a put while owning a put of the same class with an equal or longer expiration date and an equal or higher exercise price.

Covered Service—Period of employment during which an employee is a participant in an employee benefit plan.

Covering—Buying a security previously sold short.

Credentialing—Obtaining and reviewing the documentation of professional providers. Such documentation includes licensure, certifications, insurance, evidence of malpractice insurance, malpractice history and so forth.

Credit—
- —The relative financial standing of one company versus another in terms of what it will be charged to raise funds as regards the amount and interest to be paid.
- —(Canada) An entitlement to a pension benefit that is payable sometime in the future.

Credit Analysis—A report that uses the Standard & Poor's rating system to analyze the credit quality of bond holdings, with AAA being the highest rating granted. Bonds rated BBB and above are considered "investment grade."

Credit Carryover—This is created when the contribution formula calls for an annual contribution less than the maximum allowable deduction. Unused credit is carried forward and may be applied in a future year.

Credit Rating—An assessment of the factors that determine the financial soundness of a borrower. For example, a person or corporation with a strong financial position, good income prospects and a low level of indebtedness in relation to total net worth is given a high credit rating. In contrast, an entity with a weak financial position, poor income prospects and a high level of debt in relation to net worth gets a low credit rating.

Credit Splitting (Canada)—A provision in a pension plan or legislation entitling a spouse, on divorce or breakup, to a share of pension credits earned by the other during the marriage or thereafter.

Credited Projected Benefits—See Projected Benefits.

Credited Service—A period of employment before or after the effective date of the plan that is recognized as service for one or more plan purposes, such as determination of benefit amounts, entitlement to benefits and/or vesting.

Crossover Patient—A patient who has both Medicare and Medicaid coverage.

Cumulative Bulletin (CB)—A government publication in which revenue rulings and other pertinent IRS pronouncements are published. The *Cumulative Bulletin* is published semiannually and incorporates the materials that were published weekly by the IRS in its *Internal Revenue Bulletins*.

Cumulative Preferred Stock—Preferred stock having a provision that, if one or more dividends are omitted on the preferred, the omitted dividends must be paid before any dividends may be paid on the common stock. See also Convertible Preferred Stock; Noncumulative Preferred Stock; Participating Preferred Stock; Preferred Stock.

Cumulative Rate of Return—A compounded rate of return covering more than one period or year.

Cumulative Trauma Disorder—A work-related disorder which develops over time as a result of worker exposure to ergonomic hazards.

Cumulative Voting—A system under which each stockholder is able to accumulate his or her votes and cast them for less than the total number of directors being elected. For example, assume one vote per share, 100 shares owned, and six directors to be elected. Under the regular method, the shareholder can cast up to 100 votes for each candidate, for a total of 600 votes. Under cumulative voting, a shareholder can cast up to 600 votes for any one candidate. This method improves minority shareholders' chances of naming a representative to the board of directors.

Currency Devaluation—Action by the government or by the marketplace to reduce the value of a currency in relation to the currencies of other nations.

Currency Exchange Rate—See Exchange Rate.

Current Asset Value—The value of the current assets available to a particular class of security after deducting all prior liability.

Current Assets—Those assets of a company that are reasonably expected to be realized in cash, or sold, or consumed during the normal operating cycle of the business. These include cash, U.S. government bonds, receivables, money due (usually within one year) and inventories.

Current Liability—What a pension plan would owe to beneficiaries if it terminated.

Current Procedural Terminology (CPT)—A coding system developed by the American Medical Association to categorize medical procedures for billing purposes.

Current Profit-Sharing Plan—See Profit-Sharing Plan.

Current Service Benefit—

—The annuity payable for each year of participation in the plan after its adoption.

—That portion of a participant's retirement benefit that relates to his or her credited service in a contemporary period (usually a year).

Current Service (Canada)—Period of service of an employee after becoming a member of a pension plan. *Current service cost* usually refers to the cost of benefits credited to members of a plan in a given year.

Current Service Cost—See Normal Cost; Normal Actuarial Cost.

Current Value—Fair market value, where available. Otherwise, it is the fair value as determined in good faith by a trustee or a named fiduciary pursuant to the terms of the plan and in accordance with regulations of the secretary of labor, assuming an orderly liquidation at the time of such determination.

Current Yield—Annual bond interest divided by market price per bond.

Currently Insured—As applied to Social Security, a worker must have a minimum of six quarters of coverage that were earned in the most recent 13-quarter period.

Custodial Arrangement—Simple warehousing of securities by a bank for purposes of safekeeping. The bank may collect income and do simple reporting on the value of the assets. The bank does not have fiduciary responsibility.

Custodial Care—General assistance in performing the activities of daily living, as well as board, room and other services, generally provided on a long-term basis and that do not include a medical component.

Custodian—The organization (usually a bank) that holds in custody and safekeeping the securities and other assets of a mutual fund or trust. The bank does not have fiduciary responsibility.

Customary Charge—The most a Medicare carrier will approve for payment for a particular service provided by a particular physician practice, barring special circumstances. The carrier calculates this maximum from data on actual charges for a specific service performed by one physician for all his or her patients.

Customary, Prevailing and Reasonable (CPR)—A payment system used by Medicare to approve charges for Part B services. The approved charge is the lowest of the physician's actual charge, the physician's customary charge and charges by peers in the geographic area.

Cutoff Date—Date after which no prior service is credited.

Cutting a Loss—The decision to close out an unprofitable market position and take the loss involved before it becomes larger.

Cyclical Stocks—Stocks that move directly with the business cycle; i.e., generally, they advance as business conditions improve and decline when business slackens. Steel, chemical, textile and machinery stocks are included in this category. To offset cyclical factors, many companies today are striving to diversify their operations among other fields and products.

D

D—Quality rating assigned by Standard & Poor's for speculative grade bonds. A debt rated *D* is in default and payment of interest and/or repayment of principal is in arrears.

Damages—The amount claimed or allowed as compensation for injuries sustained or property damaged through the wrongful acts or the negligence of another; an award.

Day Care (Adult)—See Adult Day Care.

Day Order—An order to buy or sell (a security) that, if not executed, expires at the end of the trading day on which it was entered.

Day Surgery—See Outpatient Surgery.

De Minimis Benefit—Any property or service that an employer provides to an employee, if the value of such property or service is so minimal that accounting for it would be unreasonable or administratively impractical. The employee can exclude from income the value of these benefits.

De Minimis Rule—In the plan termination context, a rule that may reduce or eliminate small amounts of multiemployer withdrawal liability.

Dealer—An individual or firm in the securities business acting as a principal rather than as an agent. Typically, a dealer buys for his or her own account and sells to a customer from his or her own inventory.

Death Benefit—The payment made to designated beneficiaries upon the death of a participating employee. This could be the employee's share in the investment fund, the life insurance purchased for him or her, or both.

Death Rate—The proportion of persons who die within a year, usually expressed as so many per 1,000.

Debenture—A corporate obligation sold as an investment. Similar to a corporate bond but not secured by a trust deed. It is not like corporate stock.

Debenture Bonds—Bonds backed by the general credit of the issuer but not secured by a specific lien on property.

Debt—Something owed by one person to another. Debt securities are loans at a specified rate of return for a specified period of time.

Debt Limit or Ceiling—The maximum debt that can be legally created by a state or local government.

Debt Service—The sum of money required periodically to make the payments necessary to amortize a debt and interest charges, the principal and interest payments.

Debt-to-Equity Ratio—A measure of the relative amount of funds provided by lenders and owners.

$$\text{Debt/Equity Ratio} = \frac{\text{Long-Term Debt}}{\text{Stockholder's Equity}}$$

Decrement—An event that can trigger payment or nonpayment of a benefit. For example, termination can trigger a termination benefit, or prevent obtaining a retirement benefit. An actuarial assumption for this type of event is also termed a *decrement.*

Dedicated Bond Portfolio—Portfolio designed to meet a specific set of future benefit payments with the cash flow from the bonds held in a portfolio. The most common application of the dedicated portfolio concept is in funding benefits due to retired employees. Ideally, the cash flow from the portfolio exactly matches each future payment, both in amount and timing. If this exact matching is achieved, the funding of future payments will *not* depend on the level of interest rates in the future. The actuary may then raise the actuarial assumption to a market rate of interest. This reduces the actuarial liability of the plan and could substantially lower its annual funding costs.

Deductible—The amount of out-of-pocket expenses that must be paid for health services by the insured before becoming payable by the carrier. Most common in major medical policies, but also found in basic policies. See also Family Deductible; First Dollar Coverage.

Deductible Carryover—A feature whereby covered charges in the last three months of the year may be carried over to be counted toward the next year's deductible. See also Carryover Deductible.

Deed—A written instrument, signed, sealed and delivered according to the applicable law, containing some transfer, bargain or contract with respect to property; the common term for an instrument transferring the ownership of real property.

Deed of Trust—Written instrument by which title to land is transferred to a trustee as security for a debt or other obligation. See also Mortgage.

Deep-Discount Debt—Debt issued with a stated interest rate significantly less than the effective interest rate.

Default—The nonperformance of a duty, whether arising under a contract or otherwise; failure to meet an obligation when due.

Defensive Industry—An industry relatively unaffected by business cycles, such as the food industry or the utility industry.

Defensive Issues—Issues of established companies in industries relatively unaffected by business cycles.

Defensive Medicine—The practice by physicians of authorizing medically unnecessary tests and procedures, increasing hospital admissions and extending lengths of stay in an attempt to limit their exposure to malpractice suits.

Defensive Portfolio—Consists mainly of short maturity bonds, preferred stocks or other securities that are unlikely to fluctuate much in either direction. Compare with Aggressive Portfolio.

Deferred Annuity—Annuity contract providing for the initiation of payments at some designated future date or age. Contrast with Immediate Annuity.

Deferred Assets; Deferred Charges—Assets that are prepaid—such as advertising, insurance and rent, development expense, organizational expense and unamortized bond discount—which therefore are not immediately charged off, because they apply to future years' operations. That portion applicable to the next 12 months may be included as a current asset.

Deferred Compensation Plan—Any plan where employees can accumulate money on a tax-deferred basis. A qualified plan can have the option of permitting employees to withdraw assets without penalty for certain "emergency" situations specified in the plan. Many also give employees the option of taking the benefit in cash. A deferred compensation plan can be combined with other plans, such as profit-sharing plans.

Deferred Payments—Provisions in a mortgage allowing for the postponement of principal or interest payments. Mortgages on new commercial buildings or apartment houses often need a grace period in which to obtain tenants in order to build up the income stream.

Deferred Premium Plan—A funding arrangement that extends the grace period beyond the normal 31 days, usually to 60 or 90 days.

Deferred Profit-Sharing Plan—A plan established and maintained by an employer to provide for participation in its profits by its employees or their beneficiaries. The plan must provide a definite predetermined formula for allocating the contributions made to the plan among the participants and for distributing funds accumulated under the plan after a fixed number of years, the attainment of a stated age, or upon the prior occurrence of some event such as layoff, illness, disability, retirement, death or severance of employment.

Deferred Retirement—When the employee works past normal retirement age.

Deferred Vested Pension—For terminating employees, a plan offering a pension, usually deferred until retirement. Benefits are determined when employment is terminated.

Deferred Vesting—That form of vesting under which rights to vested benefits are acquired by a participant commencing on the fulfillment of specified requirements (usually in terms of attained age, years of service and/or plan membership).

Deferred Wage Concept—The forgoing of a present increase in wages for employee benefits or a pension plan.

Deficit—

—As a balance sheet item, the amount by which assets fall short of meeting the sum of liabilities plus capital stock.

—The money a government or business pays out in excess of what it takes in over a given period.

Deficit Reduction Act of 1984 (DEFRA)—One part of this act was the Tax Reform Act of 1984. DEFRA had a major impact on employee benefits in the following areas:

- 501(c)(9) trusts and experience-rated plans—prohibits tax deductions for contributions to trusts or premiums paid to experience-rated plans if reserves for benefits exceed certain limits
- Flexible benefit plans and flexible spending accounts—excludes most taxable benefits from being offered
- Health care for dependents—requires companies to give employee spouses who are senior citizens the opportunity to enroll in corporate health insurance programs.

Deficit Reduction Contribution—An amount in addition to the required minimum annual contribution if the pension plan is less than 100% funded. It consists of old liabilities (such as benefit increases granted before 1988), which are to be amortized over 18 years, and a share of new liabilities (resulting from benefit increases or plan amendments).

Defined Benefit Formulas—See Flat Benefit Formula; Flat Percentage of Earnings Formula; Percentage of Earnings Per Year of Service Formula.

Defined Benefit Limitation—The maximum annual benefit allowed by the Internal Revenue Code that a participant may receive from a qualified retirement plan.

Defined Benefit Plan—Both ERISA and the Internal Revenue Code define a *defined benefit plan* as any plan that is not an individual account plan. Under a defined benefit plan, there is a definite formula by which the employee's benefits will be measured. This formula may provide that benefits be a particular percentage of the employee's average compensation over his or her entire service or over a particular number of years; it may provide for a flat monthly payment; or it may provide a definite amount for each year of service, expressed either as a percentage of his or her compensation for each year of service or as a flat dollar amount for each year of service. In plans of this type, the employer's contributions are determined actuarially. No individual accounts are maintained as is done in the defined contribution plans. (Defined benefit plans are subject to regulation by the PBGC and are "pension plans" under the Internal Revenue Code. That is, they are designed primarily for retirement.)

Defined Benefit Plan (Canada)—An occupational pension plan that provides members with benefits directly related to their salaries and years of service.

Defined Contribution Approach (Health Insurance)—A retiree health program that commits to a specified level of annual contributions to an employee's health care account during his or her working years. The value of the account at retirement is used to provide health care benefits.

Defined Contribution Limit—The maximum contributions and additions an employer may make on behalf of a pension plan participant.

Defined Contribution Plan—A *defined contribution* or *individual account plan* is defined by the Internal Revenue Code and ERISA as a plan that provides for an individual account for each participant and for benefits based solely on (1) the amount contributed to the participant's account plus (2) any income, expenses, gains and losses, and forfeitures of accounts of other participants that may be allocated to the participant's account. 401(k), 403(b) and 457 plans are defined contribution plans. See also Individual Account Plan.

Defined Dollar Approach (Health Insurance)—A retiree health program that provides a specific value of benefits at retirement, defined in dollar terms, rather than a specified level of care as with traditional indemnity plans.

Defined Plan Limits—See Maximum Plan Limits.

Definitely Determinable Benefits—A mandatory requirement for a service benefit pension plan. For variations, see also Money Purchase Plan; Target Benefit Plan.

Deflation—A phase of the business cycle during which consumer spending is seriously curtailed, bank loans contract and the amount of money in circulation is reduced. (Antonym: inflation).

Delayed Retirement—See Deferred Retirement.

Delinquent Contributions—Failure by a participating employer to make promised payments to a multiemployer benefit fund.

Demand—The amount of a given service sought by consumers in response to their perceived need for that service.

Demand Management—The combination of strategies such as preventive health, health promotion, self-care guidelines, patient education programs and company practices that is designed to reduce actual and perceived need for health care services and promote and support informed, appropriate health care decision making, thereby reducing costs.

Demographics—The statistical study of the characteristics of a given population. May include such factors as birth rate, age and sex composition, marital status, income, employment, urban/rural distribution and mobility.

Dental Insurance—Typically a part of an employer's health insurance plan, generally covering the following dental services: diagnostic, preventive, restorative, oral and maxillofacial surgery, periodontics, prosthodontics and orthodontics.

Department of Health and Human Services (DHHS)—See Health and Human Services Department.

Department of Labor (DOL)—The nontax (regulatory and administrative) provisions of ERISA are administered by the Department of Labor. The Department issues opinion letters and other pronouncements, and requires certain information forms to be filed.

Dependent—Generally the spouse or child of a covered individual, as defined in a contract. Can be any person who relies on, or obtains coverage through, a covered individual.

Dependent Care Assistance Plan (DCAP)—Employer provides assistance to employees by reimbursing them for dependent care expenses, paying day-care centers directly or supplying dependent care services.

Dependent Care Spending Account—Employer-sponsored flexible benefits plan feature that permits employees to use pretax (tax-free) dollars from their paychecks to pay the cost of care for children or elderly dependents up to a certain legislated limit and within very specific guidelines.

Dependent Child's Benefit (Canada)—Under the Quebec Pension Plan (QPP), a monthly amount payable to each dependent child of a disability pensioner or deceased contributor.

Depletion Accounting—Natural resources, such as metals, oil, gas and timber, that conceivably can be reduced to zero over the years, present a special accounting problem. Depletion is an accounting practice consisting of charges against earnings based upon the amount of the asset taken out of the total reserves in the period for which accounting is made. A bookkeeping entry, it does not represent any cash outlay; no funds are earmarked for that purpose.

Depletion Reserve—The amount set aside that reflects the total accrued depletion to date for a particular balance sheet item (e.g., timber, ore), which sum must be subtracted from the applicable item to obtain its unamortized or net value.

Deployment—The act of committing fund money among alternative asset categories.

Depository Trust Company (DTC)—A limited purpose trust company and a member of the Federal Reserve system. The company was established to meet a recognized need for a system to reduce the volume of physical transfers of securities from vault to vault. Security holdings of a variety of financial institutions—banks, broker-dealers, investment companies and so on—are on deposit with the company so that transfers among participants can be made by relatively simple bookkeeping entries with no physical movement of securities.

Depreciation—Normally, charges against earnings to write off the cost, less salvage value, of an asset over its estimated useful life. It is a bookkeeping entry and does not represent any cash outlay nor are any funds earmarked for this purpose.

Depreciation—All Causes—Loss in value from any cause in comparison with a new item or property of like kind resulting from physical deterioration, functional obsolescence and economic obsolescence.

Economic obsolescence—Loss in value caused by unfavorable conditions usually external to the property such as the local economy, economics of the industry, encroachment of objectionable enterprises, loss of material and labor sources, lack of efficient transportation, shifting of business center, passage of new legislation, changes in ordinances and so forth.

Functional obsolescence—Loss in value caused by conditions within the property such as changes in design, materials or process resulting in inadequacy, overcapacity, excess construction, lack of utility or excess operating costs.

Physical deterioration—Loss in value caused by physical deterioration resulting from wear and tear in operation and exposure to the elements.

Depreciation Reserve—A sum that reflects the total depreciation value to date and, therefore, the expired portion of the useful life of the assets to which it is applicable. The residual value of the asset may or may not be its true market value.

Depression—A prolonged period of sharply reduced business activity characterized by widespread unemployment, low production, a contraction of credit and a drop in consumer buying.

Derivative—A financial contract to pay or receive money in the future based on the performance of some underlying asset such as a currency of a portfolio of stocks or bonds.

Determination Letter—Issued by the office of a district director of the IRS, the letter states whether or not the submitted plan meets the qualification requirements under the Internal Revenue Code.

Determination Period—The 12-month period used for computing the premium to be charged for continuation coverage under COBRA.

Diagnosis-Related Group (DRG)—A prospective hospital claims reimbursement system first implemented by the Medicare program. The reimbursement amount for an episode of care does not reflect actual cost for that care. Reimbursement is based on a predetermined classification of diagnoses, treatments, age, sex and discharge status of patients. This system is also used by some states for all payers. Also called *diagnostic related group.*

Diagnostic Center—A facility, either freestanding or hospital based, specializing in the diagnosis of illnesses and injuries.

Dialysis—A process by which dissolved substances (waste products) are removed from a patient's body by diffusion from one fluid compartment to another across a semipermeable membrane. Regular treatment for ESRD patients.

Direct Contracting—A cost-containment strategy involving an exclusive contractual arrangement between an employer and a provider for health care services, usually obtained at reduced prices for employee groups. This may be accomplished without going through a health plan.

Direct Participation Program—An investment that is managed and structured as a limited partnership rather than as a corporation so that the investment's gains, losses, income and expenses may pass directly to the individual owners. A term generally associated with a limited partnership tax shelter offering.

Direct Placement—See Private Placement.

Direct Service Plan—See Prepaid Group Practice.

Directed Brokerage Options—See Self-Directed Brokerage Accounts.

Directed Commissions—Those commissions charged by a broker for executing securities transactions that are placed by the investment manager with a particular broker, or brokers, resulting from instructions received from the client of the manager.

Directed Trust—A trust under which the trustee has less than full managerial authority. This will be the case whenever someone other than a trustee has the power to control particular actions of the trustee.

ERISA contemplates three different kinds of directed trusts. A plan may call for the shift of authority over assets, to whatever extent is desired, from the trustee to plan participants or beneficiaries in respect of the assets allocated to their own individual accounts, or to a "named fiduciary who is not a trustee," or to an investment manager.

Director—A person elected by shareholders to establish company policies. The directors appoint the president, vice president and all other operating officers. Directors decide, among other matters, if and when dividends shall be paid.

Disability—A condition that renders an insured person incapable of performing one or more duties of his or her regular occupation. Benefit plan definitions of *disability* vary. The Social Security Act defines *disability* as follows:

> (Total disability is the) inability to engage in any substantial, gainful activity by reason of any medically determinable physical or mental impairment which can be expected to result in death or has lasted or can be expected to last for a continuous period of not less than 12 months (and which precludes the claimant from performing not only his previous work, but considering his age, education and work experience any other kind of substantial gainful work which exists in the national economy regardless of whether such work exists in the immediate area in which he lives, or whether a specific job vacancy exists for him, or whether he would be hired if he applied for the work).

Disability Benefit—Periodic payments, usually monthly, payable to participants under some retirement plans if such participants are eligible for the benefits and become totally and permanently disabled prior to the normal retirement date.

Disability Income Insurance—A form of health insurance that provides periodic payments to replace a certain percentage of income lost when the insured is unable to work as a result of illness, injury or disease.

Disability Management—The proactive employer-centered process of coordinating the activities of labor, management, insurance carriers, health care providers and vocational rehabilitation professionals in order to minimize the impact of injury, disability or disease on a worker's capacity to successfully perform his or her job.

Disability Pension—The annuity that is payable in the event that an employee becomes disabled before the age of normal retirement.

Disability Retirement—A termination of employment, generally involving the payment of a retirement allowance, as a result of an accident or sickness occurring before a participant is eligible for normal retirement.

Disbursed Self-Funded Plan—In this type of self-insured or self-funded plan, employees' claims are paid directly out of the company's cash flow as part of the expense of doing business; thus, claims settlements are tax deductible when they are paid, not when they are incurred. The company sets aside no reserves and pays no premiums or expense load to an insurer. Most companies that employ a disbursed self-funded plan buy stop-loss insurance, usually in the range of 120% of expected claims, in order to protect themselves against a significantly poorer-than-expected experience. See also 501(c)(9) Trust; Self-Insurance.

Discharge Planning—A centralized, coordinated program developed by a hospital to ensure that each patient has a planned program for needed continuing or followup care.

Disclaimer—A statement denying legal responsibility for the accuracy or correctness of the presented facts.

Disclosure—The requirement of plan administrators to distribute or make available to plan participants and/or other beneficiaries materials such as summary plan descriptions and annual reports.

Discount—
- —The difference between the original offering price of a security and the price to which it may fall in the "after offering" market.
- —The amount by which a security sells below its face value (par value). A $1,000 par value bond selling at 95 (worth $950) would be selling at a $50 or 5% discount. (Antonym: premium)

Discount Bond—A bond that may be purchased below par (i.e., 1,000), thereby producing a higher yield to maturity and, in most cases, reducing the risk of call. As a general rule, the greater the discount, the lesser the chances of call and the greater the bond's attraction. Interest is paid upon presentation of the coupon attached to the bond.

Discount Factor—The factor used to calculate the present value of dollars due in the future.

Discount Rate—
- —The interest rate the Federal Reserve Bank charges to member banks for loans.
- —The percentage rate used to calculate the present value of future cash flows.

Discounted Fee-for-Service—A health maintenance organization (HMO) payment structure in which physicians are paid a certain percentage of their normal fees.

Discounted Note—On discounted notes payable, the interest is deducted from the maturity value of the note at the time the note is issued.

Discounted Restricted Stock Purchase—The employee purchases restricted stock from the employer at a price lower than the current market price of the stock.

Discounting for Mortality—The assumption that specified proportions of employees will receive retirement benefits. Contribution rates or benefit costs so calculated have been discounted for mortality.

Discretionary Account—An account in which the customer gives the broker or someone else discretion, which may be complete or within specific limits, as to the purchase and sale of securities or commodities, including selection, timing, amount and price to be paid or received.

Discretionary Formula—A profit-sharing plan contribution arrangement that enables the employer annually to determine or change the amount or the formula for its plan contribution.

Discrimination—
- —Occurs when a plan discriminates in favor of highly compensated employees, officers or stockholders; steps must be taken to avoid or rectify such discrimination in order to retain qualified status.
- —It is permissible to discriminate by group definition, such as salaried only, union employees only or hourly workers only.
- —Artificial, arbitrary and unnecessary barriers that bring about disparate treatment of certain groups, based upon race, sex, religion, national origin, age or other such classification. Discrimination also may include the failure to remedy the effects of past discrimination.

Disease Management—Comprehensive, integrated systems approach that targets costly, chronic diseases. Aims to control costs by using the most effective treatments as early as possible.

Disease Prevention—A method of protecting as many people as possible from the consequences of a particular disease or environmental hazard.

Disenrollment—Termination of an employee's health care coverage, whether voluntary or involuntary.

Disinsured—Unemployed workers no longer covered by group insurance.

Dismemberment—The loss, or loss of use, of a limb or loss of sight from an injury.

Disposable Personal Income—Income of individuals after taxes are paid.

Disqualification—Loss of tax-favored, or qualified, status.

Disqualified Benefit—In a welfare benefit fund context, a portion of the fund that reverts to the benefit of the employer or a postretirement medical or life insurance benefit provided either under a discriminatory plan or with respect to a key employee but not made from the mandatory separate account. The employer is subject to an excise tax equal to 100% of the disqualified benefit.

Disqualified Person—The IRC term roughly equivalent to *party in interest.* The term *disqualified person* also includes a highly compensated employee. See also Party in Interest; Prohibited Transaction.

Distress Termination—An underfunded pension plan that is terminated by a company with financial problems.

Distribution—A payment to a participant or beneficiary such as a mutual fund's payment to shareholders of the profits, interest or dividends it has earned on its investments.

Divergent Investments—See Socially Responsible Investments.

Diversification—The spreading of investment funds among different securities, issuers, maturity dates and localities in order to distribute the risk.

Divestiture—

—The antitrust remedy that forces a company to get rid of assets acquired through illegal mergers or monopolistic practices.

—The decision to purge a portfolio from holding the stock, or in some cases any securities issued, of corporations that do business in certain countries. The intent is to bring economic pressure to bear ultimately on the government of the country to reverse its policies in the area of human rights. In a broader sense, divestiture can apply to the purging of a portfolio of holdings whose ownership would be in contradiction to the social/political/religious/philosophical convictions of the sponsor(s), or owner(s), of the portfolio.

Dividend—

—The proportion of net earnings a corporation pays to its stockholders.

—A policyholder's share in the divisible surplus funds of an insurance company apportioned for distribution, which take the form of a refund of part of the premium on a participating policy.

—A *regular dividend* is an established dividend rate fixed by a corporation on its stock and usually paid quarterly or semiannually.

Dividend Equivalents—Some incentive plans provide payments equal to the dividends that are paid per share. Most common in phantom stock plans.

Dividend Options—Different ways an insured under a participating policy may elect to receive his or her share of surplus earnings. These are usually (1) cash, (2) reduction of premium, (3) additional paid-up insurance, (4) on deposit at interest, and (5) additional term insurance.

Dividend Reinvestment Plan—A plan in which dividends paid to a shareholder are reinvested in shares of the company through an agent for the shareholders, normally a bank.

Dividend Yield—Expressed in percent, it is calculated by dividing the dividend rate for the next 12 months by the market price of a stock. Commonly used as a value indicator.

Divisible Surplus—See Dividend.

Division of Pension Credits—See Credit Splitting.

Dollar Averaging; Dollar Cost Averaging—A policy by which the same dollar amount is placed in one or more common stocks at fixed successive intervals, thereby enabling the investor to average the purchase of his or her shares over a good many years. Assuming that each investment is of the same number of dollars, a greater number of shares are purchased when the price is low and fewer when it is high. Thus, a satisfactory average price is obtained, which precludes the investor from buying all the shares at the high levels of the market.

Dollar Temporary Annuity—See Annuity Certain.

Dollar-Weighted Rate of Return—

—This method of calculating rate of return is affected by the amount and the timing of cash flows during a given time period. This rate is an effective measure of the fund's rate of growth, giving full weight to the impact of cash flows on fund assets. The dollar-weighted rate also is referred to as the *internal, discounted cash flow* or the *real rate of return.*

—Assesses what happened to all money available to a given fund during a given period. As such, it is the best way of assessing the actual condition of the fund at any point, but it may not accurately reflect the skill of the investment manager, since he or she has no control over cash flows (deposits, etc.) as to either timing or amount.

Domestic Partner Coverage—Benefit coverage that recognizes as a family the ongoing, personal, intimate and committed relationship between two unrelated people of the same or opposite sex that is the approximate equivalent of marriage, but does not involve formal marriage. Benefit plans that recognize domestic partnerships treat the partners of participants as if they were spouses. Also known as life partners or spousal equivalents.

Double-Breasted Employer—A situation in which an employer conducts parallel business operations, one of which is union and one of which is nonunion.

Double Dipping—Variously applied to mean:

1. Qualifying for, and obtaining, pension benefits under two or more plans
2. Qualifying for, and obtaining, pension benefits under one plan while remaining employed by another employer
3. Qualifying for, and obtaining, Social Security retirement benefits while also qualifying for and obtaining retirement benefits under a civil service retirement system, particularly a federal plan.

Double Indemnity—A provision under which certain benefits are doubled when accident is due to specified circumstances, such as public conveyance accidents; in a life insurance policy, a provision that the face amount payable on death will be doubled if the death is the result of an accident.

Double Taxation—"Double taxation of dividends." The federal government taxes corporate profits once as corporate income; any part of the remaining profits distributed as dividends to stockholders may be taxed again as income to the recipient stockholders, except dividends paid from an ESOP.

Dow Jones Industrial Average (DJIA)—A popular gauge of the stock market based on the average closing prices of active representative stocks, as published by Dow Jones & Co. since July 3, 1884. Nine of the original 11 stocks were rails. The DJ Averages currently consist of 65 stocks (30 industrials, 20 transportation, 15 utilities). They include only high-quality, common stocks listed on the New York Stock Exchange.

Dow Theory—A theory of market analysis based upon the performance of the Dow Jones industrial and transportation stock price averages. The theory says that the market is in a basic upward trend if one of these averages advances above a previous important high, accompanied or followed by a similar advance in the other. When the averages both dip below previous important lows, this is regarded as confirmation of a basic downward trend. The theory does not attempt to predict how long either trend will continue, although it is widely misinterpreted as a method of forecasting future action.

Downcoding—A practice of third party payers in which the benefits code has been changed to a less complex and/or lower cost procedure than was reported.

Downsizing—The action taken by an organization in an effort to eliminate inefficient operations; or the reduction of the number of jobs in the organization.

Downtick—See Uptick.

Dread Disease Policy—A limited form of health insurance that pays for treatment of specified diseases, such as cancer.

DRG—See Diagnosis-Related Group.

DRG Payment Method—An approach to paying for hospital inpatient acute services that bases the unit of payment on the DRG system of classifying patients.

Drop-Out Months (Canada)—Under the Canada Pension Plan, certain low earnings months that are not counted in calculating average contributory earnings on which the contributor's pension is based.

Drug Formulary—A restricted list of prescription medications covered under a managed care plan, which are approved for use for specific treatments and dispensed through participating pharmacies to plan members.

Drug-Free Workplace Act—A federal law that requires employers with $25,000 or more in government contracts to certify that they are running a drug-free workplace.

Drug Testing—Urine tests administered on a pre-employment basis, for probable cause (after accidents), or at random; combinations of these models to comply with the drug-free workplace legislation and to facilitate drug-free workforces.

Drug Utilization Management (DUM)—A set of utilization management techniques for determining whether a prescribed drug therapy is the most appropriate form of therapy and also which drug is both medically appropriate and financially cost-effective for the presenting condition.

Drug Utilization Review (DUR)—A review system to monitor usage of prescriptions by enrollees, to identify potential interactions with other medications, or to identify alternative effective or cost-effective therapies.

Dual Purpose Fund—A type of closed-end investment company that offers two classes of stock: income shares and capital shares. Income shares entitle a holder to all net dividends and interest paid to the fund on both income and capital shares, but do not allow the holder to participate in any capital appreciation. The capital shares entitle the holder to profit from the growth of all the securities held by the fund.

Due Bill—A printed statement showing the transfer of a security's title or rights, or showing the obligation of a seller to deliver the securities or rights to the purchaser.

Due Date—The maturity date; the date when a bond, note or other evidence of debt becomes payable or legally demandable.

Due Diligence—Describes the careful investigation necessary to ensure that all material information pertinent to an issue has been disclosed to the public.

Due Process—Fundamental fairness. Applied to judicial proceedings, it includes adequate notice of a hearing and an opportunity to appear and defend in an orderly tribunal.

Duplication of Benefits—Overlapping or identical coverage of an insured person under two or more health plans, usually the result of contracts with different insurance companies, service organizations or prepayment plans. Synonymous with *multiple coverage.* See also Coordination of Benefits (COB).

Durable Medical Equipment (DME)—Medical equipment which is not disposable (i.e., is used repeatedly) and is only related to care for a medical condition. Examples would include wheelchairs, home hospital beds, and so forth. An area of increasing expense, particularly in conjunction with case management.

Durable Power of Attorney—A power of attorney that continues even if one becomes incompetent.

Duration—Measure of the price change of a bond to a change in its yield to maturity. It summarizes, in a single number, the characteristics that cause bond prices to change in response to a change in interest rates. The price of a bond with a duration of three years will rise by approximately 3% for each 1% decrease in its yield to maturity. That price will decrease 3% for each 1% increase in the bond's yield. Price changes for two different bonds can be compared using duration. A bond with a duration of six years will exhibit twice the percentage price change of a bond with a three-year duration. The actual calculation of a bond's duration is somewhat complicated, but the idea behind the calculation is straightforward. The first step is to measure the time interval until receipt for each cash flow (coupon and principal payments) from a bond. The second step is to compute a weighted average of these time intervals. Each time interval is measured by the present value of that cash flow. This weighted average is the duration of the bond measured in years. A table of bond maturities and durations is shown below.

Duration vs. Maturity

Coupon	14%
Yield to Maturity	14%

Years to Maturity		**Duration**	
1	Years(s)	.97	Year(s)
2	"	1.81	"
3	"	2.55	"
5	"	3.76	"
10	"	5.67	"
20	"	7.13	"
30	"	7.51	"
40	"	7.61	"

E

Early and Periodic Screening, Diagnosis and Treatment (EPSDT)—Medicaid program for participants under age 21 that pays for screening and diagnostic services to detect physical or mental problems and to provide health care, treatment and other measures needed to correct or ameliorate any defects or chronic conditions discovered.

Early Distribution—An early distribution is a distribution taken from an IRA prior to age 59½ other than because of death or disability. Early distributions are generally subject to a 10% IRS penalty.

Early Retirement—A termination of employment involving the payment of a retirement allowance before a participant is eligible for normal retirement. The retirement allowance payable in the event of early retirement is often lower than the accrued portion of the normal retirement allowance.

Early Retirement Age—An age, established by the terms of an employee pension benefit plan, that is earlier than normal retirement age, at which a participant may retire and receive benefits (usually reduced) under the plan.

Early Retirement Programs—Designed to reduce the workforce. Most plans are voluntary, waive any early retirement penalties, offer subsidies for choosing early retirement and must be accepted within a specified time. See also Window Plan.

Earmarked Accounts—Separate accounts established for each participant in a retirement plan trust, with the specific investments for each account selected and controlled by the participant.

Earned Income—Under federal income tax laws, the income of an individual from services he or she has performed, thus excluding, e.g., income from the sale or rental of property and interest income.

Earned Premium—That portion of a policy's premium payment for which the protection of the policy has already been given. For example, an insurance company is considered to have earned 75% of an annual premium after a period of nine months of an annual term has elapsed.

Earned Surplus—That part of the excess of the total net worth or stockholders' equity over the total of par or stated value of the capital stock in the amount of proprietorship reserves, which is accounted for by accumulated retained earnings.

Earning Power—That rate of earnings considered to be normal for a company under regular operating conditions. It should take the past record into consideration as well as the probabilities of that record being continued in the future.

Earnings-Based CDs—FDIC- or FSLIC-insured CDs invested in real estate and sold by brokers.

Earnings Per Share (EPS)—Net income less preferred stock dividends divided by shares of common stock outstanding.

Earnings Record—The information maintained by the Social Security Administration on each individual's Social Security and Medicare covered wages and self-employment income.

Earnings Report—A statement—also called an *income* or *profit and loss statement*—issued by a company showing its earnings or losses over a given period. The earnings report lists the income earned, expenses and the net result.

Earnings Yield—A ratio found by dividing the market price of a stock into its earnings.

Econometrics—Use of computer analysis and modeling techniques to describe in mathematical terms the relationship among key economic forces such as labor, capital, interest rates and government policies; and then test the effects of changes in economic scenarios.

Economic Benefit—The IRS uses this doctrine to determine current tax liability when there is no constructive receipt. An employer's promise to pay an amount in the future has no economic benefit to the employee unless that promise is backed by a funded instrument to which the employee has nonforfeitable rights and there is no risk of forfeiture. If the promise is backed in this way, it has economic value and a tax liability occurs. See also Constructive Receipt.

Economic Recovery Tax Act of 1981 (ERTA)—Governs specific areas of employee compensation, including incentive stock options, deductible voluntary employee contributions, tax credit ESOPs and withdrawal provisions in savings/thrift plans. Expanded IRAs and Keogh plans.

Economic Value Added (EVA)—A measure of a company's return on investment that exceeds what is predicted by the capital asset pricing model.

Economically Targeted Investing (ETI)—Investing the plan's money in an investment vehicle that directly affects the employment environment of the industries in which the participants of the plan are employed, or bolsters the economy by creating jobs or affordable housing, for example. See also Socially Responsible Investments.

Educational Assistance Plan—Program under which an employer fully or partially reimburses an employee's expenses for education and training on a predetermined basis (usually pay as you go) and is permitted a business expense deduction whether or not the reimbursement is tax free or taxable to the employee.

Educational Benefit Trust (EBT)—A tax-favored arrangement that an employer can use to accumulate funds to pay the educational expenses of its employees' children.

Effective Date—The date on which an insurance policy or retirement plan goes into effect and coverage begins.

Efficacy—Level of benefit from a fixed level of input or amount of input costs to achieve a defined level of benefit.

Efficient Market Hypothesis—The assertion that, in a market with numerous investors who prefer high returns over low returns, and low risk over high risk, "information" is of no value. In such a market, an investor can attain no more, or less, than a fair return for the risks undertaken. The three forms of the efficient market hypothesis are (1) weak form: a market in which historical price data cannot be used to predict future price changes (see also Technical Analysis); (2) semistrong form: a market in which all publicly available information is efficiently (i.e., quickly and accurately) impounded on the price of a stock and, hence, a market in which no amount or item of publicly available information can be used to predict future price changes; and (3) strong form: a market in which even those with privileged (nonpublic) information cannot obtain superior investment results.

Efficient Portfolio—A portfolio that is fully diversified. For any given return, no other portfolio has less risk; for a given level of risk, no other portfolio provides superior returns. All efficient portfolios are perfectly correlated with a general market index, except portfolios with beta coefficients above 1.0 and that do not achieve that relatively high risk by levering an efficient portfolio. Such portfolios lie on the curved frontier of portfolios consisting exclusively of risky assets.

Elapsed Time Method of Service Counting—A method for determining a worker's time in service by subtracting the hire date from the termination date.

Elder Care—Financial, emotional, and physical support to parents and older relatives, including adult day care.

Election Period—The period during which a qualified beneficiary may elect to receive continuation coverage. It must last a minimum of 60 days and begins with the date coverage terminates.

Elective Admission—An admission that can be planned or scheduled at either the patient's or the physician's convenience.

Elective Contributions—The numerator of the ADP test. The amount deferred by the employee into a cash or deferred arrangement; considered to be employer contributions. If they are from plans with the same plan year and other requirements are met, the contributions may be treated as matching contributions for ACP testing purposes. Qualified nonelective contributions and qualified matching contributions may be treated as elective contributions for ADP testing.

Elective Deferral Arrangement—A type of SEP that allows the employees of companies with 25 employees or fewer to defer taxation on a portion of their income by making voluntary contributions under the employer's SEP. This is permitted under the Tax Reform Act of 1986. See also Simplified Employee Pension Plan.

Elective Surgery—An operation or surgical procedure for a condition that is not considered an emergency or life threatening. Such surgery is subject to the choice or decision of the patient and the physician.

Electronic Claim—A claim form that is processed and delivered from one computer to another via some form of magnetic media or via telecommunications.

Electronic Data Interchange (EDI)—A generic name for electronic, computer-based networks that transmit health care data between participating organizations. For example, claims can be processed electronically using EDI, and data can be gathered for use in outcomes research, in order to improve efficiency and save costs.

Eligibility—See Participation.

Eligibility Date—The date an individual and/or dependents become eligible for benefits under an employee benefit plan.

Eligibility Period—A period of time, usually 31 days, when potential members of a group life or health insurance plan can enroll without evidence of insurability.

Eligibility Requirements—Conditions that an employee must satisfy to participate in a plan or obtain a benefit.

Eligible Employees—Those members of a group who have met the eligibility requirements under a group life insurance, health insurance or pension plan.

Eligible Employer—Qualified as a tax-exempt organization under Section 101(6) of the 1939 Internal Revenue Code or Section 501(c)(3) of the 1954 Code.

Eligible Expenses—Medical expenses for which a health insurance policy will provide benefits.

Elimination Period—See Waiting Period; Qualification Period (Canada).

Emergency Admission—An admission caused by a sudden onset of a medical condition manifesting itself by acute symptoms of sufficient severity that the absence of immediate medical attention could cause serious impairment in bodily functions or cause serious and permanent dysfunction of any bodily organ or part.

Emergency Medical Services (EMS)—Treatment of patients suffering from accidents or sudden and serious illness.

Emergicenter—See Urgent Care Center.

Eminent Domain—The right of the people or government to take private property for public use upon payment of compensation.

Employee—An individual who is compensated for services performed and whose duties are under the control of an employer.

Employee Assistance Program (EAP)—An employment-based health service program designed to assist in the identification and resolution of a broad range of employee personal concerns that may affect job performance. These programs deal with situations such as substance abuse, marital problems, family troubles, stress and domestic violence, as well as health education and disease prevention. The assistance may be provided within the organization or by referral to outside resources.

Employee Benefit Plan—A plan established or maintained by an employer or employee organization, or both. The purpose is to provide employees with a certain benefit such as pension, profit-sharing, stock bonus, thrift, medical, sickness, accident or disability benefits.

Employee Benefit Trust—A trust established to hold the assets of an employee benefit plan.

Employee Benefits—A collection of nonwage compensation elements, including but not limited to, income protection, services and income supplements for employees, provided in whole or in part by employer payments.

Employee Contributions—Made by an employee into a plan. May or may not be required for participation. See also Contributory Plan; Voluntary Contribution.

Employee Organization—Any labor union, organization, agency, or employee representation committee, association, group or plan, in which employees participate and that exists for the purpose, in whole or in part, of dealing with employers concerning an employee benefit plan, or other matters incidental to employment relationships. The term also includes any employees' beneficiary organization organized for the purpose, in whole or in part, of establishing such a plan.

Employee-Pay-All Plan—One in which employees pay all costs for the plan; the employer does not make any contributions.

Employee Pension Benefit Plan—A plan, fund or program maintained by an employer, an employee organization or both, to the extent that, by its express terms or as a result of surrounding circumstances, such plan, fund or program provides retirement income to employees or results in a deferral of income by employees for periods extending to or beyond the termination of covered employment. The method of calculating employer contributions to or benefits under the plan or the method of distributing benefits is immaterial.

Employee Retirement Income Security Act of 1974 (ERISA)—Federal statute that requires persons engaged in the administration, supervision and management of pension monies have a fiduciary responsibility to ensure that all investment-related decisions are made (1) with the care, skill, prudence and diligence that a prudent man familiar with such matters would use and (2) by diversifying the investments so as to minimize risk. This wording mandates two significant changes in traditional investment practice: (1) the age-old "prudent man" rule has been replaced by the notion of a prudent "expert"; (2) the notion of a prudent investment has been replaced by the concept of a prudent portfolio.

ERISA also established an insurance program designed to guarantee workers receipt of pension benefits if their defined pension plan should terminate. It regulates the majority of private pension and welfare group benefit plans in the United States.

Employee Stock Option Plan—See Incentive Stock Option.

Employee Stock Ownership Plan (ESOP)—A qualified stock bonus plan or a qualified stock bonus and money purchase plan. Like a stock bonus plan, the contributions need not be dependent on profits, and benefits are distributable in the stock of the employer corporation. Typically, the ESOP is used as a financing vehicle for the employer corporation: The plan borrows money from the employer or uses the employer's credit, and purchases employer stock. The borrowed money is paid to the employer for its stock. The loan is repaid with annual employer contributions. See also Stock Bonus Plan.

Employee Stock Ownership Trust (ESOT)—Holds the ESOP's assets.

Employee Stock Purchase Plan—See Stock Purchase Plan.

Employee Welfare Benefit Plan—A plan, fund or program maintained by an employer or employee organization, or both, for the purpose of providing benefits, other than pension benefits, to its participants or their beneficiaries through the purchase of insurance or otherwise. Benefits provided by such plans include medical, surgical or hospital care benefits, or benefits in the event of sickness, disability, accident, death or unemployment, or vacation benefits, apprenticeship or other training programs, or daycare centers, scholarship funds, or prepaid legal services, or any benefit described in Section 302(c) of the Labor-Management Relations Act of 1947, other than pensions.

Employee's Cost Basis—The aggregate of any amount he or she has contributed as an employee or the aggregate of the tax that he or she has paid based upon the report on Form 1099, relative to cost of insurance.

Employees Profit Sharing Plan (EPSP) (Canada)—A trusteed arrangement under Section 144 of the Income Tax Act whereby an employer makes tax deductible payments (computed by reference to profits from its business) to a trustee in trust for employees of the employer. Such payments and all profits and earnings of the trust in a taxation year must be allocated, whether absolutely or contingently (as determined by the plan text), to the individual members, and all such amounts must be included by the individuals in computing their respective incomes for the taxation year. The principle of immediate tax liability when allocations are made to a member's account distinguishes the EPSP from profit-sharing pension plans and deferred profit-sharing plans, wherein tax liability is deferred until benefits are actually received by the member. Further, employee contributions to an EPSP are distinguished by the fact that they are not tax deductible and thus must be made from after tax income. Employee contributions are therefore not taxable (as compared with employer payments) when credited to the individual member's account.

Employer—Any person acting directly as an employer, or indirectly in the interest of an employer, in relation to an employee benefit plan. The term also includes a group or association of employers acting for an employer in such capacity.

Employer Mandate—A requirement that employers offer their employees health insurance benefits.

Employer Real Property—In connection with the 10% limitation relating to acquisition and holding of employer securities and employer real property by certain plans, real property (and related personal property) that is leased to an employer of employees covered by the plan or to an affiliate of such employer.

Employer Security—In connection with the 10% limitation relating to acquisition and holding of employer securities and employer real property by certain plans, a security issued by an employer of employees covered by the plan, or by an affiliate of such employer.

Employer-Sponsored IRA—An IRA that is sponsored by the employer for purposes of helping employees make a tax deductible contribution to an IRA and to invest the funds in a particular type of investment. The employer-sponsored IRA should be distinguished from a simplified employee pension plan, which requires employer contributions and must meet certain requirements with respect to participation, discrimination, withdrawals and contributions.

Employer-Sponsored Medical Center—A medical center, often onsite, provided and paid for by the employer, where employees can go to receive medical treatment. Employer-sponsored medical centers are often costly, but are designed with long-term savings in mind.

Employment-at-Will—A legal doctrine maintaining that it is the right of an employer or employee to terminate the employment relationship at any time and for any reason. The doctrine has been successfully challenged by employees in the courts in recent years.

Employment Cost Index (ECI)—A measure of the change in the cost of labor, free from the influence of employment shifts among occupations and industries.

Employment Generating Investment—See Economically Targeted Investing.

Employment Practices—Any policies, procedures, systems, programs or actions by the employer that have a direct impact upon the terms and conditions of the employment relationship.

Encounter—An episode of service. HMOs keep encounter data, particularly where there are no claims generated, because the provider has received a capitation payment from that member.

End Stage Renal Disease (ESRD)—That stage of renal impairment that is virtually always irreversible and permanent, and that requires dialysis or kidney transplantation to ameliorate uremic systems and maintain life.

Endorsement—

—An alteration to a policy. Can either be attached to the policy or written on a page of the policy itself. See also Rider.

—A writing, usually of the name of the payee, on the back of a negotiable instrument, such as a check or note, whereby the property represented by the instrument is transferred.

Endowment Insurance—Insurance payable to the insured if he or she is living on the maturity date stated in the policy, or to a beneficiary if the insured dies prior to that date.

Enjoin—To require performance or abstention from some act through issuance of an injunction.

Enrolled Actuary (EA)—A person who performs actuarial service for a plan and who is enrolled with the federal Joint Board for the Enrollment of Actuaries.

Enrolled Group—Persons with the same employer, or with membership in an organization in common, who are enrolled in a health plan. Usually, there are stipulations regarding the minimum size of the group and the minimum percentage of the group that must enroll before the coverage is available. (Synonym: contract group)

Enrollee—Any person eligible as either a subscriber or a dependent in accordance with an employee benefit plan. (Synonyms: beneficiary, eligible individual, insured, member, participant)

Enrollment—Any process by which an individual and/or dependents become subscribers to health plan coverage. May be done either through an actual "signing up" of the individual, by virtue of a collective bargaining agreement or by conditions of employment.

Entitlement—Employee benefits that have been legislated; perception that longstanding benefits are to some extent a matter of right.

Entry Age Actuarial Cost Method—Also called *entry age normal actuarial cost method.* A method under which the actuarial present value of the projected benefits of each individual included in an actuarial valuation is allocated on a level basis over the earnings or service of the individual between entry age and assumed exit age(s). The portion of this actuarial present value allocated to a valuation year is called the *normal cost.* The portion of this actuarial present value not provided for at a valuation date by the actuarial present value of future normal costs is called the *actuarial accrued liability.* Under this method, the actuarial gains (losses) are reflected as they occur in a decrease (increase) in the unfunded actuarial accrued liability.

Entry Age Normal Actuarial Cost Method—See Entry Age Actuarial Cost Method.

Entry Date—See Eligibility Date.

Epidemiology—The study of the relationships of various factors determining the frequency and distribution of diseases in the human community.

Equal Employment Opportunity—The removal of all illegal discriminatory practices to provide all individuals the same opportunities regardless of their race, sex, religion, national origin, age or other such classification.

Equal Employment Opportunity Commission (EEOC)—The federal agency that enforces Title VII of the Civil Rights Act of 1964, ADEA, ADA and other fair employment practices legislation.

Equal Pay Act of 1963—An amendment to the Fair Labor Standards Act (FLSA) that prohibits gender-related pay differentials for jobs that are equal in terms of skill, effort, responsibility and working conditions.

Equipment Trust Obligation or Certificate—A type of security usually issued by a transportation company (e.g., railroad or airline) to pay for equipment, where title to the equipment rests in the trustee until the notes are retired. Security is usually a first lien on the equipment.

Equities—Refers to ownership of property, usually in the form of common stocks, as distinguished from fixed income-bearing securities, such as bonds or mortgages.

Equity— Anything of value earned through the provision or investment of something of value.
- —(Compensation) Any employee earns equity interest through the provision of labor on a job. Equity often is used as a fairness criterion (i.e., "equal treatment") in compensation. People should be paid according to their contributions.
- —(Accounting) On an organization's balance sheet, equity represents the book value of the owners' stake in the firm. Assets minus liabilities; also called *net worth.*
- —(Real Estate) The interest or value an owner has in real estate over and above the mortgage against it.

Equity Compensation—Stock options, deferred stock, restricted stock, stock bonuses and other stock awards given as compensation instead of cash.

Equivalency—A method of crediting employees with service based on working time, periods of employment, compensation or elapsed time.

Ergonomics—The study of human factors in production in order to create and adapt equipment and other technology to more effectively accommodate human needs and abilities.

ERISA—See Employee Retirement Income Security Act of 1974.

ERISA Liability—Statutory liability imposed upon officers or other individuals operating in a fiduciary capacity for the proper handling of pension funds or other employee benefits. It is excluded from most general liability insurance policies.

ERISAfication—A change in a pension plan to bring it in line with amendments to ERISA.

Errors and Omissions (E&O) Insurance—Professional liability insurance for individuals in professions such as accounting, insurance, law or real estate, where the exposure is primarily a property damage one as opposed to bodily injury.

Escheat—Reversion of property to the state.

Escrow—A deed or something of value delivered to a third person for the grantee to be held by him or her until the fulfillment or performance of some act or condition.

Estate—Generally refers to degree, quantity, nature and extent of the interest a person has in real property.

Estate Tax—The tax payable by the estate, after the death of a person.

Eurodollars—Interest-bearing time deposits, denominated in U.S. dollars, at banks and other financial institutions outside of the United States.

European Union (International Benefits)—A group of European countries joined together to promote trade and economic and political cooperation. The Treaty of Maastricht of 1993 established new policies for political, social and economic cohesion, including the development of a monetary union, to be completed in 1999. Formerly European Community (EC).

Evaluation—An examination of and judgment about the quality of services or programs based on predetermined criteria/standards; also sometimes used with respect to individual services.

Evergreen Contract—A contract that does not expire.

Evidence of Insurability—Any statement or proof of a person's physical condition, occupation or other factor affecting his or her acceptance for insurance. Usually not required for enrollment in group plans, and prohibited for COBRA continuation coverage.

Evidence of Participation—Usually a certificate given to each participating employee.

Ex Ante—Before the fact; distinguishes forward looking, or predicted, variables.

Ex-Dividend—A synonym for *without dividend.* The buyer of a stock selling ex-dividend does not receive the recently declared dividend. Every dividend is payable on a fixed date to all shareholders recorded on the books of the company as of a previous date of record.

Ex Post—After the fact; distinguishes backward looking, or historical, variables.

Ex-Warrants—The date after which the buyer of a security is no longer entitled to warrants that will be distributed to the security's owners.

Excess Accumulation—During a calendar year, the amount by which an individual's required minimum distribution exceeds the actual amount received. Also called an *underdistribution,* it is subject to a tax penalty of 50% of the difference between the year's minimum payment and the payment actually received.

Excess Aggregate Contributions—The amount by which aggregate contributions of highly compensated employees exceed the maximum amount of such contributions allowed under ACP testing.

Excess Benefit Percentage—The percentage of compensation at which employer-derived benefits are accrued with respect to compensation of participants above the integration level.

Excess Benefit Plan—A nonqualified plan maintained by an employer solely for the purpose of providing benefits for certain employees in excess of those which, because of Internal Revenue Code limitations on contributions and benefits, can be provided by the employer's qualified plan.

Excess Compensation—In a plan integrated with Social Security, that portion of compensation, above a specified amount, used for calculating pension benefits.

Excess Contribution—

—If the employer contributes more than the maximum amount deductible under the minimum funding rules, the excess will not be currently deductible. However, the excess may be carried over to another year or years and deducted at that time (within the maximum deduction limits).

—The amount by which elective contributions of highly compensated employees exceed the maximum amount of elective contributions allowed under ADP testing.

Excess Distribution—An annual distribution from a qualified plan such as a 403(b) plan, SEP or IRA, that exceeds a certain amount, adjusted for inflation. The IRS imposes a 15% penalty on the participant unless the excess distribution is a result of death, a QDRO, distribution of nontaxable contributions or amounts that are rolled over within 60 days of distribution.

Excess Loss Insurance—See Stop-Loss Insurance.

Excess Plan—A plan that provides benefits only with respect to earnings in excess of the maximum earnings base for Social Security benefits.

Excess Retirement Accumulation—Result of an individual having, at death, interests in qualified plans, tax-sheltered annuities and IRAs exceeding the present value of an annuity with annual payments of a specified amount. The estate may be subject to a 15% penalty tax.

Excess Return—The return derived from a security (during a specified holding period) less the return from holding a riskless security (such as a short-term government obligation) during the same period.

Exchange Rate—The price of one currency stated in terms of another currency by bankers, dealers and financial markets.

Excise Taxes—An employer that contributes to a qualified plan will be subject to an excise tax liability for failing to contribute the amount determined to be an accumulated funding deficiency (excess of total charges over total credits in the funding standard account). The tax initially is to be 5% of the accumulated funding deficiency at the end of the plan year.

Excluded Plans—Benefit plans exempt from all regulatory provisions of ERISA (reporting and disclosure, participation and vesting, funding and fiduciary responsibility). These plans include the following:

1. A governmental plan
2. A church plan for which no election has been made for coverage under the Internal Revenue Code
3. A plan maintained solely for the purpose of complying with applicable workers' compensation, unemployment compensation or disability insurance laws
4. A plan maintained outside of the United States primarily for the benefit of persons substantially all of whom are nonresident aliens
5. An unfunded plan maintained solely to provide benefits in excess of the limitations imposed on contributions and benefits for tax purposes.

Exclusion Allowance—A method for calculating the amount of compensation that may be excluded from annual income and contributed to a tax-deferred annuity on the employees' behalf, whether by an addition to or reduction of salary.

Exclusion Ratio—Refers to the taxable cost calculation of an annuity plan. It is the ratio of the employee's cost basis to his or her expected return.

Exclusions or Exceptions—Specific conditions or circumstances listed in the policy or employee benefit plan for which the policy or plan will not provide benefit payments.

Exclusive Benefit Rule—See Fiduciary.

Exclusive Provider Organization (EPO)—A more rigid type of PPO, closely related to an HMO. Provides benefits or levels of benefits only if care is rendered by institutional and professional providers within a specified network (with some exceptions for emergency and out-of-area services).

Execute an Order—To fulfill an order to buy or sell. When an execution is referred to as *good,* it generally means that both the broker and the customer are satisfied that the price obtained is fair.

Executive Perquisites—See Perquisites.

Exempt—A term referring to groups of employees that are exempt from the overtime provisions of the Fair Labor Standards Act. Includes executives, administrative employees, professional employees and those engaged in outside sales.

Exempt Jobs—Those jobs in the organization that are exempt from the Fair Labor Standards Act—typically professional and managerial level jobs. Most exempt jobs are paid on a salary basis, not on an hourly basis.

Exemption—The condition of a person or organization that is free or excused from a duty imposed by some rule of law, statutory or otherwise.

Exercise Price—The price per share at which the seller (writer) must sell the security underlying a call or purchase the security underlying a put.

Exit Fee—See Back End Load.

Expatriate—An employee assigned outside of his or her base country for a year or more.

Expected Claims—The claims forecast for a group or covered person. The expected claims level becomes the breakeven point with respect to expected premium for a period of coverage.

Expected Rate of Return—The weighted arithmetic average of all possible outcomes for an asset or portfolio; the expected value.

Expense Fund—An operating account providing for the payment of an expense of administering the retirement plan.

Experience—Usually expressed as a ratio or percentage, it is the relationship of premium to claims, coverage or benefits of a plan for a specified period of time.

Experience-Rated Premium—A premium based on the anticipated claims experience of, or utilization of service by, a contract group according to its age, sex and any other attributes expected to affect its health service utilization. Such a premium is subject to periodic adjustment in line with actual claim or utilization experience. (Antonym: community-rated premium)

Experience Rating—The process of determining the

premium rate for a group risk, wholly or partially on the basis of that group's experience. See also Community Rating.

Experience Refund—A provision in most group policies for the return of premium to the policyholder because of lower-than-anticipated claims.

Experience Study—An actuarial analysis of the plan's experience in membership age, sex, salary and service giving effect to the assumed rates of mortality, disability, employment turnover, investment earnings and other cost factors.

Experimental Medical Procedures—Health care services or treatments that are not widely accepted as effective by entities such as the Health Care Financing Administration, the American Medical Association, the National Institutes of Health or by American health care professionals; or have not been scientifically proven to be effective. Such services are excluded from most health plans.

Expiration Date—
- —The last day on which a stock option may be exercised.
- —The date the insurance master contract expires or the date an individual or employee ceases to be eligible for coverage.

Explanation of Benefits (EOB)—A statement from the insurer sent to a group member who files a claim giving specific details about how and why benefit payments were or were not made. It summarizes the charges submitted and processed, the amount allowed, the amount paid, and the subscriber balance, if any.

Exploding—A form of code gaming. A billing practice in which the provider bills separately for each test performed on a given laboratory specimen.

Exposure—The extent to which members of a retirement plan, in terms of numbers, are exposed to the probability of death, disability or separation from covered employment.

Expropriation—See Eminent Domain.

Extended Benefits—
- —Comprehensive benefits provided in excess of basic health care plans.
- —Extension of benefits for limited periods after termination of plan coverage.
- —Extension of unemployment compensation benefits during periods of high unemployment.

Extended Care Facility (ECF)—A health care facility offering skilled nursing care, rehabilitation and convalescent services for patients no longer needing hospital care.

Extended Coverage—Additional insurance at an extra premium for coverage not generally found in the normal insurance contract. Insurance for the coverage of certain specified risks, such as smoke damage, windstorm, hail, lightning, vehicle damage, riots, aircraft accidents, explosions and civil disorders.

Extended Medical Expense (Canada)—Same as major medical coverage.

External Evaluation—An evaluation performed by a person or agency not under the direct control of the individual, group or organization being evaluated.

Extra Risk Policy—See Rated Policy.

Extramarket Covariance—Tendency for the prices of related securities to move together in a way that is independent of the market as a whole.

F

Face Amount—The amount indicated on the face of a life insurance policy that will be paid in the event of death or when the contract matures. Excluded are dividend additions and amounts payable under accidental death or other special provisions.

Face Value—The value of a bond that appears on the face of the bond, unless the value is otherwise specified by the issuing company. Face value is ordinarily the amount the issuing company promises to pay at maturity. Face value is not an indication of market value. Sometimes referred to as *par value.*

Fact Finding—An alternative dispute resolution procedure in which a neutral or neutrals—known as a fact finder (or fact finding panel)—conduct a hearing at which the opposing parties define the issues in dispute and propose their prospective resolutions therefor with supporting evidence and argument. Following the hearing, the fact finder(s) issues recommendations for a solution, usually in writing. It is hoped that both parties will accept these recommendations and that the dispute will end. The recommendations are not binding, and the parties are free to accept or reject them, or to use them as a basis for further negotiation. See also Arbitration/Arbitrator.

Fair Labor Standards Act of 1938 (FLSA)—A federal law, enacted in 1938 and subsequently amended, which governs minimum wage, overtime pay, equal pay for men and women in the same type of jobs, and child labor.

Fair Market Value (FMV)—The value of property established between a willing buyer and a willing seller in an arm's length transaction.

Fair Return—A return on the investment, commensurate at least with the prevailing rate of interest at any bank or similar institution.

Fair Value—Used in financial accounting procedure. Fair value does not carry the restrictions of tax-oriented *fair market value.* Rather, it can be defined as whatever is reasonable and fairly represents the relative worth of each asset or class to another.

Family Allowances (International Benefits)—Payments made under social systems for support of one or more children in a family. Frequently funded by the social security system of the country.

Family and Medical Leave Act of 1993 (FMLA)—Requires employers with more than 50 employees to provide eligible workers with up to 12 weeks of unpaid leave each year for birth, adoptions, foster care placements, and illnesses of employees and their families.

Family Deductible—A deductible that is satisfied by the combined expenses of all covered family members. For example, a program with a $100 deductible may limit its application to a maximum of three deductibles ($300) for the family, regardless of the number of family members. An aggregate family deductible may be met by one or more family members. See also Deductible.

Family Practice—Practice of health care directed at the whole family by a family physician, a generalist who cares for patients of all ages with a variety of medical and surgical conditions.

Fannie Mae—See Federal National Mortgage Association.

Fed Funds Rate—Rate at which banks are willing to lend or borrow immediately available reserves on an overnight basis.

Federal Deposit Insurance Corporation (FDIC)—An agency created by Congress in 1933 to insure repayment of savings and time deposits if a member bank becomes insolvent.

Federal Home Loan Mortgage Corporation (FHLMC or Freddie Mac)—Created in 1970 to promote the flow of capital into the housing market by establishing an active secondary market for residential mortgages. Freddie Mac is owned by the Federal Home Loan Bank System and is under the direction of the Federal Home Loan Bank Board. It deals only with government-supervised lenders and certain mortgage bankers that meet specified criteria.

Federal Insurance Contributions Act (FICA)—The statute that requires employers and employees to pay Social Security taxes.

Federal National Mortgage Association (FNMA or Fannie Mae)—The Federal National Mortgage Association is a government-sponsored corporation established by Congress in 1938, owned entirely by private stockholders to serve as a secondary market for Federal Housing Administration, Veterans Administration or Farmers Home Administration insured or guaranteed mortgages. The association provides liquidity on mortgage investments by buying mortgages from financial institutions, such as savings and loan associations and life insurance companies, when investment funds are in short supply and selling mortgages when funds are plentiful. To finance its operations, it issues debentures, bonds and common stock, the latter being bought by institutions that sell mortgages to Fannie Mae, as well as by private investors. FNMA stock is listed on the New York Stock Exchange. The bonds and debentures are highly liquid investments that enjoy an active secondary market and have varying maturities up to 25 years. Fannie Maes come in bearer form only, in amounts of $10,000 to $500,000. The maturities on these securities vary and interest is paid semiannually by coupon.

Federal Register—The daily publication of the United States government in which federal administrative agencies officially publish their rules (including proposed rules subject to public comment).

Federal Reserve System—The central banking system

of the United States, consisting of 12 Federal Reserve Banks and supervised by the Federal Reserve Board of Governors, whose seven members are appointed by the president. It is an independent monetary authority operating outside control of Congress and the president.

Federal Savings and Loan Association—A financial institution that is federally chartered and privately owned either by stockholders or depositors. Federal Savings and Loan Associations' prime functions are twofold: (1) financing homes and, to a more limited degree, commercial properties, through conventional loans and FHA and VA mortgages and (2) providing interest-bearing savings accounts that are government insured to $100,000. All Federal Savings and Loan Associations are required to be members of their regional Federal Home Loan Bank.

Federal-State Agreement (Chapter 218 Agreement)—An agreement between the Social Security Administration and a state to provide Social Security coverage for public employees in accordance with state statutes.

Federal Unemployment Tax Act (FUTA)—An act under which employers must make contributions to finance a federal unemployment insurance program. Some states have similar laws.

Fee (Fee Simple) (Fee Simple Absolute)—These three terms are synonymous and mean that an owner has absolute, good and marketable title to the property conveyed to him or her. It is complete ownership without condition.

Fee for Service (FFS)—A traditional health benefits plan that pays benefits directly to physicians, hospitals, or other health care providers, or that reimburses the patient for covered medical services. Examples are Blue Cross & Blue Shield and Medicare.

Fee Schedule—A listing of fees or allowances for specified medical procedures, which usually represents the maximum amounts the program will pay for specified procedures. Sometimes called a *table of allowances.*

Fee Schedule Payment Structure—A fee structure used by some HMOs under which the HMO places caps or limits on the dollar amounts that it will reimburse providers for covered medical procedures and services.

Fellow of the Life Management Institute (FLMI)—Awarded by the Life Office Management Association. Holders must pass ten required education university level examinations covering various aspects of life and health insurance.

Fellow of the Society of Pension Actuaries (FSPA)—Holders must pass two examinations on pensions and actuarial practice and hold the FSPA designation.

Fiduciary—

—Indicates the relationship of trust and confidence where one person (the fiduciary) holds or controls property for the benefit of another person. For example, the relationship between a trustee and the beneficiaries of the trust.

—Under ERISA (the Employee Retirement Income Security Act of 1974), any person who (1) exercises any discretionary authority or control over the management of a plan or the management or disposition of its assets, (2) renders investment advice for a fee or other compensation with respect to the funds or property of a plan, or has the authority to do so, or (3) has any discretionary authority or responsibility in the administration of a plan.

—One who acts in a capacity of trust and who is therefore accountable for whatever actions may be construed by the courts as breaching that trust. Under ERISA, fiduciaries must discharge their duties solely in the interest of the participants and beneficiaries of an employee benefit plan. In addition, a fiduciary must act exclusively for the purpose of providing benefits to participants and beneficiaries in defraying reasonable expenses of the plan. See also Prudent Man Rule.

Fiduciary Liability Insurance—A form of errors and omissions insurance.

Final Average (Earnings) Formula (Canada)—A defined benefit formula that applies the unit of benefit credited for each year of service to the employee's average earnings for a specified number of years just prior to retirement.

Final Average Salary—A measure of a participant's level of earnings that is based on his or her average rate of salary for a specified period of time, usually the three, five or ten years immediately preceding retirement. A participant's final average salary may be one of the factors used in determining the amount of his or her benefits.

Final Pay Plan (Final Pay Formula)—A benefit formula that bases benefits on the employee's compensation over a specified number of years near the end of the employee's service period or on the employee's highest compensation periods. For example, a plan might provide annual pension benefits equal to 1% of the employee's average salary for the last five years (or the highest consecutive five years) for each year of service. A final pay plan is a plan with such a formula.

Financial Accounting Standard 87—The statement issued by FASB regarding employers' accounting for pensions.

Financial Accounting Standard 106—Requires employers to record on their balance sheets the future financial liability that they incur by promising health benefits to retirees.

Financial Accounting Standards Board (FASB)—The independent, private (nongovernmental) authority for establishing accounting principles in the United States. Successor to the Accounting Principles Board.

Financial Assets—Assets that are intangible in nature, e.g., stocks, bonds, U.S. Treasury bills.

Financial Futures—Futures contracts for interest-sensitive securities: T-bills, T-bonds, T-notes and GNMA pass-throughs.

Financial Planning—
- —The consideration and evaluation of the financial consequences of alternative economic choices and the rearrangement of one's financial affairs in light of those considerations.
- —The design of an investment program to achieve specific financial goals, such as the creation of a college fund, the purchase of a home or the establishment of a retirement nest egg.

Financial Statement—The means by which the information accumulated and processed in financial accounting is communicated. For employee benefit plans, ERISA has several special requirements that financial statements must follow.

Financing Method—The method of administering the pension program through group annuities, deposit administration, individual policies by an insurance company or a self-administered trust.

First Dollar Coverage—A benefit plan that provides reimbursement for incurred health care costs "from the first dollar," with no deductible.

First In, First Out (FIFO)—In accounting parlance, the normal way to determine the cost of inventory on hand. Sales are held to be made against the earliest purchased items. In times of rising prices, firms using the FIFO method tend to overstate profits. Contrast with Last In, First Out (LIFO).

Fiscal Agent—
- —An agent for a corporation to handle specified matters relating to taxes in connection with an issue of bonds.
- —An agent for a national, state or municipal government or government body to pay its bonds and coupons or to perform certain other duties related to financial matters.

Fiscal Intermediary (FI)—An agency, usually a Blue Cross plan or private insurance company, selected by health care providers to pay claims under Medicare. Sometimes referred to simply as *intermediary.*

Fiscal Policy—Government strategy on taxes, spending and borrowing aimed at stabilizing economic activity.

Fiscal Year (FY)—A corporation's accounting year. Due to the nature of their particular business, some companies do not use the calendar year for their bookkeeping, but rather any 12-month period.

5% Owner—Individual owning more than a 5% interest in an employer in one of the following ways: (1) the stock of a corporate employer, (2) the voting power in stock of a corporate employer or (3) the capital or profits interest of a noncorporate employer. A 5% owner is a key employee under the Tax Code. See also Key Employee; Top-Heavy Plan.

501(c)(9) Trust—
- —Used by employers and jointly administered welfare funds to provide group employee benefits governed by provisions of Section 501(c)(9) of the IRC. Only certain benefits may be provided under a 501(c)(9) program: medical, disability, term life insurance, severance compensation, vacation benefits, recreational facilities and unemployment compensation.
- —A type of self-insured or self-funded plan that is a tax-exempt trust. Under the terms of the trust,

both employer and employee contributions are paid into the fund, and claims and expenses paid from it. Excess funds are invested as reserves by the fund's trustees. In a tax-qualified fund, the employer's contributions are immediately tax deductible; the trust's investment income is tax exempt; and employees' contributions are not currently taxed. See also Disbursed Self-Funded Plan; Self-Insurance; Voluntary Employees' Beneficiary Association (VEBA).

Five-Year Averaging—A method used to determine income tax liability on a lump-sum distribution made from a qualified plan. This method often reduces the amount of income tax due to the IRS. The Tax Reform Act of 1986 generally replaced ten-year averaging with five-year averaging.

Fixed Access Charge—Flat fee charged by a PPO to allow employees and dependents to gain access to network providers.

Fixed Annuity—An annuity contract in which the insurance company makes fixed (or guaranteed) dollar payments to the annuitant for the term of the contract (usually until he or she dies).

Fixed Assets—Those assets that are acquired for use in the continuing operations of a business over a number of accounting periods rather than for resale to customers.

Fixed Benefit Retirement Plan—A type of plan providing retirement benefits only on a fixed amount or at a fixed percentage such as 1% of monthly salary times the number of years of credited employment; or 25% of the employee's average pay over the last few years prior to retirement.

Fixed Charges—
- —Expenses of a company, such as bond interest, rental expense and amortization of bond discount.
- —Fees or expenses assessed as flat amounts, not as a percentage or function of volume.

Fixed Income—Income that remains constant and does not fluctuate, such as income derived from bonds, annuities, preferred stock and royalties.

Fixed Income Fund—A mutual fund that invests in corporate, government or other issuer bonds. Despite the name, annual income is rarely fixed or guaranteed.

Fixed Rate Mortgage—A loan made on real property that has a constant interest rate over the life of the loan. See also Variable Rate or Adjustable Rate Mortgage.

Flat Benefit Formula (Flat Benefit Plan)—A benefit formula that bases benefits on a fixed amount per year of service, such as $20 of monthly retirement income for each year of credited service. A flat benefit plan is a plan with such a formula.

Flat Dollar and Service Benefit Formula—A retirement benefit formula based on years of service times a specific dollar multiplier, such as $10 per month per year of service.

Flat Dollar Benefit Formula—A retirement benefit for mula that calls for a specific pension amount without regard to income or service.

Flat Percentage of Earnings Formula—Some percentage of earnings, usually 20-40%, is selected as the measure of the pension benefit. It may be used with either career average or final average earnings, although it is used most frequently in final pay plans. This type of formula does not take an employee's service into account, except in those plans that require the employee to have completed a minimum period of service by normal retirement date and provide for a proportionately reduced benefit if the employee's service is less than the required number of years.

Flat Rate Pension (Canada)—Expressed as a dollar amount of monthly pension, this is a defined benefit not related to service or earnings. It is paid on retirement after qualifying conditions are met. See also Old Age Security.

Flat Schedule—A type of schedule in group insurance under which everyone is insured for the same benefits regardless of salary, position or other circumstances.

Flexibility—When applied to the formula of pension or profit-sharing plans, it means a plan wherein the trustees have the right to decide on larger or smaller amounts of contributions annually, as the need arises. Therefore, a fully invested program, without life insurance, would be most flexible. An insured annuity program or a plan funded with retirement income policies would be least flexible. A split funded program would be relatively flexible.

Flexible Benefit Plan/Flexible Compensation—A benefit program under Section 125 of the Internal Revenue Code that offers employees a choice between permissible taxable benefits, including cash, and nontaxable health and welfare benefits such as life and health insurance, vacation pay, retirement plans and child care. Although a common core of benefits may be required, the employee can determine how his or her remaining benefit dollars are to be allocated for each type of benefit from the total amount promised by the employer. Sometimes employee contributions may be made for additional coverage.

Flexible Spending Accounts or Arrangements (FSAs)—Many flexible benefit programs include flexible spending accounts, which give employees the opportunity to set aside pretax funds for the reimbursement of eligible tax-favored welfare benefits. FSAs can be funded through salary reduction, employer contributions or a combination of both. Employees can purchase additional benefits, pay health insurance deductibles and copayments, or pay for child care benefits with the money in their FSAs.

Flextime—Schedules permitting employees to structure their work hours around their personal responsibilities.

Float—The amount of funds tied up in checks that have been written but are still in process and have not yet been collected.

Floating Debt—Temporary or shifting short-term debt that has not been funded on a permanent basis in the longer term maturities.

Floating Interest Rate—An interest rate that fluctuates with changes in an established index, such as the prime rate.

Floating Supply—Indicates the total amount of securities believed to be available for immediate purchase offered by security dealers and other investors who wish to sell all or a portion of what they own.

Floor—The trading area where stocks and bonds are bought and sold on an exchange.

Floor Broker—A member of the stock exchange who executes orders to buy or sell listed securities received from member firms or for his or her own account on the floor of the exchange. See also Specialist.

Floor Loan—The first funding of a permanent loan. The total loan is generally funded upon achieving some predetermined minimum rental rates.

Floor Offset (Pension) Plan—A defined contribution plan is used as the primary vehicle for providing retirement benefits. Recognizing that many factors might result in the defined contribution plan providing less than adequate benefits in some situations, the employer also maintains a defined benefit floor plan. This floor plan uses a defined benefit formula to establish a minimum benefit. If the defined contribution plan provides a benefit that equals or exceeds this minimum, no benefit is payable from the floor plan. If the defined contribution benefit is less than this minimum, the floor plan makes up the difference. Thus the total benefit from both plans is equal to the minimum described in the floor plan.

Fluctuations—Variations in the market price of a security. If a stock advances or declines three points, it is said to have experienced a three-point fluctuation.

Focus Group—A group of employees brought together to discuss their attitudes and perceptions toward a proposed company initiative.

Forecast Actuarial Cost Method—See Projection Actuarial Cost Method.

Foreclosure—The legal procedures involved in enforcing payment of a debt secured by a mortgage by taking title to the applicable property or other assets and selling them. Often associated with a default of principal and interest on a loan involving real estate.

Foreign Exchange Transaction—Purchase or sale of the currency of one nation for that of another.

Foreign (or International) Fund—A mutual fund that invests only in foreign securities (differs from a *global fund,* which invests both in U.S. and foreign securities).

Foreign National—A citizen of another country who is authorized to work in the United States.

Foreign Securities—Investment in the securities issued by a company that is incorporated outside of the United States and generates a major portion of its business outside the United States, or securities issued by governments other than the U.S. government.

Forfeiture—The amount that is lost when a participant terminates employment before being fully vested under the plan's vesting schedule. In a pension plan, such amounts must be applied to reducing future employer contributions. In a profit-sharing plan, such amounts may be allocated to the accounts of remaining participants. Also applicable to flexible spending accounts.

Form 5500—A joint agency financial form developed by the IRS, DOL and PBGC that may be used to satisfy the annual reporting requirements of the IRC and Titles I and IV of ERISA.

Formulary—See Prescription Drug Formulary.

401(h) Account—A separate account of a pension plan that, under provisions of IRC Section 401(h), may be used to fund medical benefits for retirees and dependents.

401(h) Plan—A provision of a pension or annuity plan that provides for the payment of benefits for sickness, accident, hospitalization and medical expenses, of retired employees, their spouses and their dependents, subject to certain requirements.

401(k) Plan—A defined contribution plan, established by an employer. It enables employees to make pretax contributions by salary reduction agreements structured within the format of a cash or deferred plan.

401(k) Wraparound Plan—An unfunded, nonqualified deferred compensation plan to which a highly compensated employee may make pretax contributions. The employer makes matching contributions. By using this procedure, the employee avoids certain IRC limits on deferrals and compensation and is able to maximize his or her 401(k) plan. Also known as *nonqualified 401(k) plan* and *shadow 401(k) plan.*

403(b) Annuity—An annuity that provides retirement income for employees of certain tax-exempt organizations or public schools. Also known as a *tax-sheltered annuity.*

403(b) Plan—A defined contribution plan established by certain tax-exempt organizations and public schools for their employees. Similar to a 401(k) plan.

415 Limits—See Section 415 Limits.

419(a) Plan—A welfare benefit plan funded through trusts to which many unrelated employers contribute. It is referred to as a *multiple employer plan.* These plans are often structured as nondiscriminatory VEBAs or taxable trusts and offer life insurance or severance benefits.

457 Plan—An elective contribution arrangement available to states, political subdivisions of a state, or any agency or instrumentality of a state under Code Section 457.

Fractional Rule—The employee's accrued benefit on any given date is not less than the projected normal retirement benefit prorated for years of plan participation. See also Accrued Benefit.

Fractional Share—A portion of a whole share of stock. Fractional shares may be generated when stock dividends are declared or two corporations merge.

Franchise Insurance—A form of insurance in which individual policies are issued to the employees of a common employer or the members of an association under an arrangement where the employer or association agrees to collect the premiums and remit them to the insurer.

Franchise Integration (International Benefits)—A method of determining an employee's earnings, used in calculating a pension benefit to recognize the value of social security.

Fraternal Insurance—A cooperative type of life or disability insurance some social organizations offer to their members.

Fraud—An intentional misrepresentation of the truth for the purpose of deceiving another person that causes damage of some sort.

Freddie Mac—Trade name for the Federal Home Loan Mortgage Corporation.

Free and Clear—A reference to ownership of property that is free of all indebtedness. Property that never had a mortgage encumbering it or for which the mortgage has been paid in full.

Free Choice—A provision that permits the insured to choose any licensed health provider.

Freestanding Additional Voluntary Contributions (Great Britain)—Money that can be put into a pension fund outside of the company scheme or plan in order to enhance benefits.

Freestanding Emergency Medical Center—A facility offering emergency treatment or treatment for minor injuries; care is available on weekends and evenings. Charges are generally lower than those of hospital emergency rooms.

Freezing Past Service Liability—
- —Where improved benefits under a pension plan are financed from future service only rather than dividing the additional cost between past and future service.
- —Estimating the accrued liability for past service and paying into the pension fund only the interest on this amount instead of fully funding it, thus preventing this liability from increasing. Assumes plan will continue indefinitely.

Front End Load—
- —With reference to mutual funds, a system of sales charge for contractual plans that permits up to 50% of the first year's payments to be deducted as sales charges. Investors can withdraw from the plan, but there are some restrictions if this occurs.
- —The cost or commission incurred at the time an investment is acquired.

Frozen Actuarial Accrued Liability—That portion of the actuarial present value of projected benefits that is separated as of a valuation date and frozen under certain actuarial cost methods. Generally, this separate portion is the sum of an initial unfunded actuarial accrued liability and any increments or decrements in the actuarial accrued liability established subsequently as a result of changes in pension plan benefits or actuarial assumptions. Also called *frozen initial liability.*

Frozen Attained Age Actuarial Cost Method—A method under which the excess of the actuarial present value of projected benefits of the group included in an actuarial valuation, over the sum of the actuarial value of assets plus the unfunded frozen actuarial accrued liability, is allocated on a level basis over the earnings or service of the group between the valuation date and assumed exit. This allocation is performed for the group as a whole, not as a sum of individual allocations. The frozen actuarial accrued liability is determined using the unit credit actuarial cost method. The portion of this actuarial present value allocated to a valuation year is called the *normal cost.*

Frozen Entry Age Actuarial Cost Method—A method under which the excess of the actuarial present value of projected benefits of the group included in an actuarial valuation, over the sum of the actuarial value of assets plus the unfunded frozen actuarial accrued liability, is allocated on a level basis over the earnings or service of the group between the valuation date and assumed exit. This allocation is performed for the group as a whole, not as a sum of individual allocations. The frozen actuarial accrued liability is determined using the entry age actuarial cost method. The portion of this actuarial present value allocated to a valuation year is called the *normal cost.*

Frozen Initial Liability—See Frozen Actuarial Accrued Liability.

Frozen Plan—A qualified retirement plan that has stopped employer contributions and benefit accrual by participants. The plan sponsor continues to distribute plan assets and maintain the trust.

Full Disclosure Act—Another name for the Securities Act of 1933.

Full Funding Limitation—A federal tax law limit that caps the amount an employer maintaining a qualified pension plan subject to the Internal Revenue Code Section 412 Minimum Funding Standard is required or allowed to contribute on a deductible basis for a year. The full funding limitation is the lesser of (1) the accrued liability of the plan for the plan year, less the value of plan assets; or (2) 150% of the current liability over the value of the plan's assets. This limit generally will affect the level of required contributions when a plan's assets are large relative to its benefit liabilities.

Full-Time Employees—Employees of an employer who work for 1,000 or more hours in a 12-month period.

Full Vesting—That form of immediate or deferred vesting under which all accrued benefits of a participant become vested benefits.

Fully Funded—
- —A specific element of pension cost (for example, past service cost) is said to have been fully funded if the amount of the cost has been paid in full to a funding agency. A pension plan is said by some to be fully funded if regular payments are being made under the plan to a funding agency

to cover the normal cost and reasonably rapid amortization of the past service cost.

—If a specific part, or benefit, is fully paid for (such as the past service cost), then this item is fully funded. The total plan is considered fully funded if there are sufficient assets to make all payments due at particular times. This can apply to either level funding or entry age calculations, provided that both the normal costs and the conservative amount of amortization costs for the past services have been paid.

Fully Insured—Having enough quarters of coverage to qualify for Social Security benefits.

Fully Insured Plan—

—A group insurance plan in which an insurer pays all claims and assumes all risks for an employer in exchange for payment of a regular premium.

—Under a fully insured retirement plan, the policy cash value at retirement must be sufficient to provide the full benefit since no other source of funds is contemplated under the plan. Retirement income or retirement annuity contracts must be used since they are specifically designed to provide the proper ratio of insurance to income and to generate the cash value needed.

—Separate contracts are issued on the life of every employee.

Functional Obsolescence—Defects in a structure that detract from its marketability and value. When a building begins to outlive its usefulness through antiquated equipment—such as inadequate electrical wiring, outmoded elevator service, lack of or poor air conditioning, impractical design, faulty heating plant and so on—it becomes functionally obsolete.

Fund—Used as a verb, *fund* means to pay over to a funding agency (as, to fund future pension benefits, to fund pension cost). Used as a noun, *fund* refers to assets accumulated for the purpose of paying benefits as they become due.

Fund Earnings—Earnings that return to the pension trust fund for reinvestment or payment of benefits.

Funded Debt—All long-term financing of a corporation; that is, all outstanding bonds maturing in five years or longer.

Funded Plan—A funded plan under ERISA is a plan paying benefits in any manner other than through an employer's or employee organization's general assets, including an insured plan and a plan paying benefits or premiums from a trust.

Funded Ratio—Ratio of the assets of a pension plan to its liabilities.

Funded Retirement Plan—A plan under which funds are set aside in advance to provide expected benefits. The plan is not necessarily insured. In contrast to unfunded or pay-as-you-go plan.

Funding Agency—An organization or individual, such as a specific corporate or individual trustee or an insurance company, that provides facilities for the accumulation of assets to be used for the payment of benefits under a pension plan; an organization, such as a specific life insurance company, that provides facilities for the purchase of such benefits.

Funding Deficiency—See Accumulated Funding Deficiency.

Funding Excess—The amount by which the actuarial value of assets exceeds the actuarial accrued liability. Contrast with Unfunded Actuarial Accrued Liability.

Funding Instrument—A contract or an agreement describing and controlling the terms of a retirement program and the action of the funding agent. Allocated funding instruments include: individual insurance and annuity contracts, group permanent contracts and group deferred annuity contracts. Unallocated funding instruments are deposit administration contracts, immediate participation guarantee contracts and trust fund plans.

Funding Method—Any of the several techniques actuaries use in determining the amounts of employer contributions to provide for pension costs. An actuarial cost method.

Funding Policy—The program regarding the amounts and timing of contributions by the employer(s), participants and any other sources (for example, state subsidies or federal grants) to provide the benefits a pension plan specifies.

Funding Standard Account (FSA)—A requirement under ERISA. Basically, a bookkeeping account in which credits and debits are used to determine a positive or negative balance. The numbers to be used in the account originate in the actuarial valuation or the plan's actual experience for the period. The purpose of the funding standard account is to determine whether or not an accumulated funding deficiency exists. This will occur whenever the negative entries exceed the positive entries to the account.

Funding Waiver—See Waived Funding Deficiency.

Future Purchase Option Benefit—A supplemental benefit that is provided by some disability income policies and that allows the insured the right to increase the disability income benefit amount provided under the policy in accordance with increases in the insured's earnings.

Futures Contract—A transferable agreement to make or take delivery of standardized minimum quality grades, during a specific month, under terms and conditions established by a federally designated contract market upon which trading is conducted.

G

Gain—See Actuarial Gain or Loss.

Gainsharing—A form of incentive under which both employees and the organization share the financial gains according to a predetermined formula that reflects improved productivity and profitability.

Gaming—See Code Gaming.

Garnishment—A court order to an employer to withhold all or part of an employee's wages and send the money to the court or to a person who has won a lawsuit against the employee.

GASB Statement No. 2—Governmental Accounting Standards Board standard for reporting Section 457 deferred compensation assets on governmental financial statements.

Gatekeeper—The primary care provider responsible for managing medical treatment rendered to an enrollee of a health plan. Alternatively, this term has been used to describe third party monitoring of care to avoid excessive costs by allowing only appropriate and necessary care to be rendered.

General Accounting Office (GAO)—An arm of Congress that serves as the watchdog for government cost efficiency and that conducts financial studies.

General Asset Plan—A type of self-insured group health care plan in which the plan sponsor deposits the funds set aside for health care coverage into a commercial checking account or other similar account and then pays all claims out of its current operating fund. Also known as a nontrusteed plan.

General Assets—Assets owned by an employer or employee organization. They do not include employee contributions or other plan assets.

General Death Benefit—A benefit payable under a group term life insurance plan on the death of an employee, without special conditions. This type of benefit can qualify for special tax treatment under an IRC Section 79 group life insurance policy.

General Dropout (Canada)—Provision in the Canada and Quebec Pension Plans that allows members to exclude up to seven years of low earnings or no earnings for pension purposes. Parents can qualify for the child-rearing dropout in addition to the general dropout.

General Obligation (GO) Bond—A type of municipal bond that is backed by the full faith, credit and taxing power of the issuer for payment of interest and principal. Its sale finances public improvements; it is repaid by taxes.

General Partner—A person who usually is actively engaged in the trade or business of partnership and has unlimited personal liability in the partnership. See also Limited Partner.

General Partnership—A form of business whose partners include only general partners. Profits, losses and deductions are passed through to the individual partners involved in the business. See also Limited Partnership.

Generally Accepted Accounting Principles (GAAP)—Uniform minimum standards of and guidelines to financial accounting and reporting, which govern form and content of financial statements. GAAP encompass principles necessary to define accepted accounting practice at a particular time and include detailed procedures as well as broad guidelines.

Generally Accepted Auditing Standards (GAAS)—Measure the quality of the performance of auditing procedures and the objectives to be obtained through their use. Concerned with the auditors' professional qualities and judgment exercised in the performance of an audit.

Generic Equivalent Drugs—Equal in therapeutic power to the brand-name originals because they contain identical active ingredients at the same doses.

Genetic Counseling—A clinical service with informational, educational and psychological components to provide individuals and families as to the likelihood of their offspring having genetic (hereditary) conditions, defects or diseases.

Geographic Multiplier—A multiplier used for making geographic adjustments to the Medicare fee schedule. A geographic multiplier may be based on a geographic index of practice costs.

Geographic Practice Cost Index (GPCI)—An index summarizing the prices of inputs to physician services in an area relative to national average prices.

Ginnie Mae—See Government National Mortgage Association (GNMA).

Ginnie Mae is the colloquial term.

Ginnie Mae Pass-Through Securities—Under this program, principal and interest payments collected on mortgages in specified pools are "passed through" to holders of GNMA-guaranteed certificates after deduction of servicing and guaranty fees. Actual maturity of these certificates is 40 years, but the average life is approximately 12 years because of prepayments. The minimum denomination of certificates is $25,000 and issuance is in registered form only. Ginnie Maes offer investors an opportunity to participate in "pools" of government-guaranteed or -insured mortgages without having to be concerned with extensive documentation and paperwork normally associated with mortgage type investments.

Colloquial for Government National Mortgage Association (GNMA).

Glass Ceiling—Discriminatory practices that have prevented women and other protected class members from advancing to executive level jobs.

Global Budget—The overall amount spent on specific health services by all buyers of services. In some health reform plans this amount would be set each year by a governmental body.

Global Charge—The sum of the professional and technical components of a service when both are provided by the same physician.

Global Fee—A single fee charged for certain medical services that would otherwise be broken down into a number of separate fees. For example, office visits before and after a complex surgery are included in one single fee. Global fees are often developed by managed care plans for specialty procedures to protect against unbundling of claims.

Global Fund—A mutual fund that invests in stocks and bonds all over the world, including the United States. By contrast, an international fund invests all over the world except in the United States.

Globalization—An investment approach that encompasses world markets and views those markets as separate subsegments of the entire world or global market setting.

GNP Price Deflator—The price index for the Gross National Product (GNP) showing a ratio of the GNP in current prices to the GNP in constant prices. A weighted average, with all expenditures tied to a base year, is used.

Going Concern Value—Implies that a company is actively and profitably in business and, therefore, should be valued on that basis rather than on the liquidation of its assets.

Golden Handcuffs—A method of retaining executives—locking them to the corporation—through use of restricted pay devices such as deferred compensation plans.

Golden Handshakes—Additional benefits paid to employees to induce early retirement.

Golden Parachute—A substantial payment made to corporate executives who are terminated upon change or threatened change of ownership or corporate control. Such a provision in an employment contract discourages hostile takeovers and protects executives of potential target companies with monumental lump-sum bailout benefits, if they are fired.

Good Faith—Honesty in fact in the conduct or transaction concerned.

Good Will—An intangible asset on the balance sheet such as a brand name, overall corporate standing or famous association with, say, a celebrity or an event, that is carried on the books of the company at a nominal value (e.g., $1) but which is expected to generate substantial future profits.

Goods and Services Tax (GST)—A federal excise tax imposed on the provision of most goods and services in Canada.

Government National Mortgage Association (GNMA)—A wholly owned government corporation within the Department of Housing and Urban Development (HUD).

Governmental Accounting Standards Board—An organization similar to the Financial Accounting Standards Board (FASB) that was created to improve and establish standards of accounting and financial reporting for state and local government entities.

Governmental Plan—A benefit plan established or maintained for its employees by the government of the United States, by the government of any state or political subdivision thereof, or by any agency or instrumentality of the foregoing.

Grace Period—

—A specified period after a premium payment is due, in which the policyholder may make such payment, and during which the protection of the policy continues.

—A period when a mortgage payment or other debt becomes past due, and before it goes into default. Most mortgages provide for a specified period of time when it can be paid without penalty or default (commonly 30 days).

Graded Vesting—A vesting schedule that calls for partial vesting; 20% vesting is required after three years of service. The vested portion is increased 20% each year until it reaches 100%; this process cannot exceed seven years. See also Vesting Schedules.

Gradual Retirement—A program permitting workers to phase themselves out of a company over a number of years by gradually reducing their workweek, rather than going directly from full-time work into full retirement.

Graduated Benefits—Health care or other employee benefits plans in which the amount contributed by the employer is determined by the number of years the worker has been employed by the company, so shorter-term workers pay more for their coverage than those who have been with the company for many years.

Graduated Payment Mortgage (GPM)—This carries a fixed interest rate, but monthly payments are lower at the beginning and increase gradually to a fixed level after five to ten years. The GPM is intended for young people who expect their incomes to increase.

Graduated Vesting—See Graded Vesting.

Grandfather Clause—An exception to a restriction that allows all those already doing something to continue doing it even if they would be stopped by the new restriction.

Grandpa Track—Executives, senior managers and others, such as scientists and engineers, who have decided to leave the fast track and pursue a less stressful and more leisurely work pace and lifestyle. Companies have begun to accommodate these employees by implementing human resources policies to prevent them from leaving, such as elimination of responsibilities, flexible work options, sabbaticals and personal leave.

Green Card—Registration card issued to a foreign national as evidence of status as a permanent resident of the United States.

Green-Circle Rate—A rate paid to an employee that is below the established pay range minimum for a specific job. The incumbent is usually eligible for larger or more frequent base salary increases until the base salary penetrates the range minimum.

Greenmail—Substantial investor's practice of threatening a takeover until the investor subsequently accepts a premium price for his or her stock in return for a promise to walk away; a variation on blackmail.

Grievance Procedure—

—A formal process for the resolution of member or provider complaints, generally mandated by state law or federal qualification standards for HMOs.

—A formal procedure that provides for the union to represent members and nonmembers in processing a complaint.

Gross Domestic Product (GDP)—The market value of a nation's total output of goods and services.

Gross Eligible Charges—The cost of providing the postretirement health care benefits covered by a plan to a plan participant, before adjusting for expected reimbursements from Medicare and other providers of health care benefits and for the effects of the cost-sharing provisions of the plan.

Gross Income—The total of money received from income property or a business, before operating expenses, taxes, depreciation, commissions, salaries, fees and so on, are deducted.

Gross Revenue; Gross Sales—Used to identify the total business done by a company without any deductions of cost or expenses.

Gross-Up—The practice of increasing the amount of a cash payment to offset for the tax impact to the individual resulting from the cash payment.

Gross Yield—The percentage return on a security which is determined by dividing the dollar price into the annual interest payment and calculating the yield to maturity.

Group Annuity Contract—

—A contract issued by a life insurance company that may be used as the funding instrument for benefits to be made in accordance with a pension plan. A single master contract provides that the group of persons participating in the plan will receive annuities during retirement. Individual certificates stating coverage may be issued to members of the group. Forms of group annuity contracts include deposit administration, immediate participation guarantee, pension investment, deferred annuity and group permanent.

—A funding instrument wherein the insurance company, for a stipulated fee for each participant's benefit, will guarantee the purchase rates of the future annuity and will administer the plan. Also known as *group deferred annuity plan.*

Group Annuity Plan—A pension program underwritten and administered by an insurance company. Normally uses the unit benefit method of funding. Plan participants are covered under one contract; the employer pays premiums on their behalf.

Group Contract (Life and Health Insurance)—A contract of insurance made with an employer or other entity that covers a group of persons identified by reference to their relationship to the entity buying the contract: e.g., members of a trade association, employees of a common employer, members of a labor union; or members of some other group or association not formed for the purpose of buying insurance.

Group Deferred Annuity Plan—See Group Annuity Contract.

Group Enrollment Period—An annual period of at least ten working days during which employees must be given the option of enrolling in one or more HMOs or switching from an HMO to another health plan option offered by the employer.

Group Health Plan—Under ERISA, an employee welfare benefit plan providing medical care to participants and beneficiaries, directly or indirectly. Under the Internal Revenue Code, a plan maintained by an employer to provide medical care, directly or indirectly, to employees, ex-employees and their families.

Group Insurance—Any insurance plan under which a number of employees and their dependents are insured under a single policy, issued to their employer, with individual certificates given to each insured employee; the most commonly written lines are life and accident and health.

Group Legal Services Plan—An employer-funded program that provides personal legal services to employees and their spouses and dependents.

Group Model HMO—An HMO that contracts with a single multispecialty medical group to provide care to the HMO's membership. The group practice may work exclusively with the HMO, or it may provide services to non-HMO patients as well. The HMO pays the medical group a negotiated, per capita rate, which the group distributes among its physicians, usually on a salaried basis.

Group Pension Plan—A program, usually offered by an insurance company, wherein the provisions of the plan are contained in the group contract itself. Such a program will not normally employ a trust agreement.

Group Permanent Plan—

—A group insurance contract between the employer and the insurance company that usually combines life insurance with retirement benefits and uses the level premium method. Contains both cash and paid-up values.

—A program in which a policy is purchased for each participant under a group contract negotiated between an insurance company and an employer. Usually provides life insurance as well as a retirement annuity.

Group Practice—A group of persons licensed to practice medicine in a state. As a principal professional activity and as a group responsibility, it engages or undertakes to engage in the coordinated practice of medicine in one or more group practice facilities. In this connection, members share common overhead expenses (if and to the extent that such expenses are paid by members of the group), medical and other records and substantial portions of equipment and professional, technical and administrative staffs. In some cases, income is also shared.

Group Practice Prepayment Plan—In general, members of group practice prepayment plans pay regular premiums to the plan. In return, the members receive the health services the plan provides, whenever needed, without additional charges. Many prepayment plans have made arrangements with Medicare to receive direct payments for services they furnish that are covered by Part B (SMI).

Group Target Method—See Projection Actuarial Cost Method.

Group Term Life Insurance Plan—A plan qualifying under Code Section 79 to provide employees with employer-paid life insurance coverage at little or no tax cost.

Group Universal Life Plan (GULP)—A form of group life insurance that combines term protection for designated beneficiaries with an investment element for the policyholder, which can be used to create nontaxable permanent insurance or to accumulate tax-deferred capital. Participation is entirely voluntary and all premiums are paid by the employee.

Growth Fund—A type of diversified common stock fund that has capital appreciation as its primary goal. It invests in companies that reinvest most of their earnings for expansion, research or development. The term also refers to growth income funds that invest in common stocks for both current income and long-term growth of both capital and income.

Growth Income Fund—A mutual fund that seeks both capital growth and current income. The assets of these funds may be balanced (consist of both equities and bonds) or stock funds whose assets are invested in high yielding common stocks.

Growth Stock—The stock of a corporation, the earnings of which have increased consistently over a number of years and show every indication of considerable further expansion. Most growth stocks provide a relatively low dividend yield. They are primarily attractive for price appreciation potential, especially from a long-range standpoint. Growth companies should have the following characteristics:

1. A young and aggressive management team
2. Strong emphasis on research and development
3. A favorable record of sales and earnings
4. A line of essential products that seems destined to increase in popularity over the years, while new ones are constantly introduced.

Guaranteed Annual Income (Canada)—Aid provided by the majority of provinces to low-income retirees. Money is in addition to what is received from other sources, up to a guaranteed level of income.

Guaranteed Annuity (Canada)—An annuity that will be paid for the lifetime of a person, but in any event for a minimum period; e.g., if annuity is guaranteed for five years and the annuitant dies after three years, payments will be continued to a beneficiary or the estate for two more years.

Guaranteed Benefit Policy—An insurance policy or contract to the extent that such policy or contract provides for benefits the amount of which is guaranteed by the insurer. It also includes any surplus in a separate account, but excludes any other portion of a separate account.

Guaranteed Certificate of Deposit—Certificate of deposit issued by banks having flexible terms, guaranteed principal and reinvestment rate similar to the guaranteed investment contracts issued by insurance companies.

Guaranteed Income Supplement (GIS) (Canada)—See Guaranteed Annual Income.

Guaranteed Investment Certificate (Canada)—Evidences a deposit made with a financial institution. Maturities range from one to five years for amounts of at least $1,000. It is issued in registered form on an interest bearing basis.

Guaranteed Investment Contract (GIC)—A deposit arrangement entered into with an insurance company, which guarantees both the principal and interest repayments. It is a type of annuity contract, not a marketable security. The amount deposited can be a single sum or a stream of monies deposited over a specified and limited period of time. Similarly, the deposit plus the guaranteed interest paid thereon can be repaid in a single sum or installments. Expenses related to the contract arrangement can be charged against the guaranteed interest payments or paid separately by the contract holder. Also known as *guaranteed interest contract* or *guaranteed income contract.*

Guaranteed Issue Underwriting—The insurer will issue up to some stipulated amount of insurance for each individual employee without evidence of insurability. The requirements are usually based on size of group and distribution by ages, and amounts are decided on by individual insurers.

Guaranteed Renewable Contract—A contract that the insured has the right to continue in force by the timely payment of premiums to a specified age, during which time the insurer has no right to unilaterally make any change in any provision of the policy while the policy is in force, but may make changes in premium rates by policyholder class.

Guaranteed Stock—Generally, a preferred stock that has dividend payments guaranteed by a corporation other than the issuing corporation but remains the stock of the issuing corporation. Guaranteed stock is considered a dual security.

Guardian—A person appointed by the court to look after the property rights and person of minors, the insane and other incompetents or legally incapacitated persons.

Guardian Ad Litem—A special guardian appointed for the sole purpose of carrying on litigation and preserving the interests of a ward. Exercises no control or power over property.

H

Habit-Breaking Program—A type of wellness program designed to end unhealthful habits such as smoking, drinking and so forth.

Halfway House—A residential facility providing transitional care to patients between their discharge from the hospital or other treatment and their return to the community.

Hard Assets—Assets that are tangible in nature, e.g., real estate, antiques and precious metals.

Hard Dollars—Goods or services purchased with cash are said to be purchased with hard dollars. Purchases made with brokerage commissions are said to be purchases made with soft dollars.

Hardship Withdrawal—A withdrawal of an employee's contributions to a 401(k) plan prior to retirement at age 55 or attainment of age 59½. A hardship withdrawal may be made only in cases of financial emergency provided there are no other sources available to meet the need; the withdrawal is taxable as an early distribution and subject to a 10% excise tax.

HCFA Common Procedural Coding System (HCPCS)—An alphanumeric coding system for reporting physician and other provider services, procedures and supplies to Medicare patients. HCPCS includes Current Procedural Terminology (CPT) codes, and also national and local codes. It was developed by HCFA to expand the CPT code to include services such as medical equipment and ambulance services.

HCFA 1500—A form developed by HCFA for providers to bill professional fees to the Medicare program. The form has gained widespread acceptance among other payers.

Health Alliance (HA)—An organization whose basic functions are to bargain with and purchase health insurance from accountable health plans (AHPs) or other sources of health care in behalf of consumers, and to furnish information to consumers on the services provided, evaluation of their quality of care, participant satisfaction and price. Includes Health Insurance Purchasing Corporation (HIPC) and Health Plan Purchasing Cooperative (HPPC).

Health and Human Services Department (HHS)—Federal Cabinet level department responsible for Social Security, welfare and health programs (formerly HEW—Health, Education, and Welfare).

Health and Welfare Fund—See Welfare Fund.

Health Care Coalition—An organization working on broad health care concerns, including controlling costs and enhancing quality. Participants can be providers, business, third party payers and consumers; often there is government participation as well.

Health Care Cost Trend Rate—An assumption about the annual rate of change in the cost of health care benefits currently provided by the postretirement benefit plan, due to factors other than changes in the composition of the plan population by age and dependency status, for each year from the measurement date until the end of the period in which benefits are expected to be paid.

Health Care Financing Administration (HCFA)—The agency of the Department of Health and Human Services that, among other things, administers the Medicare program and works with the states to administer their Medicaid programs.

Health Care Provider—An individual or institution that provides medical services (e.g., a physician, hospital, laboratory, etc.). This term should not be confused with an insurance company which "provides" insurance.

Health Care Reform—The changes to the health care delivery system, how it is structured, how it is financed, and how people will obtain insurance and services as opposed to the current system. The term is applied to the efforts on the federal, state and local levels to make changes in the health care delivery system so that costs are reduced or contained; the uninsured population is covered; all citizens have access to health care; financing is assured; and quality of care is maintained or improved. Management options range from highly centralized, federal controls; through the setting of certain requirements at the federal or state level but allowing local innovation as to implementation; through local solutions, even if nothing is done at the state or national level.

Health Care Reimbursement Account—An option under a flexible benefits plan. Expenses paid for uninsured medical or health care services such as vision, hearing, and dental care (deductibles, copayments/coinsurance, exams, for example) are reimbursable by the employer on a nontaxable basis provided that rules established by the Internal Revenue Service are met.

Health Fair—Type of wellness program designed to increase employee awareness about unhealthy habits such as smoking or overeating and to promote healthful activities such as physical fitness programs.

Health Insurance—Protection that provides payment of benefits for covered sickness or injury. Included under this heading are various types of insurance, such as accident insurance, disability income insurance, medical expense insurance, and accidental death and dismemberment insurance.

Health Insurance Portability and Accountability Act of 1996 (HIPAA)—Federal legislation that improves access to health insurance when changing jobs by restricting certain preexisting condition limitations, and guarantees availability and renewability of health insurance coverage for all employers regardless of claims experience or business size. The law also increases the health insurance deduction for the self-employed; provides tax incentives for purchase of long-term care insurance; and establishes medical saving accounts (MSAs), which provide for tax-deductible contributions to accounts to cover medical expenses.

Health Insurance Purchasing Cooperative/Corporation (HIPC)—A managed competition reform plan for nonprofit organizations set up as collective buying agents of medical services. Also known as *health alliance.*

Health Maintenance Organization (HMO)—A prepaid medical group practice plan that provides a comprehensive predetermined medical care benefit package. The HMO can be sponsored by the government, medical schools, hospitals, employers, labor unions, consumer groups, insurance companies and hospital-medical plans. HMOs are both insurers and providers of health care.

Health Plan Employer Data and Information Set (HEDIS)—A core of performance measures designed by participating managed health plans and employers to meet employers' needs to understand the value of their health care and to hold plans accountable for performance. HEDIS is offered under the sponsorship of the National Committee for Quality Assurance (NCQA).

Health Plan Purchasing Cooperative—See Health Alliance.

Health Promotion—See Wellness (Health Promotion) Programs.

Health Risk Appraisal (HRA)—A survey used by employers to determine the likelihood of an insured experiencing death, illness or injury in the future. It helps employers decide whether wellness and other preventive care programs are necessary.

Health Stock Ownership Plan (HSOP)—The combination of an employee stock ownership plan and 401(h) account. HSOPs allow the sponsoring employer to provide for retiree medical benefits for its current employees without having to accrue such future liabilities currently for financial accounting purposes as would be required if such benefits were provided outside the qualified plan context.

Hedging—
—(Investment) The temporary purchase and sale of a contract calling for future delivery of a specific quantity of a particular commodity at an agreed-upon price to offset a present (or anticipated) position in the cash market. An operation intended to protect against loss in another operation.
—(Agriculture) The sale of a commodity by entering a contract for future delivery at an agreed price and a specific time by a farmer who has or is producing the commodity.

HEDIS—See Health Plan Employer Data and Information Set.

Heir—A person who inherits real property; to be distinguished from next of kin and from a distributee.

High Self-Insured Deductible (HSID)—Also known as shared funding, HSID is a way for employers to improve cash flow by self-funding the first tier of any employee's health care expenses. Employers can thus retain funds that would normally be paid to the insurance company to cover current and future claims.

High-Risk Pools—State-created insurance pools of individuals with extensive current or anticipated health care needs. These pools spread the risk for those individuals among the health insurance companies doing business in that state. The pools have been used by a number of states in an attempt to extend coverage to their medically uninsurable citizens.

People with a chronic disease or illness, such as diabetes or multiple sclerosis, can purchase health care insurance. Additional funds for these high-risk pools are typically taxes on health insurance premiums.

High-Yield Bonds—See Junk Bonds.

Highly Compensated Employee (HCE)—Either a 5% owner or a person who earned more than $80,000 during the current or preceding year. Repeals rule treating highest paid officer as an HCE, the top-100 rule, and family aggregation rules in both the HCE definition and the $150,000 compensation cap. Discrimination in favor of this group is prohibited.

Highly Compensated Individual—For purposes of Section 105(h), a *highly compensated individual* is (1) one of the five highest paid officers, (2) a 10% owner or (3) an employee who is among the highest paid 25% of all employees (other than the 10% owners who are not participants).

Highly Compensated Participant—As defined by IRC Section 125(e), an officer, a more-than-5% shareholder, a highly compensated employee or a spouse or dependent of one of the former.

HIPAA—See Heath Insurance Portability and Accountability Act of 1996.

Hold Harmless Clause—A contract provision in which one party to the contract promises to be responsible for liability incurred by the other party.

Holdback—Contingency provisions in a loan commitment reducing the amount disbursed if conditions are not met.

Holding Company—A corporation that owns the securities of another, in most cases with voting control.

Home Country (International Benefits)—Country of original employment, frequently that of the employee's citizenship.

Home Health Agency (HHA)—An organization providing skilled nursing and other therapeutic services in the patient's home.

Home Health Services—Items and services provided as needed in patients' homes by a home health agency or by others under arrangements made by an HHA. Can range from skilled nursing care and physical therapy to personal care and help with household chores.

Home Office—An office located in an employee's home where, for the convenience of the employer, the employee works. If certain requirements are met, the employee may be allowed to deduct home office expenses.

Homemaker Service—Agency providing services of trained homemakers for persons needing assistance in the home during illness or in situations where the parent or guardian is absent from the home.

Homeopathy—An alternative medical system that treats the symptoms of a disease with minute doses of a drug that produce the same symptoms in a healthy person as are present in the disease. This is thought to stimulate physiological defenses against the symptoms of the disease. Homeopathy as a formal system of medicine is no longer practiced in the United States. However, it may be informally practiced as an alternative therapy.

Hospice—Health care facility or service providing medical care and support services, such as counseling, to terminally ill persons and their families.

Hospital—A legally constituted institution having organized facilities for the care and treatment of sick and injured persons on a resident or inpatient basis, including facilities for diagnosis and surgery under the supervision of a staff of one or more licensed physicians and which provides 24-hour nursing services by a registered nurse on duty or call. It does not mean convalescent, nursing, rest or extended care facilities or a facility operated exclusively for the treatment of the aged, drug addict or alcoholic, whether or not such facilities are operated as a separate institution by a hospital.

Hospital Benefit Plan—A plan that makes cash payments or reimburses employees for hospital charges up to a certain amount or assumes the costs for certain specified hospital charges such as room and board, services, drugs and supplies.

Hospital Benefits—Benefits provided under a policy for hospital charges incurred by an insured person because of an illness or injury.

Hospital Confinement Policy—See Hospital Indemnity Policy.

Hospital Expense Insurance—Health insurance protection against the cost of hospital care resulting from the illness or injury of the insured person.

Hospital Indemnity Policy—A form of health insurance that provides a stipulated daily, weekly or monthly indemnity during hospital confinement. The indemnity is payable on an unallocated basis without regard to the actual expense of hospital confinement.

Host Country National—A citizen of a country who is employed in a branch or plant of a company that is located in that person's country but the company is headquartered in another country.

Hour Bank—

—A method of banking or crediting the hours worked by a worker to his or her individual account and then drawing out the required hours at each determination date, to establish or maintain the worker's eligibility for health insurance benefits.

—A variation of the system puts only the hours (or some portion of the hours) worked in excess of those required to maintain current eligibility in the hour bank account. Hour bank provisions usually specify the maximum number of hours that can be held in the account.

Hour of Service—An hour for which an employee is paid, or is entitled to payment, for the performance of services for the employer. Includes vacation, sick time and other paid leaves of absence. Measurement of time for determining a year of service.

Hours Worked—Standard hours worked in a year is 2,080 (52 weeks $\times$ 40 hours per week).

HR 10 Plan—See Keogh Plan.

Human Immunodeficiency Virus (HIV)—The virus which causes acquired immune deficiency syndrome (AIDS).

Human Resource Information System (HRIS)—A computer-based system for gathering, storing, manipulating, analyzing, retrieving and distributing relevant timely and accurate data and information regarding the staff of an organization, for both organizational effectiveness and legal compliance.

Hurdle Rate—A minimum standard rate of return for acceptability as an investment.

Hybrid HMO—A type of HMO which includes service features of indemnity insurance, such as coinsurance, deductibles, experience rating, open panel of providers, in addition to the various utilization, cost, and access controls and structures of prepaid HMO-type health plans. Sometimes called a mixed model managed care plan.

Hybrid Pension Plan—A qualified retirement type plan that has characteristics typical of both defined benefit and defined contribution plans.

Hypothecate—To give something as security without parting with possession.

Hypothetical Tax (International Benefits)—The amount deducted from an expatriate's salary that is the equivalent of what an expatriate would pay for income tax if at home. The amounts deducted are used by employers to satisfy expatriate tax obligations worldwide.

I

Immature—An actuarial concept referring to newly established companies, or growing organizations, wherein all employees as yet are active and no one has retired. See also Deferred Annuity; Mature.

Immediate Annuity—An annuity under which income payments begin one annuity period (e.g., one month or one year) after the annuity is purchased.

Immediate Basis—An actuarial concept that recognizes the actuarial gains and losses as they occur.

Immediate Participation Guarantee (IPG) Contract—
—A group insurance contract under which the employer's unallocated account is credited with its share of actual investment income for the year. There is generally no guarantee of principal or a minimum rate of interest. Annuity payments are charged directly against the account as they are paid. See also Investment-Only (IO) Contract; Modified Immediate Participation Guarantee Contract.
—A funding instrument offered by insurance companies wherein all dollars paid by the employer and dividends credited are immediately participating in the investment program.

Immediate Vesting—That form of vesting under which rights to vested benefits are acquired by a participant, commencing immediately upon his or her entry into the plan.

Immunization (Bonds)—The design of a bond portfolio to achieve a target level of return in the face of changing reinvestment rates and price levels. It is the combining of short- and long-term bonds in the same portfolio to produce a predictable rate of return regardless of movements in interest rates. See also Dedicated Bond Portfolio.

In and Out Rule—An exception to the general rules on transfers between multiemployer plans and single employer plans, designed to protect multiemployer plans that merge with, but later spin off from single employer plans.

Incapacity—See Disability.

Incentive Compensation—Rewarding the performance of an individual in an institution with added compensation, typically in the form of bonuses or percentage increments above the base salary.

Incentive Fees—See Performance-Based Fees.

Incentive Plan—An employee health benefit plan that offers employees a financial incentive to use preferred providers, which serve to contain overall plan utilization and/or promote healthier lifestyles. For example, deductibles may be lowered or the out-of-pocket limit may be reduced in exchange for using a preferred provider.

Incentive Program (Dental)—A benefits program that pays an increasing share of the treatment cost, provided that the covered individual utilizes the benefits of the program during each incentive period (usually a year) and receives the treatment prescribed.

Incentive Stock Option (ISO)—Gives an executive a right to pay a fixed price for company stock at a future time. Tax is not due until the shares are sold.

Incidental Rules—Limit qualified plans in providing ancillary or supplemental benefits, which are benefits not directly related to a lifetime retirement income. See also Supplemental Benefits.

Incidents of Ownership—Rights that will result in the inclusion of life insurance policy proceeds in the policyholder's estate for federal estate tax purposes.

Income Account—See Profit and Loss Statement.

Income and Service Benefit Formula—A retirement benefit formula based on income and credited service, such as 1% of average annual income multiplied by the years of service.

Income Averaging—A method of determining how much tax is owed on a lump-sum distribution from a qualified pension plan. An individual who receives such a distribution and includes it in taxable income may be eligible to treat the tax liability as if the distribution had been received over a five- or ten-year period. Certain requirements must be met.

Income-Based Benefit Formula—A retirement formula based solely on income, such as 50% of the final yearly salary.

Income Investment—An investment whose main objective is to generate income in the form of interest or dividend payments, rather than to grow principal. For example, a bond fund is an income investment.

Income Manager—A common stock manager whose style places emphasis on the receipt of dividend yield.

Income Protection Insurance Policy—A disability income policy which specifies that an insured is disabled if he or she suffers an income loss caused by a disability, therefore qualifying him or her for benefits under the policy.

Income/Replacement Ratio—The amount of gross income that is replaced by the retirement plan.

Income Statement—See Profit and Loss Statement.

Incontestable Clause—An optional policy clause making the contract indisputable regarding any statements made in the application after a specified period (usually two or three years) has elapsed. Can be used in noncancelable or guaranteed renewable health insurance contracts.

Incurred but Not Reported (IBNR)—Claims that have been incurred but have not been reported to the insurer as of some specific date. Often a disputed figure since carriers must estimate this liability for accounting purposes based on their experience with claims lags.

Incurred but Unreported Claim (IUC) Reserve—Reserve accumulated by an insurance company to cover IUCs.

Incurred Claims—Incurred claims equal the claims paid during the policy year plus the claim reserves as of the end of the policy year, minus the corresponding reserves as of the beginning of the policy year. The difference between the year-end and beginning of the year claim reserves is called the *increase in reserves* and may be added directly to the paid claims to produce the incurred claims.

Incurred Losses—The losses occurring within a fixed period, whether or not they were reported or adjusted during that period.

Indemnify—Literally, "to save harmless." Thus, one person or organization agrees to protect another against loss.

Indemnity—A benefit paid by an insurer for a loss insured under a policy.

Indemnity Contract—A contract in which the amount of the benefit is based on the actual amount of financial loss as determined at the time of loss.

Indemnity Plans—In these traditional fee-for-service group health insurance plans, the patient chooses whichever doctor and hospital he or she wants to use. The employer pays premiums to the health insurance company to cover the costs of providing benefits and administering claims. The employee may pay a portion of the monthly insurance premiums, an annual deductible and/or copayments per medical visit. These plans are usually experience rated, and health care providers are paid on a cost-plus, retroactive reimbursement system. The insurance carrier uses the premiums to pay claims and for retention fees, including state premium taxes, administrative expenses, commissions, risk charges and claims processing. The employer has no liability for a deficit.

Indenture—A mutual agreement in writing between or among two or more parties whereof usually each party has a counterpart or duplicate. Originally so called because the parts were indented by a notched cut or line so the two parts could be fitted together.

Independent Contractor—As distinguished from an employee by the IRS, a person who works for another whose labor and how it is performed is largely determined by the worker, not the employer. Independent contractors pay their own taxes; the employer does not, for example, pay Social Security or unemployment taxes for the worker.

Independent Living Program (ILP)—A program of housing assistance, job retraining and other types of assistance to help disabled individuals live as independently as possible.

Independent Practice Association—See Individual Practice Association.

Index—A statistical model expressed in terms of percentages of a base year or years that serves as a reference in judging investment performance. For instance, the BLS Wholesale Price Index uses as its base period 1967 equals 100; the June 1974 index figure was 155.7, indicating that wholesale prices had risen by almost 56% since 1967. The index most often used for stock market performance is the Standard & Poor's 500 Index, which measures the average performance of 500 widely held common stocks. Over periods of 15 years or longer, the stock market, as measured by the S&P 500 Index, historically has earned an average 10% annual return. Other frequently used indexes are the Dow Jones Industrial Average; the Russell 2000, used for smaller company stocks; the Wilshire 5000, used for the entire U.S. stock market—including both the big company stocks that make up the S&P 500 Index and the smaller stocks represented in the Russell 2000; and the Morgan Stanley Capital International Europe, Australia, Far East Index (EAFE), which is used as a benchmark for foreign company stocks.

Index Fund—An investment fund (or account) composed of securities the characteristics of which will produce a return that will duplicate (or substantially duplicate) a designated securities index.

Index Option—An option based on the market value of a particular group of stocks. Unlike stock options, index options—when exercised—are settled in cash.

Indexing (International Benefits)—A form of automatic adjustment of benefits that are in the course of payment, based on the change in consumer prices, cost of living, average wages and so on.

Individual Account Plan—A defined contribution plan or profit-sharing plan that provides an individual account for each participant; allows participants to choose, from a broad range of investment options, how their accounts will be invested; and whose benefits are based solely on the amount contributed to the participant's account, including income, expenses, gains and losses. Defined contribution retirement plans such as 401(k) plans are examples of individual account plans. See also Defined Contribution Plan.

Individual Aggregate Actuarial Cost Method—See Individual Spread Gain Actuarial Cost Method.

Individual Annuity—A contract by which an insurance company undertakes to pay an individual a specified annuity. Two main types are the retirement annuity policy and the retirement income policy. When used for pension plans, the policies are usually held in trust until the employee retires. Generally used when the number of covered employees is too small to permit the use of group annuities.

Individual Health Care Account (IHCA)—A proposed method of financing health care costs by giving tax advantages to individuals who establish and maintain such accounts, which are similar to individual retirement accounts (IRAs). Money placed in an IHCA would be excluded from the individual's taxable income and would be invested, with principal and income to be used only for specified health care. Synonym(s): health IRA, medical savings account (MSA).

Individual Level Actuarial Cost Method; Individual Level Premium Actuarial Cost Method—A method under which the actuarial present value of each increment of an individual's projected benefits is allocated on a level basis over the future earnings or service of the individual between the age at which such increment is first recognized and the exit age(s). The portion of this actuarial present value allocated to a valuation year is called the *normal cost.* Each individual's portion of the actuarial accrued liability should be determined on a consistent basis, usually as the retrospective accumulation of the individual's prior actuarial accrued liability and prior normal cost, using the valuation actuarial assumptions.

Individual Life Insurance and Annuity Contracts—Individual life insurance contracts generally provide for paying the face amount in a lump sum upon the death of the insured while the insurance is in force. The insurance may be continuous throughout the lifetime of the insured, for a specified number of years or to a specified age. A medical examination is generally required for insurance under individual contracts, but if the amount of insurance is not large, a statement by the applicant as to his or her physical condition and medical history may be accepted by the insurer.

Individual Mandate—A health care financing option that would require individuals to buy their own insurance if employers do not provide it.

Individual Pension Plan (Canada)—A personalized, employer-sponsored registered pension plan that provides a guaranteed lifetime pension. When used with an RRSP, the plan can boost tax-sheltered retirement savings. The plan can be structured in either defined benefit or defined contribution format; it is primarily used for executives.

Individual Practice Association (IPA)—A type of health care provider organization composed of physicians, in which the physicians maintain their own practices but agree to furnish services to patients who have signed up for a prepayment plan in which the physician services are supplied by the IPA. An IPA is not a health maintenance organization (HMO), a health care organization (HCO), or a preferred provider organization (PPO).

Individual Projected Benefit Cost Method—The individual category of projected benefit cost methods is characterized by the assumed allocation of the actuarial cost in respect to each employee individually, generally as a level amount or as a percentage of earnings, over all or part of his or her period of service, period of coverage under the plan or some other appropriate period uniformly applied. Under individual cost methods, the total actuarial cost is generally separable as to the various participants, i.e., costs are individually calculated for each employee, or are calculated by group methods in such a way as to produce essentially the same total result as though individually calculated.

Individual Retirement Account (IRA)—A specific type of retirement account, usually with a bank, savings and loan, or credit union, for individuals to which yearly tax deductible contributions up to a specified limit can be made. The amounts contributed are not taxed until withdrawal. Withdrawal is not permitted, without penalty, until the individual reaches age 59½. See also Individual Retirement Plans.

Individual Retirement Plans—Effective for tax years beginning after December 31, 1981, employees and self-employed persons receiving compensation can establish their own individual retirement plans, even if they are already covered under tax-qualified plans (including HR 10 or Keogh plans), government plans or certain annuities.

Individual Spread Gain Actuarial Cost Method; Individual Aggregate Actuarial Cost Method—A method under which the actuarial present value of each increment of an individual's projected benefits is allocated on a level basis over the future earnings or service of the individual between the age at which such increment is first recognized and the exit age(s). The portion of this actuarial present value allocated to a valuation year is called the *normal cost*. The actuarial value of assets is deemed to be assigned to individuals on a reasonable and consistent basis; for example, such individual's share may be the accumulation of his or her prior normal costs and any prior actuarial gains (losses) allocated to the individual. Actuarial gains (losses) are allocated to the individuals in proportion to the assigned actuarial value of assets, or on any other reasonable and consistent basis. The actuarial accrued liability for an individual equals the assigned portion of the actuarial value of assets.

Individual Stop-Loss Coverage—Insurance coverage that may be purchased to limit an employer's liability for paying claims on behalf of a covered individual after the employer has paid claims of a given amount for that individual.

Industry Life Cycle—The evolvement of industries through stages, including the pioneering, expansion and stabilization stages.

Infertility Benefits—Insurance coverage for treatments to enable human reproduction where that capacity is reduced or absent. Can range from diagnostic tests, to treatment of underlying causes of infertility to in vitro procedures.

Inflation—A phase of the business cycle characterized by abnormally high prices, a decrease in the purchasing power of money, and spiraling costs and wage rates. Inflation may occur when purchasing power is in excess of goods and services for sale, and/or buyers stampede to convert money into commodities; or when production costs and prices advance to consecutively higher levels. The opposite of *deflation*.

Informal Plan—The employer has no legal obligation and the employee has no legal rights regarding retirement benefits. There is no set level of benefit payments and no particular method of funding.

Informally Funded Arrangement—A retirement program wherein the reserve carried against the future liability under the program remains the sole property of the employer during the deferred period.

Initial Actuarial Liability—See Initial Past Service Liability.

Initial Past Service Liability—The actuarial value (single sum) of the past service benefits as of the effective date of the establishment of the plan, or at the date of the latest liberalization. The maximum annual past service contribution allowable for tax deduction is the amount required to amortize past service liabilities and other supplementary pension or annuity credits over ten years. Also referred to as *initial supplemental liability* or *past service liability*.

Initial Public Offering (IPO)—The original sale of a company's securities to the public.

Initial Supplemental Liability—See Initial Past Service Liability.

Injunction—A writ of judicial process by which a party is required to do a particular thing or to refrain from doing a particular thing. Imposed when the complaining party will suffer irreparable injury as a result of unlawful actions by the other party.

Injury Management—The processes of injury prevention, injury control, injury-related cost containment, and integration of persons with disabilities in the workplace through ergonomics.

Inpatient—A person who occupies a hospital bed, crib or bassinet while under observation, care, diagnosis or treatment for at least 24 hours. (Antonym: outpatient)

Inpatriates (International Benefits)—Employees of foreign corporate parents or subsidiaries of U.S. companies who are transferred to the United States on a temporary or permanent basis.

In-Service Distribution—Profit-sharing plans may allow a plan participant to take a distribution from the plan prior to the time the participant incurs a traditional triggering event.

In-Service Withdrawal—A withdrawal of plan benefits prior to separation from service with an employer. No in-service withdrawals are permitted from a pension plan.

Insider—A shareholder who owns 5% or more of a company, a member of the board of directors or an elected officer of a corporation, or anyone else who possesses information that is not publicly known about the company, but which is important in valuing its stock. Securities and Exchange Commission (SEC) regulations place restrictions on stock purchases and sales by insiders.

Insourcing—Administering benefit plans, such as flexible benefits, internally. This permits valuable access to and control of data.

Institutional Investor—An organization the primary purpose of which is to invest its own assets or those held in trust by it for others. Includes pension funds, investment companies, universities and banks.

Insurable Interest—A person's or party's interest—financial or emotional—in the continuing life of an individual; a person or party must have an insurable interest in the life of a proposed insured in order to purchase an insurance policy on the proposed insured's life.

Insurable Risk—The conditions that make a risk insurable are (1) the peril insured against must produce a definite loss not under the control of the insured, (2) there must be a large number of homogeneous exposures subject to the same perils, (3) the loss must be calculable and the cost of insuring it must be economically feasible, (4) the peril must be unlikely to affect all insureds simultaneously and (5) the loss produced by a risk must be definite and have potential to be financially serious.

Insurance—A means of providing or purchasing protection against some of the economic consequences of loss.

Insurance Companies Act (Canada)—The primary federal law that governs insurance companies operating in Canada. It is designed to break down barriers among the various financial service sectors, increase competition and bring about change in the insurance industry.

Insurance Contract—An irrevocable contract in which the insurance company unconditionally undertakes a legal obligation to provide benefits in return for a premium, thereby transferring risk from the employer (or the plan) to the insurance company.

Insurance Guaranty Fund—A fund maintained by the state guaranty association, financed by contributions from insurers, which pays claims of insolvent insurance companies. A few states now have HMO guaranty funds.

Insurance Reform—A package of legislative provisions that would regulate the marketing practices of health insurance companies. Typically, insurance reforms attempt to address either access to coverage and/or affordability of coverage for the small group market.

Insured—In life insurance, the person on whose life an insurance policy is issued; in property and liability insurance, the person to whom or on whose behalf benefits are payable under the policy.

Insured Event—An occurrence that causes the PBGC to assume responsibility for benefit payments. Termination of a single employer plan or an insolvent multiemployer plan are insured events.

Insured Pension Plan—A plan funded through contracts with a life insurance company, which guarantees payment of the annuities.

Insurer—An organization, insurance company or other, that assumes the risk and provides the policy to the insured.

Intangible Assets—Capital assets carried on the balance sheet that are not physical or financial in character and that often are shown at cost or having nominal value assigned to them which usually does not reflect their substantial contribution to earning power. Examples would be patents, good will, trademarks, copyrights, franchises and unamortized discounts.

Integrated Health Delivery Network—A group of hospitals, physicians, other providers, and insurers and/or community agencies that work together to coordinate and deliver a broad spectrum of cost-effective services to their community. Also known as *integrated delivery system* or *integrated service network.*

Integrated Plan—A plan that makes adjustments in contributions or benefits for amounts available through Social Security. See Permitted Disparity.

Integrated Provider (IP)—A health care group that provides comprehensive and coordinated care, and typically includes hospitals, group practices, a health plan and other related services. Physicians may either be employees of the IP or keep their own practice.

Integration Level—The compensation level below which, under a plan's benefit formula, compensation is excluded in the computation of benefits or contributions.

Integration With OAS, CPP/QPP (Canada)—The usual option provides a larger pension from the plan from retirement until eligibility for these government benefits, reducing at that age by the amount of the government benefits; it thus provides a level total pension throughout retirement.

Integration With Social Security—

—A plan wherein the benefits are integrated with the Social Security benefit. Under regular corporate plans, the regulations define the percentages applicable to the various benefits. Under a self-employed program, the only offset permissible is the amount of the Social Security tax paid for the employee. If more than one plan is instituted for the same company, only one program may be integrated.

—The basic concept of integration is that the benefits of the employer's plan must be dovetailed with Social Security benefits in such a manner that employees earning more than the taxable wage base will not receive combined benefits under the two programs that are proportionately greater than the benefits for employees earning less than the taxable wage base. See also Permitted Disparity.

Intensive Care Unit (ICU)—A unit of a hospital especially designed and staffed to meet the specific needs of critically or seriously ill patients. These patients are under constant personal observation by a nurse who has all necessary lifesaving equipment, drugs and supplies immediately available.

Interactive Benefits Communication—Use of technologies for communicating employee benefits such as touch-tone phones, personal computers and multimedia kiosks. Forms of interactive communication include interactive voice response (IVR) systems, desktop personal computers, multimedia personal computers and public kiosks.

Interest—

—The return earned or to be earned on funds invested or to be invested to provide for future pension benefits. In calling the return *interest,* it is recognized that, in addition to interest on debt securities, the earnings of a pension fund may include dividends on equity securities, rentals on real estate and gains or (as offsets) losses on fund investments.

—The amount a borrower pays to a lender for the use of its money. Interest is paid by a corporation to its bondholders for the use of their money.

—Regular interest is a rate of interest to be used in accumulating contributions under the retirement plan and in making actuarial computations.

Interest Rate Risk—When interest rates rise, the market value of fixed income contracts (such as bonds) declines. Similarly, when interest rates decline, the market value of fixed income contracts increases. Interest rate risk is the risk associated with these fluctuations.

Interest Table—A listing of the present or accumulated value of $1 at compound interest or of periodic payments of $1 at intervals of one year or other specified periods.

Interest Yield—The uniform rate of interest on investments computed on the basis of the price at which the investment was purchased, giving effect to the periodic amortization of any premiums paid or the periodic accrual of discounts received.

Intergenerational Day Care—A day-care program in which children and elderly relatives are cared for at the same facility.

Intermediate Care Facility (ICF)—An institution licensed under state law to provide, on a regular basis, health care and services to individuals who do not require the degree of care and treatment that a hospital or a skilled nursing facility is designed to provide. The individuals must, however, require care and services above the level of room and board. Federal payment for intermediate care facility services is limited to Medicaid.

Intermediate-Term Bonds—Bonds with between five and ten years to maturity.

Intern—A person who has had formal training in a profession who is now obtaining supervised professional training. As applied to medicine, a physician intern is now called a *first year resident physician.*

Internal Medicine—The branch of medicine that deals especially with diagnosis and medical (nonsurgical) treatment of disorders and diseases of the internal structures of the body.

Internal Revenue Code (IRC)—As amended, this code is the basic federal tax law.

Internal Revenue Service (IRS)—Part of the Treasury Department, the IRS is the government agency charged with the collection of taxes, including those related to employee benefit plans. The IRS is also responsible for administering the requirements for qualified pension plans as well as other retirement and welfare plans. It assesses penalties for failure to comply with certain reporting and disclosure requirements.

***International Classification of Diseases,* Ninth Revision, Clinical Modification (ICD-9-CM)**—The classification in current use for coding of diagnoses and operations, for compiling hospital statistics, and for submitting bills. The *International Classification* is a publication of the World Health Organization (WHO).

International Compensation—Pay practices covering employees who move across national borders, including headquarters expatriates, third country nationals and inpatriates. The definition sometimes is extended to include domestic pay practices in foreign countries.

International Fund—See Global Fund.

Internet—A worldwide network of computer networks that can share information because a common set of language protocols is used by all. The Internet was created by the U.S. government in the late '60s to link defense researchers and contractors. Now computer systems at universities, libraries, government agencies, schools, businesses and homes with personal computers with Internet access are all connected.

Internist—A physician who practices internal medicine.

Interrogatories—Written questions sent by one party in a lawsuit to the opposing party, in preparation for trial.

Intervention—A formal process where the counselor (and often with a team consisting of supervisor, coworkers and family members) confronts an individual, breaks through denial and convinces him or her to enter treatment.

Intestate—Dies without a will.

Intranet—An internal computer network accessible to employees only.

These private networks combine text, graphics and even video to distribute news, answer employee questions, update personnel records and connect workers in remote locations.

Inventory—

—Current assets representing the present stock of finished merchandise, goods in process of manufacture, raw materials used in manufacture and sometimes miscellaneous supplies such as packing and shipping materials. These are usually stated at cost or market value, whichever is lower.

—Those tangible assets on the balance sheet valued at cost or market, whichever is lower, consisting of raw materials, semifinished and finished goods, and expected to be disposed of within a year, from which a company hopes to derive a profit.

Invested Capital—The sum of a company's long-term debt, capital stock and all surplus.

Investment—The process by which money is transferred from one owner to another for the purpose of making more money in the form of capital gains or additional income or a combination of both.

Investment Adviser—A professional who is selected, usually by the trustees of a plan, to manage plan assets in a trust. Advisers are generally required to register with the SEC.

Investment Advisers Act of 1940—As amended in 1960, a law that established a pattern of regulation of investment advisers and is similar in many respects to Securities Exchange Act provisions governing the conduct of brokers and dealers. It requires, with certain exceptions, that persons or firms engaging for compensation in the business of advising others with respect to their securities transactions shall register with the commission and conform their activities to statutory standards designed to protect the interests of investors.

Investment Banker—Also known as an *underwriter*. He or she is the middleman between the corporation issuing new securities and the public. The usual practice is for one or more investment bankers to buy outright from a corporation a new issue of stocks or bonds. The groups form a syndicate to sell securities to individuals and institutions. Investment bankers also distribute very large blocks of stocks or bonds, perhaps held by an estate. Thereafter, the market in the security may be over the counter, on a regional stock exchange, the American Exchange or the New York Stock Exchange.

Investment Company or Trust—A company or trust managed by investment professionals that invests its capital in other companies for purposes of diversification, the two principal types of which are the *closed- end* and *open-end* or *mutual fund. Closed-end funds* have a fixed capitalization, and are usually listed and traded on the New York Stock Exchange like any other security, and may sell at a premium or discount to net asset value. *Open-end funds* whose shares are not listed stand ready to sell new shares continuously to investors and to redeem them when called upon to do so.

Investment Consultant—An individual or firm that provides—for a fixed fee based on a percentage of assets or a fee derived from brokerage commissions—investment advice. Such advice generally includes analyzing portfolio constraints, setting performance objectives, counseling on allocation of assets, educating the investment manager, and selecting and monitoring services. It may or may not include performance measurement services.

Investment Contract—An investment method for insured pension plans that is similar to an immediate participation guarantee contract (IPG).

Investment Earnings—Investment income on contributions, which is not normally subject to federal income tax for employee benefit plans.

Investment Education—The provision of educational materials and information to assist plan participants in planning for their retirement. Topics can include specific plan information; general financial and investment information such as risk and return, diversification and compound return; hypothetical asset allocation models using different time horizons and risk profiles; and interactive investment material such as questionnaires, worksheets and computer programs for estimating retirement needs, and the impact of asset allocation. Care must be taken to leave decision making in the hands of participants; giving actual investment advice places the employer under ERISA fiduciary liability. See Investment Consultant.

Investment Gain/Loss—The realized or unrealized increase (decrease) in market value of a portfolio at the end of a time period as compared to its market value at the beginning of that period.

Investment Manager—Any fiduciary other than a trustee or named fiduciary that (1) has the power to manage, acquire or dispose of any asset of a plan; (2) is registered as an investment adviser under the Investment Advisers Act of 1940, is a *bank* as defined in that act or is an insurance company licensed in more than one state to perform investment managing services; and (3) has acknowledged in writing that it is a fiduciary with respect to the plan.

Investment Objectives—Long-term, risk-return targets developed principally from careful consideration of plan sponsor factors, investment factors and a forecast of the future. Critical in the adoption of investment objectives is the asset allocation decision.

Investment-Only (IO) Contract—A modification of an IPG contract. The benefit payments are not guaranteed by the insurance company past the current year and investments may be made in the insurance company's general account or in its various separate accounts. See also Immediate Participation Guarantee (IPG) Contract.

Investment Policy—Commonly used to describe how contributions to an employee benefit plan are utilized from the time they are received until benefits are paid. Under ERISA, a written investment policy is required.

Investment Policy Statement—The statement of policy is the communication of a *risk policy* to the fund's investment manager(s). It states unambiguously the degree of investment risk that fiduciaries are willing to undertake with pension trust assets. A statement of investment policy differs importantly from a statement of investment objectives. An investment *policy* prescribes acceptable course of action; a policy can be acted upon, implemented. An investment *objective* (such as a performance standard) is a desired result. A manager cannot implement an objective; a manager can only pursue a course of action, consistent with investment policy, which the manager believes offers a reasonable likelihood of realizing the objective. Therefore, in drafting instructions for an investment manager, primary emphasis should be on stating the investment, or risk, policy clearly.

Investment Portfolio—A securities portfolio in which is held securities whose principal is considered relatively safe and that provides a fair return.

Investment Return—See Yield.

Investment-Sensitive Life Insurance—See Variable Life Insurance.

Investor—Someone whose principal purpose is to invest money prudently and productively over the longer, as opposed to the shorter, run with the investment objective being protection of principal, obtaining a reasonable return and capital appreciation to preserve purchasing power. Compare with Speculator; Trader.

IRA—See Individual Retirement Account.

Irrevocable Beneficiary—An unalterable beneficiary. The owner gives up the right to change the beneficiary designation without the beneficiary's consent.

J

Jackson Hole Group (JHG)—A group of health care experts, executives and others interested in problems in the health care system that meets periodically at the home of Dr. Paul Ellwood, M.D., a group member in Jackson Hole, Wyoming to develop solutions. The group gained national attention with the 1991 release of a plan entitled "The 21st Century American Health System: The Jackson Hole Group Proposals for Health Care Reform Through Managed Competition." In this model, large health insurance purchasing cooperatives would be created for small employers and individuals. Accountable health partnerships would act as both insurer and provider, and a national health board would develop and oversee a standard benefits package.

January Effect—The observed tendency for stock returns to be higher in January than would be expected.

Job Lock—Remaining in a particular job for fear of losing one's health insurance coverage. This is caused by waiting periods for preexisting conditions, high rates and outright denials of coverage.

Job Sharing—Two people, typically in career-oriented professional positions, performing the tasks of one full-time position in order to enjoy more flexibility in their personal schedules, typically for child or dependent care. Salary and benefits are prorated.

Job Shoppers—Retired workers who are hired part time to work with new recruits as mentors and trainers.

Joint Administration (Canada)—Provision for a union-management committee or board of trustees to assume supervisory functions relating to administration of an employee benefit plan.

Joint and Several Liability—Used when compensation for liability may be obtained from one or more parties either individually or jointly, whichever may be most advantageous. Example: Partners are responsible for their own and the others' actions in business.

Joint and Survivor Annuity—A contract that provides income periodically, payable during the longer of the lifetimes of the two persons. The benefit payable may be adjusted to account for the extended life expectancy of the couple, and the benefit amount may decrease when one or the other dies. The contingent annuitant is usually the spouse. See also Automatic Survivor Coverage and Contingent Annuity Option.

Joint and Survivor Option—A pension plan provision in which, based on the age of a designated survivor (usually one's spouse), a reduced pension is paid as long as one of the two parties is living.

Joint Commission on Accreditation of Healthcare Organizations (JCAHO)—An accrediting body that periodically evaluates and awards accreditation status to facilities such as hospitals, skilled nursing facilities and health maintenance organizations in recognition of satisfactory performance. Most managed care plans and some state and federal programs require JCAHO certification.

Joint Tenancy Estate—The ownership of property by two or more persons in equal shares with the rights of survivorship.

Joint Venture—The joining of two or more people to carry out a specific business venture; a cooperative endeavor. Sometimes called a *joint adventure.*

Jointly Trusteed Single Employer Plan—An employee benefit plan that is administered by a board of trustees consisting of an equal number of employee and employer representatives.

Judicial Review—The power of courts to declare laws and executive actions unconstitutional. The review is limited to conclusions of law; findings of fact are excluded unless they are not supported by the evidence.

Junior Mortgage—A mortgage second in lien to a previous mortgage. Also called a *subordinate mortgage.*

Junk Bonds—Bonds that are initially issued as low-quality securities, often in conjunction with takeovers, leveraged buyouts and restructurings. They offer high interest and high risk. These securities generally lack the characteristics of a desirable investment. The rights of the bondholder are subordinated to senior debtholders. Assurance of interest and principal payments in the future is limited. Repayment often depends on asset sales rather than on the ongoing profitability of the business. Also called *high-yield bonds.*

Jury Duty Pay—Pay to employees to supplement the small stipend provided by local governments for jury duty service. Jury duty pay, whether provided by the government or employer, is taxable income to the employee.

Just-in-Time (JIT) System—A system of inventory control in which a manufacturer coordinates production with suppliers so that raw materials and components arrive just as they are needed in the production process.

Juvenile Insurance Policy—An insurance policy that is issued on the life of a child but is owned and paid for by an adult.

K

Keogh Plan—A qualified retirement plan for self-employed persons and their employees to which yearly tax deductible contributions up to a specified limit can be made, if the plan meets certain requirements of the Internal Revenue Code. Keogh plans, also known as HR 10 plans, include defined benefit and defined contribution plans.

Key Employee—A criterion used to describe highly compensated officers or owners of companies and to establish whether a defined benefit pension plan is top-heavy; if it is, special requirements for vesting, contributions and benefits must be met to retain tax qualifications. Specifically, a key employee is a participant who, at any time during the plan year or any of the four preceding years: (1) earned at least $45,000 and was an officer, (2) earned more than $30,000 and was one of the ten employees owning the largest interest in the employer, (3) owned more than 5% of the employer, or (4) earned more than $150,000 and owned more than 1% of the employer. All dollar limits are adjusted for cost of living on an annual basis.

Key Employee Insurance—Protection of a business firm against the financial loss caused by death or disability of a vital member of the firm; a means of protecting the business from the adverse results of the loss of an individual possessing special skills or experience. See also Business Continuation Insurance.

Kiosk—A computer-based interactive system installed in high-traffic employee areas to perform a range of functions such as accessing general information about benefits, checking the status of savings plans, making calculations of benefits coverage, and changing the mix of benefits in a flexible benefit program. Employees can access the kiosk in passing and interact through a touch screen or mouse.

Knowledge-Based Pay—A system of salary differentiation based on the formal education, related experience or specialized training a professional employee has that qualifies the individual to deal with specific subject matter or work effectively in a specific field. Salary level may not be dependent on whether the employee utilizes the knowledge.

L

L—Long-term funds; includes M_3 bankers acceptances, commercial paper, Eurodollar holdings of U.S. nonbank residents and marketable liquid Treasury obligations.

Labor Force—All persons at least 16 years of age employed as civilians, the unemployed and those in the armed forces. Does not include people not looking for work, those engaged in housework in their own homes, full-time students and unpaid family workers laboring fewer than 15 hours a week.

Labor Law—Dictates the rules and regulations that govern the relationship between labor and management, defining the rights, privileges, duties and responsibilities of each.

Labor-Management Relations Act of 1947 (Taft-Hartley Act)—See Taft-Hartley Act.

Labor-Management Reporting and Disclosure Act of 1959—Required the reporting and disclosure of union financial records and administrative acts, to prevent union officials from failing to fulfill their proper roles; also established procedures for the orderly conduct of union elections.

Lag—The period of time between the incurring of a claim and the payment of that claim.

Lapse—Termination of a policy upon the policyholder's failure to pay the premium within the time required.

Last In, First Out (LIFO)—Used in inventory accounting terminology to reflect the fact that sales are made against the latest inventory purchases, which tends to minimize inventory profits and losses. Contrast with First In, First Out (FIFO).

Lease—A contract between landlord and tenant setting forth the rights and obligations of both parties.

Leaseback—A transaction in which a seller remains in possession as a tenant after completing the sale and delivering the deed.

Leased Employee—A three-party relationship whereby the user business purchases services of a worker, on a more or less full-time basis, from a business that pays the worker's salary. Any interrelationship between these parties can lead to an *affiliated service group* or *controlled group* relationship, which is treated separately.

Leasehold—A right to occupy a property for a stated number of years at a stipulated annual rental. Where a bonus is paid to obtain the lease, the excess amount paid should be carried on the balance sheet and amortized over the life of the lease.

Leasehold Improvement—The sums expended to improve or upgrade the property over a period of years. Because such improvement normally accrues to the landlord or owner at the expiration of the lease, their costs must be amortized over the life of the lease.

Least Expensive Alternative Treatment (LEAT)—A limitation in a benefits plan that will only allow benefits for the least expensive treatment. Also referred to as Least Expensive Professionally Acceptable Alternative Treatment (LEPAAT).

Legal Services Plan—A group benefit plan that provides convenient and affordable legal assistance in exchange for a contribution, usually from the employee. The plan can be part of a cafeteria plan or linked to an EAP. Examples of covered services are legal advice, drafting of wills and house closings.

Legend Drugs—Drugs that must be obtained by doctor prescription, as opposed to those prescribed by a doctor but available over the counter.

Lender—Here used to denote an institution, such as an insurance company, bank, savings and loan association, pension fund or savings bank, that lends monies at interest for investment purposes, which loan is usually collateralized by the property for which the funds are lent.

Lending of Securities—A practice whereby owners of

securities either directly or indirectly lend their securities to primarily brokerage firms for a fee, and against which either cash, securities or a letter of credit is pledged to protect the lender. Securities are borrowed to cover fails of deliveries or short sales, provide proper denominations and enable brokerage firms to engage in arbitrage trading activities.

Length of Stay (LOS)—The number of days that elapse between admission and discharge from a hospital or health care facility.

Length of Stay Legislation—Legislation to safeguard against substandard care so that patients are not discharged until it is medically appropriate (for example, for mothers and infants after childbirth, legislation has been passed that sets a minimum length of stay; the opposition states that clinical decision making should be free of politics).

Lessee—The person, corporation or other legal entity to whom or to which property is leased.

Lessor—The person, corporation or other legal entity that leases property to a lessee.

Letter Ruling—A private ruling issued by the IRS in response to a request from a taxpayer about the tax consequences of a proposed or completed transaction. Private Letter Rulings are published informally by several publishers. They are not considered to be precedents for use by taxpayers other than the one who requested the ruling, but they do give an indication of the current attitude of the IRS toward a particular type of transaction.

Level Annual Premium Funding Method—

—The cost of providing a pension where the contributions for any employee remain constant until normal retirement age.

—A method of accumulating money for payment of future pensions under which the level annual charge for a particular benefit is determined by the actuary for each age of entry and is payable each year until retirement, at which time the benefit is fully funded.

—See also Actuarial Cost Method.

Level Premium—A premium that remains unchanged throughout the life of a policy. In a level premium plan, reserves accumulate in the early years of the policy because the actual cost of coverage is less than the premium charged.

Leveling—Means of correcting a failed nondiscrimination test. The highest contribution ratios of the highly compensated employees are reduced until the group percentage falls within acceptable limits. See also Recharacterization.

Leverage—

—Means of enhancing return or value without increasing investment, e.g., buying securities on margin.

—A condition where wide changes in earnings and market value of a company's common stock may be expected because of a heavy preponderance of debt and/or preferred stock in a company's capitalization, which necessitates substantial interest and preferred dividend payments be absorbed before anything is left for the common. Works to the advantage of common shareholders when earnings are good, and to their disadvantage when they are bad. Where a company has no outstanding debts or preferred stock, as in the case of most insurance companies, no leverage exists as earnings flow to the common stockholders.

—In real estate, the term means the effective use of money by investing the least amount of capital possible when acquiring property in order that it may bring the maximum percentage of return by mortgaging the property to the highest amount that is practical.

Leverageable ESOP—An ESOP that is permitted to leverage under the terms of the plan documents but has not done so by a given date.

Leveraged Buyout (LBO)—The purchase of assets or stock of a privately owned company, a public company, or a subsidiary or division of a private or publicly held company in which the purchaser uses a significant amount of debt and very little or no equity capital. This is accomplished primarily by utilizing the purchased assets for collateral and the acquired earnings stream to amortize the debt.

Leveraged ESOP—An ESOP in which money is borrowed by the ESOP trust for the purpose of buying stock of the employer. The stock is normally held as security by the lender and released for allocation to participant accounts as the loan is paid off.

Liabilities—The amount of money that a business, government or individual owes to others. Includes amounts owed for mortgages, supplies, wages, salaries, accrued taxes and other debts. Also includes future obligations.

Liability Insurance—A type of insurance that provides a benefit payable on behalf of a covered party who is held legally responsible (liable) for harming others or their property.

Liability Reserve—A reserve established by a company that appears on the right side of the balance sheet to reflect a potential charge, the existence of which is undisputed but the proper amount of which cannot now be ascertained.

Libel—A defamatory statement made in writing about another person. See also Slander.

Licensure—The process by which an agency of government—usually state government—grants permission to an individual or organization to engage in a given occupation or business upon finding that the applicant has attained the competency necessary to ensure that the public health, safety and welfare will be reasonably well protected. See also Accreditation; Certification.

Lien—The right in law of one person, usually a creditor, to keep possession of, or control, the property of another for the purpose of satisfying a debt. See also Mechanic's Lien.

Life Care—A long-term care arrangement in which all care required for the lifetime of the participant is provided. A retirement home that agrees to provide not only facilities for independent living, but also nursing care and hospitalization to residents as needed is a *life care community.*

Life Cycle Benefits—Benefits designed to meet the needs of employees throughout the stages of life: when they are single, married, with the birth or adoption of a child, as the child grows, when they are responsible for elderly parents, before they retire, after they retire and at death.

Life Cycle Pension Plan—A defined benefit plan that expresses benefits as a lump-sum benefit rather than as an annuity. There are no account balances for the plan participants. In addition, this plan recognizes final average salary in the benefit calculation. Under the life cycle plan, a participant earns credits for each year of service. Age is not directly a factor, except as it pertains to how much service an individual could accrue. The total of these credits is considered a percentage, which is multiplied by the annual final average salary of the participant to determine what lump sum will be paid at retirement. Also known as *retirement bonus plan* and *lump-sum plan.*

Life Expectancy—Length of time a person of a given age is expected to live. The period is a statistical average, based on mortality tables showing rate of death at each age. It does not seek to predict the life span of any particular individual. See also Mortality Rate.

Life Insurance—A type of insurance that provides a sum of money if the person who is insured dies while the policy is in effect.

Life Support—Maintenance of vital body functions, e.g., breathing and heartbeat, to sustain life.

Life Years (International Benefits)—A measure used in some multinational pools to determine when a dividend may be paid, e.g., one person insured for one year equals one life year.

Lifestyle Cost Index (LCI)—A methodology that uses a combination of company-specific health claims experience and health risk factor analysis to pinpoint specific health problems at any given company.

Lifestyle Plan—A type of wellness plan that penalizes employees who do not meet certain types of physical evaluations or standards (overweight, smoking, etc.) and rewards those who do.

Lifetime Aggregate—The major medical maximum lifetime benefit under a plan.

Lifetime Disability Benefit—A payment to help replace income lost by an insured person as long as he or she is totally disabled—even for a lifetime.

Limit of Risk—The maximum amount a company is willing to insure under a given form of contract on any particular life.

Limitations—Conditions or circumstances for which benefits are payable or are limited. Detailed information about limitations and exclusions can be found in the certificate of insurance.

Limited Coverage (Dread Disease) Policy—A type of medical expense policy designed to cover only those medical expenses incurred by an insured who has contracted a specified disease, such as cancer, that is named in the policy.

Limited Liability—The creditors of the corporation

have a claim against the assets of the corporation but not against the personal property of the stockholders.

Limited Liability Company (LLC)—A corporation designed to be taxed as a partnership. It provides for partnership agreements and liability protection of the owners. For 401(k) plan purposes, the members of an LLC are treated like partners and the non-members are treated like partnership employees. In a medical setting, an LLC is an excellent way to share risk and equity between hospital systems and physician practices.

Limited Partner—An investor who has limited personal liability in a partnership. See also General Partner.

Limited Partnership—An unincorporated business owned both by general partners, having unlimited liability; and by limited partners, whose liability is limited to their investment in the firm.

Liquid Assets—Those assets shown on the left side of the balance sheet that are most susceptible to being turned promptly into cash or the equivalent, usually within the course of a year.

Liquid Market—A market where selling and buying can be accomplished with ease, due to the presence of a large number of interested buyers and sellers willing and able to trade substantial quantities at small price differences.

Liquidated—A claim is liquidated when it has been made fixed and certain by the parties concerned.

Liquidated Damages—A fixed sum agreed upon between the parties to a contract, to be paid as ascertained damages by the party who breaches the contract.

Liquidation—
- —The dissolution of a company, with all cash remaining after the sale of its assets and payment of all indebtedness being distributed to the shareholders.
- —The process of converting, securities or other property into cash.

Liquidity—
- —The measure of how quickly an investment can be turned into cash. Mutual funds and Treasury notes are liquid investments, while real estate is illiquid. See also Marketability.
- —An actuarial concept that prescribes that sufficient cash, or cash-like securities, be available at times of disbursement for retirement, disability or separation.
- —The capacity of the marketplace to accommodate a given supply of and/or demand for a security without unreasonable price changes resulting. Liquidity is a vital requirement of a healthy capital market. Also refers to maintenance of short-term reserves held for special purposes.

Listed Stock—The stock of a company that is traded on a recognized securities exchange, and for which a listing application and a registration statement, giving detailed information about the company and its operations, have been filed with the Securities and Exchange Commission, unless otherwise exempted, as well as with the exchange itself.

Living Benefits—Permit life insurance policyholders to access the face amounts of their polices before death under certain circumstances, such as diagnosis of a terminal illness or confinement to a nursing home. See Viatical Settlement.

Living Will—A document that allows a person to state in advance his or her wishes regarding the use or removal of life-sustaining or death-delaying procedures in the event of a terminal illness or injury.

Load—
- —A sales charge paid when purchasing or selling fund shares. A front end load, assessed when money is initially invested, effectively reduces the amount invested by 2-8.5%. A back end load, sometimes referred to as a *redemption* or *exit fee,* is a charge for withdrawing money and may be levied as a percentage of the redemption amount or at a flat rate. Loads may also be charged when dividends are reinvested.
- —The amount added to the net or pure premium for any type of insurance or pension program for administrative expenses, taxes, contingency reserves and profits.

Loan Broker—See Mortgage Broker.

Loan Provisions—The terms under which loans may be granted, the interest to be paid and the maximum repayment period.

Local Area Network (LAN)—The hardware and software allowing two or more computers to be connected together over a small geographic area (typically an office or one building).

Local Nationals (International Benefits)—Employees hired by a local subsidiary or branch in the country of operation. Usually nationals of that country but may be citizens of any country.

Lockbox Plan—A procedure used to speed up collections through the use of post office boxes in payers' local areas.

Locked In—
—A situation where, because of the capital gains tax liability, an investor elects not to sell a long-term stock position, thereby substantially reducing both the efficient movement of capital and market liquidity. Often called a *retrogressive tax*.
—A term used to describe the situation of members of a health plan who are restricted to certain doctors, hospitals or other health care providers. A nonplan provider will not be covered by the plan.

Lockout—Strategy by which the employer denies employees the opportunity to work by closing its operations.

Long—Signifies an ownership position in securities with the actual certificate held by the investor and/or his or her custodian. As opposed to short.

Long-Term Bonds—Bonds with more than ten years to maturity.

Long-Term Care (LTC)—Includes all forms of services, both institutional and noninstitutional, that are required by all people with chronic health conditions.

Long-Term Care Benefit—An accelerated death benefit provided by some individual life insurance policies under which the insurer agrees to pay a monthly benefit to an insured who requires constant care for a medical condition.

Long-Term Care Insurance—Coverage designed to pay some or all of long-term costs, thereby preventing depletion of the policyholder's assets.

Long-Term Disability (LTD)—A significant period of disability generally ranging from six months to life.

Long-Term Disability Income Insurance—Insurance issued to an employer (group) or individual to provide a reasonable replacement of a portion of an employee's earned income lost through serious and prolonged illness or injury during the normal work career.

Loss—See Actuarial Gain or Loss.

Loss of Benefits—An employee's right to accrued benefits from personal contributions is not subject to forfeiture under any circumstances. However, a plan may provide for the forfeiture of vested benefits derived from employer contributions in the event of the employee's death before retirement. This forfeiture rule does not apply if the employee continued to work after retirement eligibility and if a joint or survivor annuity was to be provided. A limited forfeiture may take place if a retiree returns to work for his or her employer (or returns to work in the same industry, in the case of a multiemployer plan).

Loss-of-Income Benefits—Payments made to an insured person to help replace income lost through inability to work because of an insured disability.

Loss Ratio—The ratio of paid and incurred claims plus expenses to premium.

Loss Reserve—As stated on a financial statement, an amount representing the estimated liability for unpaid insurance claims (losses) that have occurred as of a given date. Includes losses incurred but not yet reported (IBNR), claims being adjusted and amounts known to be payable in the future (e.g., long-term disability). On an individual basis, loss reserve represents an estimate of the total amount ultimately to be paid out on that claim.

Low-Volume DRGs—DRGs with five or fewer patients in a hospital's base year.

Lump Sum—The capital accumulation in a plan, with or without interest, that may or may not be paid to the plan member on resignation or retirement. Most plans do not allow full cash payment on retirement but permit a small portion to be paid as a lump sum.

Lump-Sum Compensation—Refers to a lump-sum payment to employees negotiated by an employer and a union; often in lieu of general pay increases.

Lump-Sum Distribution—A distribution that qualifies for forward averaging or rollover treatment. The basic requirements are that the distribution be made within one taxable year of the recipient, that it include the entire balance to the credit of the employee, and that it be made on account of the employee's death, attainment of age 59½, separation from service (except for the self-employed), or disability (self-employed persons only).

Lump-Sum Plan—See Life Cycle Pension Plan.

M

M_{1B}—Currency plus demand deposits and other checkable deposits.

M_2—M_{1B} plus savings and small (under $100,000) time deposits at commercial banks and thrift institutions, overnight repurchase agreements, overnight Eurodollars issued by Caribbean branches of U.S. member banks to U.S. nonbank customers and money market mutual funds.

M_3—M_2 plus large (over $100,000) time deposits at all depository institutions plus repurchase agreements issued by commercial banks and savings and loans.

MacBride Principles—Developed by human rights activist Sean MacBride to lay the foundation for justice in the workplace, these principles call on U.S. companies with operations in Northern Ireland to promote fair employment practices there.

Magnetic Resonance Imaging (MRI)—A noninvasive diagnostic procedure of imaging soft tissues using a powerful magnet and radio waves to produce computer-processed images of the inner body.

Mail-Order Drug Program—A method of dispensing medication directly to the patient through the mail by means of a mail-order drug distribution company. Offers greatly reduced costs for prescriptions, especially for long-term therapy.

Maintenance—A necessary expense incurred in maintaining plant and equipment in proper operating conditions.

Maintenance of Benefits (MOB)—A type of coordination of benefits that limits the total reimbursement for all health plans to a given individual for a program of treatment.

Major Diagnostic Categories (MDCs)—Broad classifications of diagnoses that apply to DRGs.

Major Medical Coverage—Type of coverage that usually pays only a portion of the expense for all covered services (generally involving major illnesses and injuries) and specifies a deductible that the insured must first pay. Full reimbursement is often provided once the expenses paid by the individual reach a certain level. Although the maximums that limit total benefits are usually substantial, maximums are generally specified and mean that most policies do not provide completely unlimited protection. Internal limits on particular services, such as psychiatric care, may also be specified. See also Basic Medical Benefits; Comprehensive Major Medical Coverage; Supplemental Major Medical Coverage.

Making a Market—When a dealer stands prepared to buy or sell at the bid and offer prices that he or she quotes, the dealer is said to be making a market. The market is maintained when the dealer continues to quote bids and offerings over a period of time. See also Specialist.

Malpractice—A dereliction from professional duty or failure of professional skill or learning that results in death, injury, loss or damage to the patient.

Managed Care—Health care programs that impose some controls on the utilization of health care services, the providers who offer such care, and/or the fees charged for such services. Managed care can be provided through HMOs, PPOs and managed indemnity plans. The primary goal is to deliver cost-effective health care without sacrificing quality or access.

Managed Care Network—National or regional organization of health care providers (owned by commercial insurance companies or other sponsors) offered to employers either as an alternative to or total replacement for traditional indemnity insurance.

Managed Competition—A health care reform strategy that blends government regulation with competition among health care organizations on quality and cost. The basic idea is to band employers and individuals into large health plan purchasing groups and require health care providers to compete through price and health outcomes to win consumers.

Managed Fund (International Benefits)—An investment vehicle used by funds that are too large to require insurance guarantees but too small to operate independently in terms of direct investments.

Funds may be pooled with those of other plans; selection is frequently offered with different portfolio mixes.

Management—In corporate language, the operating officers of a company appointed by the directors themselves who are elected by the stockholders.

Management Fee—The amount paid by a mutual fund to the investment adviser for its services. The average fee industrywide is about one-half of 1% a year of the fund's assets.

Management Information System (MIS)—A computer-based network that integrates the collection, processing and transmission of information.

Management Services Organization—Provides administrative and practice management services to medical groups, which are typically owned by physicians; it is usually a subsidiary of the group. It owns all business assets, but the clinic assets stay with the medical group.

Manager—With reference to mutual funds, the entity responsible for investment advisory services.

Managerial Accounting—The segment of accounting concerned with the needs of users who are internal to the firm. (Antonym: financial accounting)

Mandated Benefits—A specific set of benefits required by law to be provided by all insurance carriers and reimbursed under all insurance policies.

Mandatory Employee Contribution—A contribution that is made by employees in order to participate in the plan, share in employer contributions or in some way receive more favorable treatment than those not contributing.

Mandatory Retirement—See Compulsory Retirement.

Manipulation—The illegal act or effort designed to artificially influence, either up or down, the price action of a security for the personal benefit or aggrandizement of a few insiders at the expense of the other shareholders and the public at large.

Manual Rate—Premium rate for group insurance coverage from the company's standard rate tables; based on the experience of an average group, not any particular group. It is used to determine the premium for a small group.

Margin—The sum of money required, expressed as a percent of 100, to carry stocks and/or bonds listed on a national exchange with the balance being loaned by the brokers at interest. Controlled by the Federal Reserve Board, the amount of margin required to carry stocks over the past 20 years has ranged from 40-100% of the purchase price.

Margin Account—An account wherein one can buy securities by initially paying only a portion of their purchase price and the balance at a later date.

Margin Call—A call from a clearinghouse to a clearing member, or from a brokerage firm to a customer, to bring margin deposits up to a required minimum level.

Margin of Profit—Calculated by dividing the operating income by the sales. Nonoperating income received and interest paid are excluded when arriving at operating income.

Market Excess Return—Forecast of annual expected return (%) in excess of risk-free rate of return derived from predicted market return.

Market Letter—Any publication that comments on securities and is prepared for distribution to the organization's clients or to the public.

Market Order—An order to buy or sell a security at the most advantageous price available after the order reaches the trading floor.

Market Portfolio—Includes all risky assets in proportion to their market value. In the capital asset pricing model (CAPM), the optimum portfolio of risky assets for all investors.

Market Price—With reference to a security, the last reported price at which the stock or bond sold. The highest price a buyer, willing but not compelled to buy, would pay; and the lowest a seller, willing but not compelled to sell, would accept.

Market-Related Value of Plan Assets—A balance used to calculate the expected return on plan assets. Can be either fair market value or a calculated value that recognizes changes in fair value in a systematic and rational manner over not more than five years. Different ways of calculating market-related value may be used for different classes of assets, but the manner of determining market-related value shall be applied consistently from year to year for each asset class.

Market Replicator—A common stock manager whose style of management results in a broadly diversified portfolio with sector weightings comparable to the market as a whole.

Market Risk—Risk engendered by the day-to-day fluctuations in prices at which a security can be bought or sold.

Market Timer—A common stock manager whose primary emphasis is on percentages of the equity portfolio to be allocated to cash and stocks.

Market Value—The price an investor will pay for each share of common stock at any given time. Market value is determined by the laws of supply and demand.

Market Value per Share—The current price at which a stock is trading in the open market.

Marketability—Term synonymous with salability and meaning the degree of investment or speculative interest that underlies any security; the ease with which it can be sold. See also Liquidity.

Marketable Securities—Securities for which there is always a ready market. Temporary investments in stocks, bonds and other securities that are readily salable and that are intended to be held for only a short period.

Marketplace Reform—A health care reform strategy based on marketplace dynamics of competition and price rather than government regulation, government management or price rate setting.

Mass Withdrawal—The withdrawal of substantially all employers from a plan within a specified period.

Master Contract—A life insurance policy that insures a number of people under a single insurance contract; a contract between an insurance company and a group policyholder in which the individuals insured are not parties to the contract.

Master Limited Partnership—A form of limited partnership primarily used as an investment vehicle for a large number of investors. Interests in master limited partnerships are usually listed and traded on national or regional stock exchanges. In many large business transactions, they may enjoy tax advantages over corporations.

Master Plan—A defined benefit or defined contribution plan that has been prepared by a sponsoring organization and that provides a single trust account in which all adopting employers must invest their plan contributions; the sponsoring organization must have the plan approved by the Internal Revenue Service. See also Prototype Plan.

Master Trust—A pooling of directed and/or discretionary trusts (a *discretionary trust* is one in which the bank is trustee and also has investment responsibility for all or part of the assets). The "pure" definition is pooling of one sponsor's assets which include multiple managers and multiple plans under one trust agreement.

Matching Contributions—Made by an employer to a plan on an employee's behalf when the employee makes elective or nonelective contributions.

Material Information—Anything of material fact that could affect an investor's decision to buy certain securities.

Material Modification—A change in information required to be in an SPD or the terms of the plan considered important to plan participants.

Material Safety Data Sheets (MSDS)—Documents that contain vital information about hazardous substances.

Materiality Concept—Judgment decision by an auditor about the relative importance of an item for disclosure in financial statements.

Maternity Benefits—See Length of Stay Legislation.

Mature—An employee group is said to be mature if the age distribution of the employees, including the ages of employees who have retired and are drawing pensions, is stable and is expected to be duplicated year after year through the effect of new entries and dropouts (deaths and withdrawals). This condition is typical of a company whose pension plan has long been in effect and whose workforce is neither increasing nor decreasing. Newly established companies and growing companies ordinarily have immature employee groups. Employee groups covered by pension plans recently adopted also tend to be immature.

Maturity—The date on which a loan, bond, mortgage or other debt/security becomes due and is to be paid off.

Maturity Funding Contracts—Group single premium immediate annuity contracts to be used for noninsured pension, profit-sharing and savings plans. Both fixed dollar and variable annuities are available under these contracts.

Maturity Value—The amount that the holder of note is entitled to receive at the due date, including the principal plus any accrued interest.

Maximization—Manipulation of data to optimize hospital reimbursement.

Maximum Age—A company that maintains a defined benefit plan may be discouraged from hiring older employees because of the cost of funding benefits for them. Consequently, ERISA permits a defined benefit plan to exclude an employee who is within five years of normal retirement age at the time when service begins. However, the plan must comply with coverage and antidiscrimination rules.

Maximum Allowable Actual Charge (MAAC)—A method of regulating the fees that nonparticipating providers may charge Medicare patients.

Maximum Allowable Cost (MAC) List—A list health plans distribute to their participating pharmacies describing the maximum amount the plan will pay for specific medications.

Maximum Benefit—

—The highest annual or lifetime benefit that can be paid by a qualified defined benefit plan.

—(Canada) The highest amount an individual may receive under an insurance contract.

Maximum Fee Schedule—A compensation arrangement in which a participating physician agrees to accept a prescribed sum as the total fee for one or more covered services.

Maximum Out-of-Pocket Payment—The maximum amount of money a person will pay in addition to premium payments. The out-of-pocket payment is usually the sum of the deductible and coinsurance payments.

Maximum Plan Limits—The maximum amount payable under a health plan. There are three types of limits: defined, per cause (disability) maximum and all-causes maximum.

Defined: In general, the limit is the maximum amount the plan will pay for covered medical expenses.

Per Cause (Disability) Maximum: The maximum limit applies separately to each accident or illness incurred by a covered person. For example, if a covered person under a per cause plan is receiving treatment for both a psychiatric illness and a heart condition, the overall maximum limit under the plan would apply separately to each. Often, separate dollar limits are applied for psychiatric causes only in terms of maximum limits per year or lower lifetime maximum for psychiatric causes.

All-Causes Maximum: The maximum limit applies to all covered expenses incurred by a covered person or persons during a specified period of coverage.

Mean—A simple arithmetic average obtained by adding a set of numbers and then dividing the sum by the number of items in the set.

Means Test—

—A regulation that eligibility for aid and the amount of aid provided do not depend, for example, on past employment or earnings but on specified levels of income and/or assets of those requesting aid.

—(International Benefits) Provides for a reduction in social security disability benefits if other income exceeds minimum levels. Also applies in other forms to other benefits, e.g., surviving spouse benefits.

Mechanic's Lien—A lien created under statute to assist laborers and suppliers in collecting their accounts and wages. It subjects the real property of the owner to a lien in the event of nonpayment for contracted improvements. State laws vary as to procedures and the degree of protection accorded. See also Building Lien.

Median—The middle item in a set of ranked data points containing an odd number of items. When an even number of items are ranked, the average of the two middle items is the median.

Mediation—Arises when a third party, called the *mediator,* comes in to help the adversaries with their negotiations. He or she may either be designated by the government or selected by the parties themselves. In seeking to narrow the differences between the parties, the mediator may meet with them jointly and/or separately. He or she continues to function only as long as the parties both agree to his or her presence. The mediator will remove himself or herself from a case when (1) agreement is reached, (2) one of the parties requests his or her departure, (3) the agreed-upon time comes for appeal to the next step in the procedure or (4) he or she feels his or her acceptability or effectiveness is exhausted. The mediator can make proposals for settlement and operates without any authority to compel an agreement, depending instead upon his or her ability to persuade the parties to come together and upon the parties' own overriding need to do so.

Medicaid (Title XIX)—A medical benefits program administered by the states and subsidized by the federal government that pays certain medical expenses for those who meet income and other guidelines. See also Title XIX.

Medical Care—Under the IRC definition, diagnosis, cure, mitigation, treatment or prevention of disease or affecting any structure or function of the body; also travel for or incidental to medical care. Insurance for medical care is treated as medical care; so is the cost of prescription drugs and insulin.

Medical Case Management (MCM)—This option, often offered by insurance companies, provides coordinators to handle high-cost claims and recommend specialized care and services targeted to an individual's treatment goals and needs. MCM is most often used to deal with catastrophic illnesses. The MCM coordinator helps to oversee overall management of the patient, from the onset of the illness or injury into acute care hospitalization, specialized care programs and followup treatment.

Medical Child Support Order—See Qualified Medical Child Support Order.

Medical Expense Reimbursement Plan (MERP)—The employer pays its employees' out-of-pocket medical expenses.

Medical Insurance—Protection that provides benefits for the cost of any or all of the numerous health care services normally covered under various health care plans.

Medical IRA—An individual plan to save funds to pay for postretirement health care costs.

Medical Loss Ratio (MLR)—An index which compares the costs of delivering health benefits with the revenues received by the plan.

Medical Reimbursement Plan—An employer plan that reimburses employees for medical expenses directly from employer funds, and not through a policy of health or accident insurance.

Medical Savings Account—An individual account to which employees contribute pretax money. Used to pay uncovered health care expenses like deductibles and exclusions. Often used in conjunction with a high-deductible catastrophic health insurance policy. Can also accept employer contributions.

Medical Spending Account—A type of flexible spending account that reimburses the employee for out-of-pocket medical expenses; is part of a flexible benefit plan.

Medically Indigent (MI)—Unable to pay—either directly or through an insurance program—the full cost of his or her own health care and not eligible for Medicare or Medicaid. This term is used to describe people who do not have health insurance; it is not related to income, employment or housing.

Medically Necessary—Describes services required to prevent harm to the patient or an adverse effect on the patient's quality of life, as judged against generally accepted standards of medical practice. The term is usually used to determine whether or not a procedure or service is covered by insurance. The reasonable and appropriate diagnosis, treatment and followup care as determined and prescribed by qualified, appropriate health care providers in treating any condition, illness, disease or injury.

Medically Needy Program—States receive federal funds to provide care for blind or disabled individuals or families and children who are otherwise eligible for Medicaid except that their income is too high.

Medicare—

—Administered by the Social Security Administration, Medicare is the U.S. federal government plan for paying certain hospital and medical expenses for those who qualify, primarily those over 65. Benefits are provided regardless of income level. The program is government subsidized and government operated. Part A, Hospital Insurance (HI), provides for inpatient hospital services and posthospital care. Part B,

Supplementary Medical Insurance (SMI), pays for medically necessary doctors' services, outpatient hospital services and a number of other medical services and supplies not covered by Part A. Enrollment in Part B is voluntary and available for a small premium. See also Title XVIII.
—(Canada) Provincial government plans that cover hospital care and services, as well as physician fees.

Medicare Catastrophic Coverage Act of 1988 (MCCA)—Added significant catastrophic coverage and substantially increased the cost of Medicare. The MCCA was repealed in 1989.

Medicare Economic Index—Based on estimates of the expenses of producing physician office services and a measure of increases in earning levels in the economy as a whole, it is used to determine limits on physicians' prevailing charges.

Medicare Secondary Payer Program—The law now provides that Medicare is the secondary payer for three categories of beneficiaries, if these beneficiaries are also covered by their employer's group health plan. The three categories are (1) individuals with end stage renal disease (up to the first 18 months); (2) those over age 65 and currently employed (including the spouse of an employed individual); and (3) those who are disabled but active (including disabled dependents of active individuals).

Medicare Supplement Policy—A voluntary, contributory private insurance plan available to Medicare eligibles to cover the costs of deductibles, coinsurance, physicians' services and other medical and health services not covered by Medicare. Also called *Medigap.* See also Carve-Out.

Medigap Policy—See Medicare Supplement Policy.

Member—See Plan Participant.

Member Bank—A state or federal bank that belongs to the Federal Reserve System. All national banks are required to be members; state-chartered commercial banks and mutual savings banks may elect to do so.

Member Corporation—A securities brokerage firm, organized as a corporation, with at least one member of the New York Stock Exchange who is a director and a holder of voting stock in the corporation.

Member Firm—A securities brokerage firm organized as a partnership and having at least one general partner who is a member of the New York Stock Exchange.

Member Organization—Includes a New York Stock Exchange member firm and member corporation. The term participant, when used with reference to a member organization, includes general and limited partners of a member firm and holders of voting and nonvoting stock in a member corporation.

Member, Society of Pension Actuaries (MSPA)—Holder must pass seven examinations on general mathematics, probability and statistics, employee benefits, regulations and so forth.

Merger—A combining of two or more companies or corporations. Called an *amalgamation* in Canada.

Merger of Plans—In the case of a merger or consolidation of plans, each participant must be entitled to receive a benefit after the merger at least equal to the value of the benefit he or she would have been entitled to receive before the merger. The before and after merger benefits are determined as if the plan had been terminated. If a multiemployer plan is involved, this rule will apply only to the extent that the Pension Benefit Guaranty Corporation determines that this provision is necessary for the protection of the participants.

Minimum Annuity—A special annuity provision in a retirement plan that prescribes a rate of annuity payable to an employee upon attainment of a specified age or upon completion of a specified period of service, or both, irrespective of the amount of annuity provided by the regular formula.

Minimum Benefits—Some plans provide that a minimum amount of annuity will be paid if the regular benefit formula produces less. This minimum is usually payable only if certain service requirements are met at retirement.

Minimum Compensation Level—The amount of compensation an employee must earn before being eligible to participate in a plan.

Minimum Contribution Requirement—Under the Multiemployer Pension Plan Amendments Act of 1980, the sum of the vested benefits charge and the increase in normal cost for the plan year determined under the entry age normal funding method that is attributable to plan amendments adopted while the plan was in reorganization, less the amount of overburden credit.

Minimum Funding—The minimum amount that must be contributed by an employer that has a defined benefit, money purchase or target benefit pension plan. If the employer fails to meet these minimum standards, in the absence of a waiver from the IRS, an excise tax will be imposed on the amount of the deficiency.

Minimum Funding Standard—See Accumulated Funding Deficiency; Funding Standard Account.

Minimum Group—The least number of employees permitted under a state law to effect a group for insurance purposes; the purpose is to maintain some sort of proper division between individual policy insurance and the group forms.

Minimum Participation Rules—IRS rules prescribing conditions for employees to participate in most retirement plans.

Minimum Participation Standards—In general, the maximum amount of time a qualified retirement plan can require an employee to work before becoming eligible to participate is one year of service and the highest age a plan may require a participant to have attained before being admitted is 21. There are exceptions made for plans maintained by tax-exempt educational institutions and for plans that have an immediate vesting upon participation feature.

Minimum Premium Plan (MPP)—Under this approach, the employer and the insurance company or the service plan agree that the employer will be responsible for paying all claims up to an agreed-upon aggregate level, with the carrier responsible for the excess. This level is usually based on the amount of claims paid in the past two or three years, adjusted by projected increases in claims due to inflation and greater utilization. The carrier usually is also responsible for processing claims and administrative services.

Minority Interest—Used in a consolidated income statement to describe the extent of the interest of the minority stockholders of a subsidiary in the earnings of that subsidiary. With reference to a balance sheet, it represents the equity of the minority stockholders in the net worth of the subsidiary.

Minus Tick—See Uptick.

Miscellaneous Hospital Expenses—A provision for the payment on a blanket basis or schedule basis of hospital services (other than room and board, special nursing care and doctor fees) up to a stipulated maximum amount. Also called *ancillary charges.*

Mistake of Fact—Ignorance or forgetfulness of a fact that is material to the creation of a legal obligation.

Mistake of Law—An erroneous conclusion or interpretation as to the legal effect of known (i.e., not disputed) facts.

Mixed Model—A managed care plan using more than one type of delivery system, such as an HMO that has both closed panel and open panel delivery systems.

Mode—As a statistical average, the observation that occurs with the greatest frequency.

Model Plans—Plans prepared by the Internal Revenue Service for small employers. Model plans are easy and inexpensive to implement due to the simple IRS procedure required for qualification.

Modern Portfolio Theory (MPT)—The theoretical constructs that enable investment managers to classify, estimate and control the sources of risk and return. In popular usage, the term is not limited to portfolio theory. Instead, MPT encompasses all notions of both modern investment theory and portfolio theory.

Modification—An amendment to the federal-state agreement relative to Social Security coverage for public employees, entered into between the state and the Social Security Administration pursuant to authority granted under the state Social Security enabling law. Whenever an additional governmental unit adopts Social Security for its employees, a modification in the federal-state agreement must be made to effect coverage for these employees. Such modification is proposed by the state agency administering the Social Security enabling law and must be approved by the Social Security Administration. The term *modification* is also used in connection with any revision of a retirement plan.

Modifications—Changes to a job to accommodate an employee or to make a job safer. See also Accommodation.

Modified Immediate Participation Guarantee Contract—A group insurance contract under which the active life fund is maintained on an immediate participation basis, but single premium immediate annuities are actually purchased for each participant upon retirement. Also known as *direct rated deposit administration contract.* See also Immediate Participation Guarantee (IPG) Contract.

Modified Indemnity Plan—Like traditional indemnity plans, modified plans pay providers on a fee-for-service basis, allow patients to have full freedom of choice of providers and require patients to pay a portion of the cost of care through deductibles, coinsurance and contributions. The insurer bears the majority of the financial risk. Cost-containment/utilization review controls are used.

Modified Refund Annuity—An arrangement commonly used under a contributory pension plan. If an employee dies after retirement, his or her beneficiary or his or her estate will receive a sum equal to the accumulated value of the employee's own contributions to the pension fund, with or without interest up to his or her retirement date, less the total retirement benefits he or she received prior to death. See also Refund Annuity.

Modular Plan—A type of flexible benefits plan that offers a choice of benefits packages rather than a selection of individual levels of coverage.

Monetary Policy—The policies of the Federal Reserve Board that determine the size of the money supply and the level of interest rates. Meant to improve employment, economic growth and price stability.

Money Follows the Man—See Reciprocal Agreement; Reciprocity.

Money Market—That segment of the securities market that deals in short-term (less than one year) debt and equity issues.

Money Market Fund—A mutual fund that seeks maximum current income through investment in securities whose maturities are less than one year, and allows investors to write checks against their accounts. Such securities may include bank CDs, bankers acceptances, T-bills, repurchase agreements (repos) and commercial paper.

Money Market Instruments—Fixed income securities that mature in less than one year. Also known as cash equivalents since their marketability and characteristics provide easy liquidity access to ready cash, as needed. Included in this category are U.S. government securities, negotiable certificates of deposit, commercial paper, short-term investment fund accounts, bankers acceptances and mutual funds.

Money Purchase Plan—A type of defined contribution plan in which the employer's contributions are determined for, and allocated with respect to, specific individuals, usually as a percentage of compensation. The benefits for each employee are the amounts that can be provided by the sums contributed to his or her account. Unlike a profit-sharing plan, however, forfeitures are not added to participants' accounts; they are used to reduce the employer's contributions.

An individual account plan, as defined in Section 3(34) of ERISA, other than a profit-sharing plan or a stock bonus plan, in which the employer's contributions are fixed or determinable.

Money Purchase Plan (Canada)—An occupational pension plan that lacks the specific guarantees of retirement income that are found in defined benefit plans. When members of money purchase plans retire, whatever money has been built up over the years in their names is used to buy them annuities.

Money Supply—A measure of the amount of money in circulation. See also L, M_{1B}, M_2 and M_3.

Morbidity—The relative incidence (number of cases) and severity of disease, usually used with respect to specific disease conditions, e.g., tuberculosis morbidity refers to the number of cases of tuberculosis. A term used for sickness.

Morbidity Table—Shows the average number of illnesses befalling a large group of persons. It indicates the incidence of sickness the way a mortality table shows the incidence of death.

Mortality—The number of deaths resulting from each specific type of illness or disease.

Mortality Assumption—Death Rate—An actuarial assumption involving the probability of death at given ages; used in estimating the amount of future retirement benefits that will become payable.

Mortality Experience—The rate at which participants in a pension or insurance plan actually die. Also the financial effect of such deaths upon the operation of the plan.

Mortality Rate—Number of persons out of a large group (usually 100,000) who, experience shows, will live to reach each age up to the death of the last survivor; inferentially establishing the expectancy of life of the average person of each age. See also Life Expectancy.

Mortality Table—Shows how many members of a group, starting at a certain age, will be alive at each succeeding age. It is used to calculate the probability of dying in, or surviving through, any period, and the value of an annuity benefit. To be appropriate for a specific group, it should be based on the experience of individuals having common characteristics, such as sex or occupational group.

Mortgage—An instrument by which the borrower (mortgagor) gives the lender (mortgagee) a lien on property (commonly real property) as security for the payment of an obligation. The borrower continues to use the property; when the obligation is fully extinguished, the lien is removed. If the subject matter of the lien is personal property other than securities (such as machinery, tools or equipment), the mortgage is known as a chattel mortgage. Investors may buy whole loans, participating interests in a loan or a security representing a participating interest in a pool of loans. The seller of a loan typically services the loan for a fee, relieving the buyer of the paperwork burden. Mortgage loans are used in connection with single family structures, condominiums, multifamily structures, office buildings, large commercial centers and industrial plants or even undeveloped land.

Mortgage Banker—An organization that deals in mortgage loans by originating and then selling these loans to investors. A mortgage banker usually retains the servicing for the loan sold and derives income from originating and servicing fees. The mortgage banker typically borrows the funds used for the loan origination and pays off these borrowings when the loan is sold.

Mortgage Bonds—A debt obligation secured by a property pledge. These are liens or mortgages against the issuing corporation's properties and real estate assets.

Mortgage Broker—An individual or company that, for a fee, brings together a borrower and lender. A second type of mortgage broker is one that specializes in bringing together sellers and buyers of mortgage loans. A mortgage broker works on a commission basis. Also called a *loan broker.*

Mortgage Correspondent—An agent of a lending institution authorized to handle and process loans.

Mortgage Pass-Through Securities—A security consisting of a pool of residential mortgage loans with monthly distribution of 100% of the interest and principal to the investor. There are nongovernment-sponsored issues of these securities, as well as the government versions, Freddie Macs and Ginnie Maes.

Mortgage Redemption Insurance—Decreasing term life insurance that provides a death benefit amount corresponding to the decreasing amount owed on a mortgage.

Mortgage REIT—A real estate investment trust formed for the purpose of purchasing mortgages and lending money on real estate.

Mortgagee—The one to whom a mortgage is given—the lender.

Mortgagor—An owner who conveys his or her property as security for a loan—the debtor.

Multiemployer Plan—Under ERISA, a multiemployer plan is one that requires contributions from more than one employer and is maintained pursuant to a collective bargaining agreement. They are also known as jointly administered or Taft-Hartley plans. The Multiemployer Pension Plan Amendments Act of 1980 (MPPAA) made substantial changes to ERISA and the Internal Revenue Code which had the effect of enhancing the funding requirements for multiemployer pension plans, providing new rules for multiemployer plans and revising the termination insurance provisions applicable to these plans.

Multimanagement System—The use of more than one investment manager by the plan sponsor in order to provide diversification of management as well as diversification of styles and classes of investments.

Multinational Corporation (International Benefits)—A firm with independent business units operating in multiple countries.

Multinational Dividend (International Benefits)—The surplus resulting from the second stage accounting of a multinational pool.

Multinational Employee (International Benefits)—A person working in a country other than his or her own for a company based in a country other than his or her own. May also be called a *multicountry employee* or a *third country national.*

Multinational Pooling (International Benefits)—Arrangement that links together the worldwide insured benefit plans of a multinational company to secure cost savings, improved financial information, and improved service and facilities.

Multiphasic Screening—A rapidly administered medical examination that involves a battery of laboratory tests using automated equipment.

Multiple Coverage—See Duplication of Benefits.

Multiple Employer Group—One master plan covering employees of two or more employers that are not financially related.

Multiple Employer Plan—A postretirement benefit plan maintained by more than one employer allowing them to pool their plan assets for investment purposes and to reduce the cost of plan administration. A multiple employer plan maintains separate accounts for each employer so that contributions provide benefits only for employees of the contributing employer. There are no collective bargaining agreements requiring contributions in a multiple employer plan.

Multiple Employer Trust (MET)—Self-funded or insured corporate group benefit plan that covers medical and dental insurance and pensions, generally geared toward small employers (sole proprietorships and partnerships with several principals and few employees). Not a jointly administered, union-management multiemployer plan.

Multiple Employer Welfare Arrangement (MEWA)—A noncollectively bargained arrangement or plan maintained to benefit employees of two or more employers that are not under common control. ERISA generally does not preempt state law with regard to MEWAs. Small employers participating in MEWAs may be exempt from COBRA's continuation coverage requirement, and other special rules apply under COBRA.

Multiple Funding—See Conversion Fund.

Multiple Qualifying Events—When qualified beneficiaries already receiving continuation coverage experience another qualifying event, entitling them to an additional period of coverage (except in the case of divorce or legal separation, death of a covered employee or loss of dependency status).

Multiplier Doctrine—The concept that investments increase national income by a multiplied amount.

Municipal Bond Fund—A mutual fund that seeks to provide shareholders tax-free income through investment in bonds issued by state and local governments.

Municipal Bonds—Long-term promissory notes issued by state and local governments and public agencies. In general, interest paid on municipal bonds is exempt from federal income taxes and state and local income taxes within the state of issue. See also Revenue Bonds; Special Assessment Bonds; Tax-Exempt Securities.

(Canada) Bonds backed by city governments and sold in the municipal markets.

Mutual Fund Custodian—Usually a national bank, trust company or other qualified institution that physically safeguards securities. It does not act in a managerial capacity; its function is solely clerical.

Mutual Funds (Investment Companies)—Companies or trusts that use their capital to invest in the securities of other companies, with the two principal types being the closed end and the open end trust. Shares of closed end funds are often listed on the New York Stock Exchange, and are traded like any other security. Capitalization of these funds remains fixed for the most part. See also Investment Company or Trust.

Mutual Insurance Company—Has no capital stock structure. Members contribute premiums to a common fund, from which each is entitled to indemnity in case of loss. Its policyholders constitute its membership, who elect a board of directors or trustees through whom business is conducted. Earnings belong to the policyholders as a group and are distributed to them as dividends. In years when the loss experience is unfavorable, assessments, in addition to their normal premiums, may be made against the policyholders.

N

Named Fiduciary—A fiduciary who is named in the plan instrument or who, pursuant to a procedure specified in the plan, is identified by an employer and/or employee organization with respect to the plan and is given the express authority to control plan operations.

National Association of Insurance Commissioners (NAIC)—An organization that assists state insurance departments in promoting national uniformity in the regulation of insurance. A major function is the drafting of model laws.

National Committee on Quality Assurance (NCQA)—An independent, private sector group that reviews care quality and other procedures of managed care organizations to render an accreditation. Its membership includes health care quality experts, employers, labor union officials and consumer representatives.

National Council on Health Planning and Development (NCHPD)—Department of Health and Human Services advisory council that sets national health policies and guides health development.

National Health Insurance—Any system of socialized health insurance benefits, covering all or nearly all citizens, established by federal law, administered by the federal government and supported or subsidized by taxation.

National Labor Relations Act of 1935 (NLRA) (Wagner Act)—A federal law giving employees the right to self-organize, form or assist labor organizations, bargain collectively through representatives of their own choosing, engage in other concerted activities and refrain from any or all such activities except for requiring membership in a labor organization as a condition of employment.

National Labor Relations Board (NLRB)—The board of five members administering the Wagner Act and the Taft-Hartley Act. The board conducts elections to determine bargaining agents, determines bargaining units and adjudicates unfair labor practice charges. The board seeks enforcement of its orders through the court system.

Needs Test (Canada)—Method of assessing a person's or family's expenditure requirements in relation to other income or means to determine amount of income support to be provided under a government program.

Negative Election—A 401(k) plan design feature that provides for enrollment as soon as the employee meets the plan's eligibility requirements, with fixed pretax salary reductions ranging from 1-3% of compensation being taken automatically from the employee's paycheck. Enrollment and salary reduction can be prevented only if the employee makes an active election to opt out of the plan. Also known as *automatic enrollment.*

Negligence—The failure, through omission or commission, to act as an ordinary, reasonable and prudent person would act. Consideration must be given to the specific situation, the circumstances and the knowledge of the parties involved.

Negotiable—A stock or bond certificate, or other evidence of debt, the title to which is freely transferable at delivery, i.e., coupon bonds, bankers acceptances and so on.

Negotiable Certificate of Deposit (CD)—See Certificate of Deposit.

Negotiable Instrument—Property that includes cash, checks, coupon bonds, stock certificates with stock powers attached, promissory notes and so on, where title passes at delivery and is not subject to challenge when owned by a holder in due course and in good faith.

Negotiated Plan—See Collectively Bargained Plan.

Negotiation—In the labor context, refers to the practice of adversarial parties meeting together for the purpose of reaching agreement on the items that are in dispute between them. This format of face-to-face discussion is usually carried on between the parties without any third party presence. It is normally the first step in collective bargaining but will probably recur at such other times in the impasse procedure as the parties feel will be helpful to settle all or a portion of their differences.

Neighborhood Health Center—Facility rendering health services to entire families in readily accessible geographic locations.

Neonatal Mortality Rate—Number of infants under 28 days old dying per 1,000 births during the same calendar year.

Neonatal Period—The interval from the time of birth up to the time the infant becomes 28 days old.

Net Asset Value (NAV)—The value of a mutual fund share determined by deducting the fund's liabilities from the total assets of the portfolio and dividing this amount by the number of shares outstanding. This is calculated once a day, based on the closing market price for each security in the fund's portfolio.

Net Assets Available for Benefits—The difference between a plan's assets and its liabilities. For purposes of this definition, a plan's liabilities do not include participants' accumulated plan benefits.

Net Cash Value—The amount the policy owner will actually receive when surrendering a policy for its cash value. The net cash value is the cash value, minus such items as policy loans, and plus such items as accumulated dividends.

Net Current Assets (Working Capital)—Current assets less current liabilities.

Net Income—The money remaining after all expenses are subtracted from the gross income. The profit.

Net Incurred Claims Cost—The employer's share, net of retiree contributions, of the cost of providing postretirement health care benefits, after adjusting for reimbursements from Medicare and other providers of health care benefits and for the effects of cost-sharing provisions such as deductibles and co-insurance.

Net Net Income—In real estate dealings the word *net* is sometimes repeated for emphasis, stressing actual profit after all expenses are paid, including mortgage reduction payments (principal and interest). What remains is cash flow, or money available for use.

Net Periodic Pension Cost—The amount recognized in an employer's financial statements as the cost of a pension plan for a period. Components of net periodic pension cost are service cost, interest cost, actual return on plan assets, gain or loss, amortization of unrecognized prior service cost, and amortization of the unrecognized net obligation or asset existing at the date of initial application of this statement. This statement uses the term *net periodic pension cost* instead of *net pension expense* because part of the cost recognized in a period may be capitalized along with other costs as part of an asset, such as inventory.

Net Quick Assets—Net current assets minus inventory.

Net Replacement Ratio (Canada)—Measurement of adequacy of retirement income by relating it to income immediately before retirement, taking into account income taxes, tax credits, etc.

Net Return—Yield after taxes.

Net Worth (NW)—
- —The amount by which actual assets are greater than actual liabilities.
- —The amount of equity available for stockholders as shown on the company's books, which consists of common stock, capital surplus, earned surplus and accumulative retained earnings as well as intangible assets. Intangibles are excluded in calculating book value.

Network Model HMO—An HMO model that contracts with multiple physician groups to provide services to HMO members; may involve large single and multispecialty groups.

New Issue—A stock or bond sold by a corporation for the first time. Proceeds may be used to retire outstanding securities of the company, for new plants or equipment, or for additional working capital.

New Issue Market—The market for new issues for securities (as opposed to the secondary market on securities already issued).

New York Stock Exchange (NYSE)—An unincorporated, voluntary association founded in 1792 and existing under a written constitution and bylaws. Membership must be approved by a Committee on Admissions, and is obtained by purchasing a seat from a retiring, deceased or expelled member. Privileges include the right to buy and sell securities on the trading floor of the exchange for one's own account or for others.

New York Stock Exchange Composite Index—A capitalization-weighted index of all stocks listed on the New York Stock Exchange. The value of the index varies with the aggregate value of the common equity of all companies with common stock listed on the NYSE.

No-Fault Insurance—A type of insurance that will pay benefits whether or not the insured is at fault.

No-Load Fund—A mutual fund that charges little or no commission (load charge) to the buyer of its shares. No sales organization is involved. The shares are sold directly to the public by the sponsoring firm.

No-Par Stock—Stock without a par value.

Nominal Interest—The actual interest rate paid or received, or the yield to maturity (not adjusted for inflation). This is commonly understood when one says "the interest rate."

Nominal Return—The rate of return on an asset expressed in monetary terms; i.e., unadjusted for any change in the price level. The nominal return is contrasted with the real return, which is adjusted for changes in the price level.

Nominal Yield—The interest rate stated on the face of a bond not including any paid discount or premium.

Nominee Name—The registered name issued by the comptroller of the currency into which a bank or a trust company registers the securities it holds as custodian and/or investment agent for its trust department portfolios, thereby facilitating the making of "good" delivery to brokers at time of sale or exchange.

Non-Key Employee—Any employee who does not meet the criteria for being considered a key employee.

Nonadmitted Insurance (International Benefits)—Insurance written by a carrier that is not licensed or chartered to underwrite business in the country where the coverage will be issued.

Noncancelable; Noncancelable and Guaranteed Renewable Policy—A policy that the insured has the right to continue in force to a specified age—such as to age 65—and at a guaranteed rate by the timely payment of premiums. During the specified period, the insurer has no right to unilaterally make any change in any provision of the policy while it is in force.

Noncompliance Period—Under COBRA, the period beginning on the date a violation first occurs. The period is used to compute the penalty excise tax imposed on employers that violate COBRA rules.

Nonconfining Sickness—An illness that prevents the insured person from working but does not confine the insured to a hospital or to his or her home.

Noncontributory Provision—A term applied to employee benefit plans under which the employer bears the full cost of the benefits for the employees.

Noncore Coverage—Dental, vision and other types of benefits, as opposed to core coverage, which usually means medical benefits.

Noncumulative Preferred Stock—A type of preferred stock that does not have to pay any dividends in arrears to the holders. See also Convertible Preferred Stock; Cumulative Preferred Stock; Participating Preferred Stock; Preferred Stock.

Nondetachable Warrant—See Warrant.

Nondisabling Injury—An injury that may require medical care but does not result in loss of working time or income.

Nondiscrimination Rules—The requirements in Section 105(h) of the IRC that self-funded employee benefit plans not provide significantly greater benefits to higher paid employees and owners than to lower paid employees. Although some disparity is permitted, there are limits which, if crossed, result in the benefits being deemed taxable income to the beneficiaries.

Nonduplication of Benefits Provision—A type of coordination-of-benefits provision under which the benefits payable by an insured's secondary insurance plan are limited to the difference, if any, between the amount paid by the primary plan and the amount that would have been payable by the secondary plan had that plan been primary.

Nonelective Contribution—Any employer contribution (other than a matching contribution) for which (1) the employee may not elect to have the contribution paid to the employee in cash instead of being contributed to the plan and (2) the contributions are nonforfeitable when made and are ineligible for withdrawal prior to the attainment of certain conditions.

Nonexempt Employees—Employees who are subject to the minimum wage and overtime pay provisions of the Fair Labor Standards Act. Most are paid on an hourly basis.

Nonforfeitable; Nonforfeitability—The condition wherein contributions are vested as of the moment they are made into the plan. Under ERISA, all employee contributions are nonforfeitable.

Nonforfeitable Pension Benefit—A claim obtained by a pension plan participant or beneficiary to that part of an immediate or deferred benefit arising from the participant's service, which is unconditional and which is legally enforceable against the plan.

Nonguaranteed Life Insurance—See Variable Life Insurance.

Nonhighly Compensated Employees (NHCE)—Employees eligible to participate in the plan who do not meet the definition of *highly compensated employees.*

Noninsured Plan—See Self-Funding.

Nonmarket Risk—Volatility of returns from portfolio securities, not related to the movement of the market in general.

Nonoccupational Death Benefit—A benefit payable upon the death of an employee, resulting from any cause other than that occasioned by the performance of an act or acts of duty.

Nonoccupational Disability Benefit—A benefit payable on account of the disability of an employee incurred from any cause other than that occasioned by the performance of an act or acts of duty.

Nonoccupational Policy—A contract that insures a person against off-the-job accident or sickness. It does not cover disability resulting from injury or sickness covered by workers' compensation. Group accident and sickness policies are frequently nonoccupational.

Nonprofit Facility—Any facility owned and operated by one or more nonprofit corporations or associations, no part of the earnings of which benefits any private shareholder or individual.

Nonprofit Health Plan—A prepaid health plan under which no part of the net earnings inures, or may lawfully inure, to the benefit of any private shareholder or individual.

Nonprofit Insurers—Persons organized under special state or provincial laws to provide hospital, medical or dental insurance on a nonprofit basis. The laws exempt them from certain types of taxes.

Nonprofit Organizations—Includes churches, foundations and trade associations.

Nonpublic Enterprise—An enterprise other than one (a) whose debt or equity securities are traded in a public market, either on a stock exchange or in the over-the-counter market (including securities quoted only locally or regionally), or (b) whose financial statements are filed with a regulatory agency in preparation for the sale of any class of securities.

Nonqualified Deferred Compensation Plan—An agreement whereby one person (or legal entity) promises to compensate another for services rendered currently with actual payment for those services delayed until sometime in the future. Such agreements are almost invariably reduced to writing, and are mutually supported by the employer's promise to pay deferred benefits and the employee's promise to render services in exchange therefor. Such plans do not receive tax advantages.

Nonqualified Plan—An employer-sponsored plan that does not meet the requirements of Section 401(a) of the 1954 Internal Revenue Code and that, as a result, suffers distinct disadvantages from a tax standpoint.

Nonrecourse Loan—A secured liability for which the borrower is not personally liable.

Nonresident Alien—A foreign national who does not meet the U.S. lawful permanent resident (green card) test or the substantial presence (days of physical presence in the United States) test, and is therefore considered an alien for federal tax purposes.

Nonstandardized Plan—A prototype qualified plan that allows an adopting employer increased latitude in plan eligibility criteria, vesting, etc. An employer adopting a nonstandardized plan should seek a favorable determination letter from an IRS key district office.

Normal Cost; Normal Actuarial Cost—The cost assigned, under the actuarial cost method in use, to a given year subsequent to the inception of a pension plan. It may or may not include adjustments for actuarial experience gains or losses but does not include any portion of the supplemental cost or interest thereon. That portion of the actuarial present value of pension plan benefits and expenses allocated to a valuation year by a given actuarial cost method. The presentation of normal cost should be accompanied by a reference citing the actuarial cost method used.

Normal Form of Benefit—A distribution from a qualified plan that for a married individual is a joint and survivor annuity of at least 50%. For a single individual the normal form of benefit is typically a life annuity, or in a contributory plan, a modified cash-refund annuity.

Normal Pension Costs—See Funding Standard Account.

Normal Retirement—A termination of employment involving the payment of a regular formula retirement allowance without reduction because of age or service and with special qualifications such as disability.

Normal Retirement Age—The age, as established by a plan, when retirement normally occurs. Since unreduced Social Security benefits currently are available at 65, that is the most common normal retirement age. See also Social Security Retirement Age.

Normal Retirement Benefit—The greater of the early retirement benefit under the plan or the benefit commencing at normal retirement age.

Normal Retirement Date (NRD)—The earliest date at which a participant qualifies for normal retirement under the plan.

Normal Service Cost—See Normal Cost.

Norms—Numerical or statistical measures of usual observed performance when related to health care provided to a given number of patients over time.

Notary—A public officer authorized to administer oaths by way of affidavits and depositions. Attests deeds and other formal papers, in order that they may be used as evidence and be qualified for recording.

Note—See Bond.

Notice of Completion—Notice recorded after completion of project, the filing of which starts the statutory time limit for filing mechanic's liens.

Nuclear Medicine—The scientific and clinical discipline concerned with diagnostic, therapeutic and investigative uses of radionuclides (radioactive forms of chemical elements).

Nurse Practitioner—A registered nurse who has completed a nurse practitioner program at the master's or certificate level and is trained in providing primary care services. Generally, nurse practitioners provide services at a lower cost than primary care physicians.

Nursing Home—See Skilled Nursing Facility.

O

Objective (Health Care)—A quantitative statement of desired health status or health system performance expressed as an indicator level to be achieved within a specified period. Objectives are derived from and express partial (or total) attainment of goals.

Obsolescence—The deteriorating value of a capital asset resulting from new inventions and better manufacturing techniques and developments, which render the asset unusable.

Occupancy Rate—The ratio of actual patient days to the maximum patient days, as determined by bed capacity, during any given period.

Occupational Death Benefit—A benefit payable upon death of an employee resulting from his performance of an act or acts relating to the duties of his position in the employer's service.

Occupational Disability Benefit—A benefit payable on account of disability arising out of and in the course of employment.

Occupational Disease—A disease or condition of health resulting from performance of an occupation. In most states, occupational disease is now covered under workers' compensation.

Occupational Hazards—Occupations that expose the insured to greater-than-normal physical dangers by the very nature of the work in which the insured is engaged, and the varying periods of absence from the occupation, due to disability, that can be expected.

Occupational Health Services—Employer-sponsored services designed to protect the physical health and safety of employees at work.

Occupational Illness—Impairment of health caused by conditions in the work environment.

Occupational Pension Plan—Pension plan sponsored by an employer, labor union or professional organization. Occupational plans can be called private pension plans, company pension plans, registered pension plans or employer-sponsored pension plans.

Occupational Safety and Health Act (OSHA)—Federal statute establishing national standards for health and safety conditions in the workplace. Enforced by the Labor Department, the act also provides for the reporting and compiling of statistics pertaining to occupational illnesses and injuries.

OCONUS (International Benefits)—Outside the Continental United States. Used for assigning values to certain fringe benefits such as travel and meal allowances.

Odd Lot—An amount of stock less than the established 100-share unit or ten-share unit of trading: from one to 99 shares for the great majority of issues; one to nine for so-called inactive stocks. Odd lot prices are geared to the auction market. On an odd lot market order, the odd lot dealer's price is based on the first round lot transaction that occurs on the floor following receipt at the trading post of the odd lot order.

Offer—The price at which a person is willing to sell.

Offering Price—With reference to mutual funds, the price an investor will pay per share. The offering price is the net asset value plus a sales charge (for funds that have a sales charge). See also Asked (or Asking) Price.

Office of Management and Budget (OMB)—Arm of the executive branch of the federal government responsible for cost-efficient management.

Office Visit—A formal face-to-face contact between the physician and the patient in a health center, office or hospital outpatient department.

Officer—An executive, key employee or highly compensated employee who is in regular and continued service with an employer.

Offset—The liquidation of a purchase of futures through sale of an equal number of contracts of the same delivery month, or the covering of a short sale of futures through the purchase of an equal number of contracts of the same delivery month. Either action cancels the obligation to make or take delivery of the commodity.

Offset Integration (Canada)—Provision in a pension plan for directly reducing a plan benefit by all or a portion of pensions payable to the individual from a government program.

Offset Plan—A plan under which (1) no employee is ineligible to participate because his or her compensation does not exceed a minimum level, (2) no portion of compensation is excluded in computing benefits and (3) all the provisions including the benefit rates apply uniformly to all covered employees regardless of compensation, except that an employee's benefit otherwise computed under the plan formula is reduced or offset by a stated percentage of such employee's old age insurance benefit under the Social Security Act.

Old Age Security (OAS) (Canada)—A monthly pension to qualified Canadian residents regardless of past earnings or current income. This pension is indexed to the Consumer Price Index. This benefit is taxed back wholly or partially for those with incomes over a certain level.

Old-Age, Survivors, Disability, and Health Insurance (OASDHI)—Benefits provided under the Social Security program in the United States.

Older Workers Benefit Protection Act (OWBPA)—Restores the requirement for equal benefits or equal cost in employee benefit plans that provide different treatment based on participants' ages. The law also added some employer requirements and covers all companies subject to ADEA except the federal government. The law addresses early retirement window plans, severance pay and disability benefits, health benefits, cost determinations and waivers of age discrimination rights.

Omnibus Budget Reconciliation Act (OBRA)—Annual tax and budget reconciliation acts of Congress, most of which impact managed care or Medicare.

Omnibus Budget Reconciliation Act of 1986 (OBRA '86)—Key provisions: Made changes to Medicare reimbursement to physicians and hospitals. Amended COBRA to make the loss of retiree health coverage because of a firm's Chapter 11 bankruptcy filing a qualifying event for continuation of health insurance coverage for retirees and their dependents. Required that employers with pension plans provide pension accruals or allocations for employees working beyond age 64, and for newly hired employees who are within five years of normal retirement age.

Omnibus Budget Reconciliation Act of 1987 (OBRA '87)—Key provisions: Allowed states to extend Medicaid coverage to pregnant women and infants in families with incomes up to 185% of poverty level. Contained provisions affecting the minimum funding standards, including the Pension Protection Act of 1987.

Omnibus Budget Reconciliation Act of 1989 (OBRA '89)—

—Key provisions: Allowed COBRA continuees who become covered under another plan to continue their former employer coverage for a health problem considered to be a preexisting condition under the new plan. Extended the continuation period for individuals who are disabled at termination of employment and raised the premium for the extended period.

—Partially repealed the interest exclusion on ESOP loans. Imposed mandatory Labor Department civil penalties on violations by qualified plan fiduciaries and created a tax penalty for substantial overstatement of pension liabilities in determining deductibility Required that various forms of deferred compensation be included in determination of average compensation and, in turn, the Social Security taxable wage base.

Omnibus Budget Reconciliation Act of 1993 (OBRA '93)—Key provisions: Impacts many direct and indirect components of pay (such as qualified retirement plan limits), increases the Medicare tax base, eliminates the deduction for executive pay in excess of $1 million under most circumstances, and extends the tuition reimbursement exclusion.

On the Money—An option whose exercise price is the same, or at least very close to, the stock's current price.

133⅓% Rule—Under ERISA, one of three permitted methods for calculating benefit accrual. This rule may be used only by plans that continue to accrue benefits at least until the participant is eligible to retire (at normal retirement age or early retirement age) with actuarially unreduced benefits. The basic element of the rule is that the accrual rate for a later year must not be more than 133⅓% of that for the current year. See also Accrued Benefit.

1% Owner—An individual owning, directly or indirectly, at least 1% of the employer's stock. If the employer is not a corporation, the individual's capital or profits interest in the employer is considered. See also Key Employee; Top-Heavy Plan.

One-Year Break in Service—As used in connection with the minimum vesting standards, a calendar year, plan year or other consecutive 12-month period designated by the plan during which the participant has not completed more than 500 hours of service.

One-Year Term Cost—The actuarial present value, as of a valuation date, of all benefits expected to become payable in the future as a result of an event or events expected to occur during a valuation year.

Open-End Funds—

—Issue their own shares to investors continuously, and stand ready to repurchase them as required. They are not listed on a national exchange. Within the group, there are load and no-load funds, the former involving a charge to cover sales commissions and all of the costs of distribution, while in the latter case, there is no charge, the shares being offered at net asset value.

—Participants buy and sell in at a unit price based on appraised value of total assets. Participants can leave and enter at any time. Properties continually are added to the fund. See also Investment Company or Trust.

Open-End Investment Company—See Investment Company or Trust.

Open-End Mortgage—A mortgage that permits the borrower to reborrow the money paid on the principal, usually up to the original amount.

Open-Ended HMO—An HMO that provides benefits for medical care obtained from providers who do not belong to the HMO's network of providers. Also known as *point-of-service (POS) plan.*

Open Enrollment—A period during which subscribers in a health benefit program have an opportunity to select an alternate health plan being offered to them; or a period when uninsured employees and their dependents may obtain coverage without presenting evidence of insurability.

Open Group/Closed Group—Terms used to distinguish between two classes of actuarial cost methods. Under an open group actuarial cost method, actuarial present values associated with expected future entrants are considered; under a closed group actuarial cost method, actuarial present values associated with future entrants are not considered.

Open Interest—The total number of futures contracts of a given commodity that have not yet been offset by opposite futures transactions or fulfilled by delivery of the commodity; the total number of open transactions. Each open transaction has a buyer and a seller, but for calculation of open interest, only one side of the contract is counted.

Open Market Operations—The buying and selling of government securities by the Federal Open Market Committee (FOMC) for the purpose of increasing or decreasing the money supply.

Open Mortgage—A mortgage that can be paid off at any time before maturity without penalty.

Open Order—An order to buy or sell at a stipulated price that remains effective until it is executed, canceled or changed to a different price.

Open Panel—A managed care plan (such as an HMO) that contracts with physicians who operate out of their own offices.

Opening Price—The first price at which a transaction in a security takes place each day. Also refers to the first quoted price of a new issue of securities.

Opinion Letter—A written statement issued by the IRS as to the acceptability of the form of a prototype retirement plan.

Option—

—Where the employee has the right to exercise various choices as to the type of annuity desired.

—An agreement or privilege that conveys the right to buy (receive) or sell (deliver) a specific security or property at a stipulated price and within a stated period of time. If not exercised during that time, the money paid for the option (but no more than that amount) is forfeited. See also Call Option; Put Option; Puts and Calls—Options.

Option Agreement—The agreement a customer must sign within 15 days of his or her approval for options trading. In it the client agrees to abide by the rules of the listed options exchanges and not to exceed the exchanges' position limits.

Option Expiration Date—The date the put or call option expires.

Optionee—The person who received an option on property; buyer.

Optioner—Person who gives an option on his or her property; seller.

Ordinary Care—The prudent man standard, under the circumstances of a given case.

Ordinary Life Insurance—A form of whole life insurance usually issued in amounts of $1,000 or more with premiums payable on an annual, semiannual, quarterly or monthly basis to the death of the insured or to the end of the mortality table employed, whichever occurs first and at which time (benefits) proceeds are due. The term is also used to mean *straight life insurance.*

Ordinary Life Pension Trust—A trust-funded pension plan that provides death benefits through the purchase of ordinary or whole life insurance contracts for employees covered. The trust pays premiums on the insurance coverage until the employee reaches retirement age. The trust also accumulates, in an auxiliary fund, the additional sums necessary to purchase the retirement benefits of the plan for the employees, using the paid-up cash value of the life insurance policy for each employee as part of the purchase price of the annuity.

Organization Expense—The out-of-pocket costs associated with beginning a new company. Primarily consists of legal fees, corporation fees, licenses and taxes. It can be shown on the balance sheet as a deferred asset, in which case it is usually written off against the initial few years of earnings.

Osteopathic Medicine—A system of medicine that emphasizes the theory that the body can make its own remedies, given normal structural relationships, environmental conditions and nutrition. Osteopathic physicians are granted the Doctor of Osteopathy (DO) degree.

Other Diagnosis (DRG Use Only)—All conditions that exist at the time of admission or develop subsequently that affect the treatment received and/or the length of stay in a hospital. Diagnoses that relate to an earlier episode, which have no bearing on the present hospital stay, are to be excluded.

Out-of-Area Benefits (HMO)—Those benefits that the plan supplies to its subscribers when outside the geographical limits of the HMO. These benefits usually include emergency care benefits plus low indemnity payments for nonemergency benefits. Most plans stipulate that area services for emergency care will be provided until the subscriber can be returned to the plan for medical management of the case.

Out-of-Pocket Maximum (OOP Maximum)—See Maximum Out-of-Pocket Payment.

Outcomes Management—The optimization of health outcomes through the continuous development of clinical guidelines and interventions as well as the monitoring and evaluating of data.

Outcomes Measurement—The collection and use of data to show how well a given medical intervention is meeting the health and cost goals of plan sponsors as well as those of patients.

Outliers (DRG Use Only)—Patients displaying atypical characteristics relative to other patients in a DRG, i.e., low and high length of stay, death, leaving against medical advice, admitted and discharged the same day, clinical outliers and low-volume DRGs.

Outpatient—A person who visits a clinic, emergency room or health facility and receives health care without being admitted as an overnight patient. (Antonym: inpatient)

Outpatient Services—Medical and other services provided by a hospital or other qualified facility or supplier, such as a mental health clinic, rural health clinic, mobile X-ray unit or freestanding dialysis unit. Such services include outpatient physical therapy services, diagnostic X-ray and laboratory tests, X-ray and other radiation therapy.

Outpatient Surgery—Same day surgery without anticipation of the overnight stay of patients. Often performed at an ambulatory care facility. (Synonyms: ambulatory surgery; day surgery)

Outpatient Surgical Facility—A freestanding center or entity within the hospital that is approved and licensed by the state to perform outpatient diagnostic services or surgical treatment of an illness or injury.

Outplacement Assistance—Employment counseling, employment agency services and other aid for employees who are dismissed when an organization downsizes or modifies its business strategy.

Outsourcing—

—The practice of purchasing parts or finished goods from domestic nonunion shops or from foreign companies.

—Means of eliminating in-house management, administrative and/or clerical duties associated with a particular employee benefit plan by contacting with an external service provider specializing in that particular benefit area.

Over the Counter (OTC)—

—Pharmaceutical products available without a prescription.

—A market for securities made up of securities dealers who may or may not be members of a securities exchange. Over the counter is mainly a market made over the telephone. Thousands of companies have insufficient shares outstanding, stockholders or earnings to warrant application for listing on the New York Stock Exchange. Securities of these companies are traded in the over-the-counter market between dealers who act as either principals or brokers for customers. The over-the-counter market is the principal market for U.S. government and municipal bonds.

Overbought—With regard to stock market price levels, an expression implying that the market is vulnerable to a correction. Also may be applied to a stock that has risen too high too fast in relation to its intrinsic earning power.

Overcoding—Reporting a more complex and/or higher cost procedure than was actually performed.

Overfunded Plan—A defined benefit plan in which the company's current contributions exceed both current liabilities and projected future liabilities.

Overhead Insurance—Reimburses insured for specified, fixed monthly expenses, normal and customary, in the operation and conduct of the insured's business or office.

Overinsurance—When persons covered under one or more plans can recover total benefits that exceed their actual medical expenses.

Oversold—A very depressed stock market level relative to past norms—also applies to a single issue.

Overtreatment—Providing more services than are consistent with or justified by diagnosis and treatment plan; being neither necessary nor appropriate; often used with or synonymous to overutilization. See also Undertreatment.

Owner-Employee—Self-employed individual who owns the entire interest in an unincorporated business, or a partner who owns more than 10% of the capital or profit interest of the partnership. If the owner-employee established a plan just for his or her employees but does not cover himself or herself, the rules for qualification and tax treatment of contributions and benefits are the same as those plans established by corporate employers. The requirements and limitations of HR 10 apply when a self-employed individual is included.

Owners' Equity—The owners' financial interest in a company, consisting of the difference between the company's assets and its liabilities.

Ownership of the Policy—The person or entity that pays for and owns the insurance policy. Unless otherwise specified, the owner's estate will be the beneficiary.

P

P/E Ratio—See Price/Earnings (P/E) Ratio.

Paid Claims—

—The dollar value of all claims paid (e.g., hospital, medical, surgical) during the plan year, regardless of the date that the services were rendered. Measures a plan's performance.

—(Canada) Most commonly defined as the benefit checks dated within the policy year. Can also mean the benefit checks that cleared the bank within the year.

Paper Profit—A profit still existing in the security on paper, which has not yet been sold and therefore realized. An unrealized profit.

Paperless Claims System—The process under which employees do not have to submit a claim for the payment of benefits from the medical plan. The claim is made directly by the provider to the insurer.

Par, Parity, Par Value—When applied to common stock, it refers to an arbitrary dollar amount assigned to each share by the company's charter, which has little significance to the actual market value of a stock. In the case of preferred stock, and bonds, it is important, however, because the preferred dividend and interest on the bond are often based on par value assigned to each issue. An 8% bond is a promise to pay that percentage of the bond's par (100% of face value) value annually. Also, the amount to be received at maturity in case of a bond.

Parachute—An arrangement with an employee, particularly an officer or executive of a corporation, which protects the employee financially in the event of change of control of the corporation or loss of employment. The arrangement may be a stipulated severance payment, an employment contract with a substantial notice of severance requirement, insurance or other protection.

Parent Company—A company that owns a majority or controlling interest in another company; a holding company.

Parental Leave—Leave benefits for mothers or fathers offered by employers voluntarily or as mandated by the federal Family and Medical Leave Act of 1993, state-mandated disability insurance or an agreed-upon collective bargaining provision.

Parity Rule—A break-in-service rule that says a participant loses pension rights if the break in service exceeds the greater of five years or the length of time worked.

Parol (pronounced "payroll") Evidence—Legal proof based on oral statements; with regard to a document, any evidence extrinsic to the document itself.

Part A; Part B—See Medicare.

Part-Time Employees—Refers to employees who work less than 1,000 hours for an employer in a year. Such employees may be kept from participating in qualified retirement plans.

Partial Disability—An illness or injury that prevents an insured person from performing one or more of the functions of his or her regular job.

Partial Hospitalization—Therapeutic program that provides less than 24-hour care (usually during the day) for mental health patients in transition from full-time inpatient care to outpatient care and a return to the community.

Partial Termination—Reducing benefits or making participation requirements less liberal although not amounting to a complete termination of the plan, may be considered a partial termination, resulting in the vesting of accrued benefits for at least part of the plan. To the extent that the benefits under a defined plan are underfunded at the time of termination, the benefits may be insured by the PBGC.

Partial Vesting—That form of immediate or deferred vesting under which a specified portion of the accrued benefits of a participant becomes a vested benefit.

Partial Withdrawal—An employer does not completely withdraw from a multiemployer plan, but a specified event occurs that significantly reduces the employer's obligations for contributions under the plan.

Participant—See Plan Participant.

Participant-Directed Plan—A plan under which participants determine the investment of their account balance.

Participating Annuity Contract—An annuity contract that provides for the purchaser to participate in the investment performance and possibly other experience, both favorable and unfavorable (for example, mortality experience) of the insurance company. See also Annuity.

Participating Preferred Stock—A type of preferred stock that offers the holder a share of the earnings remaining after all senior securities have been paid. This payment is made in addition to the fixed dividend received. Dividends may be cumulative, noncumulative or convertible. See also Convertible Preferred Stock; Cumulative Preferred Stock; Noncumulative Preferred Stock; Preferred Stock.

Participation—Membership in a plan.

Participation Requirements—Most pension and other employee benefit plans provide that a new employee must wait a specified length of time before he or she is eligible to participate in the plan. Under ERISA, in general, the maximum permissible service requirement is one year, although up to two years may be used in pension plans (without CODAs) that provide for full and immediate vesting. The highest minimum age that can be used is 21. See also Minimum Participation Standards.

Partition—The segregation of a portion of the assets and liabilities of a multiemployer plan ordered by the PBGC. The segregated portion of assets and liabilities is held as a separate plan after the partition.

Partnership—Co-ownership of a business by two or more people. Each owner is responsible for the debts of the whole business, not just a share.

Party in Interest—A person who is prohibited from engaging in certain transactions with the plan. Defined as (1) a fiduciary, counsel or employee of the plan; (2) a person who provides services to the plan; (3) an employer any of whose employees are covered by the plan; (4) an employee organization any of whose members are covered by the plan; (5) a 50% or more owner of an employer or employee organization; (6) a relative of any of the foregoing except item 4; (7) a corporation, partnership, trust or estate 50% or more owned by persons in items 1-5 above; (8) an employee, officer or director of the plan or of a person in items 2-5 and 7 above; and (9) a 10% or more shareholder, partner or joint venturer of a person described in items 2-5 and 7 above. See also Disqualified Person; Prohibited Transaction.

Passive Management—A style of investment management that seeks to attain average risk-adjusted performance.

Pass-Through Securities—These represent undivided interests in pools of mortgages. The sponsoring organization, for example, the Government National Mortgage Association (GNMA), passes through interest and principal payments to the certificate holders as these payments are received on a monthly basis. This results in an uneven cash flow because of prepayments caused by foreclosures or delinquent payments. Pass-through securities are offered by private organizations also.

Past Service Benefit—Credit toward a pension, provided by the employer, for all or part of a participant's years of service with the company before the adoption or amendment of a pension plan, or before the employee's entry into the plan.

Past Service Cost—See Actuarial Accrued Liability; Amortization.

Past Service Funding—Method of funding the past service liability. This cost may be amortized over a period of years. The Internal Revenue Code specifies that the employer may not deduct more than one-tenth of the original liability in any one year for income tax purposes. The minimum contribution that must be made for past service is the payment into the pension fund of interest on the unfunded past service liability.

Past Service Liability—See Initial Past Service Liability.

Patient Care Evaluation Study—A process, usually performed retrospectively, in which an in-depth assessment of the quality and/or nature of the utilization of an aspect of health care services is conducted, often by means of record audit or observation.

Patient Days—Accumulated total, for the reporting period, of the number of patients in a hospital each day (excluding newborns). A patient day is one patient in one hospital bed for one day.

Pattern Plan—A form of prototype plan that has been prepared by an organization, such as a law firm, for use by its clients and that has been approved by the Internal Revenue Service. See also Master Plan.

Pay As You Go—

—Paying pension benefits as they become due without advance funding. See General Asset Plan.

—(Canada) Also called a *pay-go plan.* A modified pay-as-you-go plan is partially funded.

Pay for Knowledge—See Skill-Based Pay.

Pay or Play—A proposal that would require all employers either to provide health insurance for their workers or to pay a tax that would enable the government to provide insurance. Employers can either "pay" (pay into the public health insurance program) or "play" (provide coverage for their employees in the private market).

Pay-Related Plan—A plan that has a benefit formula that bases benefits or benefit coverage on compensation, such as a final pay plan.

Payer—In health care, generally refers to entities, other than the patient, that finance or reimburse the cost of health services. In most cases, refers to insurance carriers, other third party payers and/or health plan sponsors (employers or unions).

Payroll Audit—

—An examination of the insured's payroll records by a representative of the insurer to determine the premium due on a policy. Some insurance, notably workers' compensation, charges its premium on the basis of the policyholder's payroll. The company sends out "payroll auditors" to de-termine the accuracy of the policyholder's figures.

—In the multiemployer plan context, frequently a part of the collections enforcement procedure, in which the payroll records of a contributing employer are audited by a trust fund representative or fund employee to ensure that contributions are being made in accordance with the provisions of the collective bargaining agreement.

Payroll-Based Stock Ownership Plan (PAYSOP)—An ESOP eligible for tax credits based on employee payroll; replaced TRASOPs in 1983. The tax credits were repealed by the Tax Reform Act of 1986. See also Employee Stock Ownership Plan.

Peer Review—A process established to provide for review by unbiased physicians of the effectiveness and efficiency of care provided under a plan's benefits.

Penny Stocks—Low-priced stock selling at less than a dollar, usually highly speculative and volatile in terms of price movements and trading volume, but periodically very rewarding.

Pension—

—A series of periodic payments, usually for life, payable monthly or at other specified intervals. The term is frequently used to describe the part of a retirement allowance financed by employer contributions. Compare with Annuity.

—A regular payment, usually monthly, to a person who has retired from employment because of advanced age or disability.

Pension Adjustment (PA) (Canada)—The value of pension benefits accruing to a plan member during a year as defined in the Income Tax Act. The PA is subtracted from the member's comprehensive retirement contribution limit (18% of pay, subject to specified dollar limits) to determine the maximum RRSP contribution allowed for the following year.

Pension Administrator—See Administrator.

Pension and Welfare Disclosure Act—A 1958 law requiring companies to file certain pension information with the Department of Labor.

Pension Benefit Formula (Plan's Benefit Formula or Benefit Formula)—The basis for determining payments to which participants may be entitled under a pension plan. Pension benefit formulas usually refer to the employee's service or compensation or both.

Pension Benefit Guaranty Corporation (PBGC)—The federal agency, established as a nonprofit corporation, charged with administering the plan termination provisions of ERISA Title IV and the Multiemployer Pension Plan Amendments Act of 1980. Employers pay premiums to the PBGC, which guarantees benefits up to a specified maximum for participants and beneficiaries when defined benefit plans terminate.

Pension Benefits Acts (Canada)—Legislation of the federal government and the provinces regulating private pension plans. Included are the federal Pension Benefits Standards Act, Quebec's Supplemental Pension Plans Act and Alberta's Employment Pension Plans Act, as well as the acts in effect in other provinces.

Pension Committee—In general, persons other than the trustees designated by management and/or the union to pass on the eligibility of employees to receive a pension.

Pension Cost(s) (Actuarial Cost)—See Normal Cost; Amortization.

Pension Plan—A plan that provides benefits, after retirement, from a trust or other separately maintained fund, by the purchase of insurance, or from general assets (unfunded plan). The amount of benefits is either specified or can be calculated in accordance with a set formula based on various factors such as age, earnings and service, but not profits. The amount of annual contributions needed to provide the specified benefits can be estimated actuarially and does not depend upon profits.

Pension Reform Act—See Employee Retirement Income Security Act of 1974.

Pension Reserve—An actuarial computation of the financial obligation for future payments to be made on account of a pension or retirement allowance or benefit.

Pension Simplification Act—A provision of the Small Business Job Protection Act of 1996. The Pension Simplification Act encourages small businesses to offer retirement plans and establishes simplified small employer pension plans known as savings incentive match plans for employees (SIMPLE). SIMPLE plans may be in the form of an IRA or part of a 401(k) plan.

Pension Trust—A fund consisting of money contributed by the employer and/or the employee plus earnings to provide pension benefits.

Pensionable Salary (International Benefits)—The salary used to calculate a pension. May be the average of a number of years prior to retirement or of the last year's salary.

Per Cause (Disability) Maximum—See Maximum Plan Limits.

Per Diem Rate—

—The rate set in advance to cover hospital or other health care facility costs on a daily basis. Sometimes includes only room and board charges and not ancillary service charges.

—Methods of calculation include dividing the total of operating costs, finance charges and depreciation by the number of inpatient days in a hospital or health care facility, as well as applying a uniform overall charge.

Percentage of Earnings Per Year of Service Formula—A formula that gives specific recognition for service as well as earnings is considered by many pension practitioners to produce the most equitable results in terms of a benefit formula that provides benefits for employees in relation to their value or contributions to the firm. A formula producing this result often is called a *unit credit* or *past and future service formula.*

Percentage of Occupancy—The ratio of actual patient days to the maximum possible patient days, as designated by bed capacity, during any given period.

Percentage Participation Clause—See Coinsurance.

Percentage Test—The requirement that at least 70% of all nonhighly compensated employees be covered by a plan. One of the IRS minimum coverage tests.

Percentile—A range of a distribution of provided charges determined by a third party payer for specific medical/dental services. For example, if the third party uses a 90th percentile, maximum payment may be made for any charge at or below that level.

Performance-Based Fees—Investment management fees that are related to investment results, not to the size of assets managed. Also known as *incentive fees.*

Perinatal—Referring or relating to the fetus or newborn, especially the human infant during the first week of life.

Period Certain—See Annuity Certain.

Perjury—False swearing upon an oath properly administered in some judicial proceedings.

Permanent Disability—Employee's inability to work at any job, rather than at the specific job held at the time the disability was incurred. Permanent disability is typically covered by insurance for those employees who become disabled before reaching age 60.

Permanent Life Insurance—Any form of life insurance except term; generally insurance, such as whole life or endowment, that accrues cash value.

Permanent Loan—A permanent loan or take-out loan is a long-term loan generally supplied by an insurance company. It is funded after completion of construction.

Permissive Aggregation Group—To determine top-heavy group status, an employer may elect to expand the aggregation group to take into account any other plan maintained by the employer if the expanded aggregation group continues to satisfy the coverage and nondiscrimination rules.

Permitted Disparity—

—A term for the Social Security integration method of allocating employers' contributions. A qualified pension or profit-sharing plan maintained by a private employer for the benefit of its employees is permitted to be integrated with benefits available to employees under the federal Social Security system. The effect of integration is to reduce the employer's cost of contributing to the plan, due to the credit available for the employer's Social Security contribution for plan participants. Permitted disparity can be an important factor in formulating the plan's participation standards in that the required inclusion of a particular employee may result in no obligation to actually make contributions for such person's benefit.

—The allowable difference between benefit and contribution rates for highly compensated and nonhighly compensated participants in qualified pension plans as permitted by IRS regulations.

Perquisites (Perks)—Special benefits for top executives and other managerial employees. Treated as taxable income to the employee. Examples include legal counseling, special parking and club memberships.

Person—An individual, partnership, joint venture, corporation, mutual company, joint stock company, trust, estate, unincorporated organization, association or employee organization.

Personal Earnings and Benefit Estimate Statement—This statement provides workers with information about their individual Social Security records, showing them the earnings that have been reported for them over the years and estimates of the different types of benefits for which they may qualify.

Personal Insurance—See Individual Insurance.

Personal Pension (Great Britain)—Individual policy that enables a person to save for retirement if he or she has contracted out of the state earnings-related pension scheme or does not have access to an occupational plan.

Personal Property—Movable property; all property that is not real property.

Phantom Stock Plan—

—A nonqualified deferred compensation plan under which deferred compensation units are created, assigned a value equivalent to the value of the company's stock and awarded to certain key employees.

—*Full value:* a long-term executive incentive plan in which the participant receives a payment in cash, representing the value of a number of shares of phantom stock, using the company's actual stock price as the value determinant and the valuation date specified in the plan or award.

—*Incremental value:* the same as the full value phantom stock grant except the amount is paid in stock or cash, and is equal to the increase in value of the company's shares from the time of the grant of the phantom stock to the date of payment.

Pharmacy Benefits Manager/Management (PBM)—Refers either to an individual or to a company that manages pharmacy benefits. Company services typically include development of formularies and drug utilization review to help contain costs.

Physical Therapy—Treatment of disease and injury by physical means, including exercise, manipulation, electricity, heat, cold and water.

Physician Adviser—A physician who provides advice on medical necessity and other medical issues in the context, for example, of preadmission authorization or concurrent review, claims that are questioned for medical necessity or other medical questions.

Physician-Hospital Organization (PHO)—Alliances between physicians and hospitals to help providers attain market share, improve bargaining power and reduce administrative costs. These entities sell their services to managed care organizations or directly to employers.

Physician's Assistant (PA)—An allied health professional who is trained to perform certain medical procedures previously reserved to the physician, and who works under the supervision of a physician.

Piecework—Work compensated according to the number of units produced.

Pink Sheets—Quotation lists of various over-the-counter securities published daily on pink paper by the National Quotation Bureau, Inc.

Plan—An arrangement under which employer and employee contributions, if any, are deposited with a trustee who is responsible for the administration and investment of these monies and the income earned on accumulated assets of the fund, and who is normally responsible for the direct payment of benefits to eligible participants under the plan. Benefits are often paid by an insurance company with transfers from the trust fund as required. The trustee may be a corporate trustee (trust company) or an individual.

Plan Administrator—See Administrator.

Plan Amendment—See Amendment.

Plan Assets—Stocks, bonds and other investments, including securities of the employer if they are transferable, that have been segregated and restricted (usually in a trust) so they can only be used to provide for postretirement benefits. Plan assets include amounts contributed by the employer (but not amounts accrued and unpaid), amounts contributed by plan participants for a contributory plan and amounts earned from investing the contributions, less benefits, income taxes and other expenses incurred.

Plan Document—For purposes of qualified retirement plans, a definite written program maintained by an employer for the benefit of employees or beneficiaries that is intended to be permanent and is communicated to employees. Sets forth the benefits available under an employee benefit plan and the eligibility requirements. This document is often separate from the trust agreement in order to allow plan modifications without frequent trust agreement amendments.

Plan Liabilities—Include normal costs, accrued liability, past service liabilities and experience losses. Plan liabilities are to be determined under the funding method used generally to determine costs under the plan. Experience gains and any decreases in plan benefits that reduce plan liabilities are also subject to this rule. Plan costs must be determined on the basis of actuarial assumptions that, in the aggregate, are reasonable.

Plan Participant—Any employee or former employee of an employer, member or former member of an employee organization, sole proprietor, or partner in a partnership who is or may become eligible to receive a benefit of any type from an employee benefit plan, or whose beneficiaries may be eligible to receive any such benefit. See also Active Participant; Participation Requirements.

Plan Sponsor—The party that establishes and maintains the plan, which is (1) the employer, in the case of an employee benefit plan maintained by a single employer; (2) the employee organization, in the case of a plan maintained by an employee organization; or (3) the association, committee, joint board of trustees or other similar group of representatives of the parties involved, in the case of a plan maintained by one or more employers and one or more employee organizations.

Plan Suspension—An event in which the pension plan is frozen and no further benefits accrue. Future service may continue to be the basis for vesting of nonvested benefits existing at the date of suspension.

The plan may still hold assets, pay benefits already accrued and receive additional employer contributions for any unfunded benefits. Employees may or may not continue working for the employer.

Plan Termination—
—When the plan ceases to exist and benefits are settled. Replacement with another plan is not a termination. ERISA requires that all accrued benefits (to the extent funded) must be fully vested upon the termination or partial termination of a plan. (A partial termination might result from a large reduction of the workforce or a sizable reduction of benefits under the plan.)
—(Canada) Voluntary or involuntary discontinuance of a plan. The Pension Benefits Act regulates the windup procedure.

Plan Termination Date—If the plan is terminated by the plan administrator, the termination date is the date established by the administrator and agreed to by the Pension Benefit Guaranty Corporation. If the plan is terminated by the PBGC, it is the date established by the PBGC and agreed to by the administrator. In either case, if the administrator and PBGC cannot agree, the date will be set by the court.

Plan Termination Insurance—Insurance protecting pension plan participants from loss of pension benefits due to plan termination. The federal program set forth under Title IV of ERISA insures defined benefit pension plans against the failure of the employer to properly fund. It is administered by the Pension Benefit Guaranty Corporation. All defined benefit pension plans are subject to these regulations. The Multiemployer Pension Plan Amendments Act of 1980 extended mandatory Title IV coverage to multiemployer plans (such coverage was discretionary under ERISA as originally enacted) and adjusted the multiemployer per participant premium.

Plan Year—The calendar, policy or fiscal year on which the records of the plan are kept.

Plant Closing Bill of 1988—Requires employers that anticipate a major layoff to notify the affected workers 60 days in advance.

Play or Pay—See Pay or Play.

Plus Tick—See Uptick.

PM/PM—Per member per month; the revenue or cost of a risk payment that is typically made to providers by HMOs for providing a defined amount of care for each enrolled patient each month.

Point—
—In the case of shares of stock, a point means $1. If ABC shares rise three points, each share has risen $3.
—In the case of bonds, a point means $10, since a bond is quoted as a percentage of $1,000. A bond that rises three points gains 3% of $1,000, or $30 in value. An advance from 87 to 90 would mean an advance in dollar value from $870 to $900 for each $1,000 bond.
—In the case of market averages, the word *point* means merely that and no more; its value is relative and is assigned arbitrarily. If, for example, the Dow Jones Industrial Average rises from 870.25 to 871.25, it has risen a point. A point in this average, however, is not equivalent to $1.
—The term is frequently used when referring to mortgage premiums and is 1% of the principal amount. It is a method used by lenders to obtain additional revenue over the legal interest rate.

Point-of-Service Plan (POS)—A health plan that allows members to choose to receive services from a participating or nonparticipating network provider, usually with a financial disincentive for going outside the network. More of a product than an organization, POS plans can be offered by HMOs, PPOs or self-insured employers.

Poison Pill—An attempt by a company's management to insulate the firm from either a two-tier bid or a low-ball bid by creating additional equity at very low prices, thereby substantially increasing the acquiring company's acquisitions cost. It is an antitakeover ploy.

Policy—The contract between the insurance company and the policy owner under which the insurance company agrees to pay the policy benefit when specific losses occur, provided the insurer receives the required premiums.

Policy Dividend—See Dividend.

Policyholder—The owner of the policy. Under a group purchase plan, the policyholder is the employer, labor union or trustee to whom a group contract is issued. In a plan contracting directly with the individual or family, the policyholder is the individual to whom the contract is issued.

Political Investments—See Socially Responsible Investments.

Pool—In some cases refers to a large number of small groups that are analyzed and rated as a single large group. Risk pools may be any account that attempts to find the claims liability for a group with a common denominator.

Pooled Trust—A common trust fund generally sponsored by one employer and used to accumulate the assets of different plans of the employer and its subsidiaries.

Pop-Up Option—A variation of the usual joint and survivor option in which, if the participant survives the contingent annuitant, the amount of benefit payable reverts back (or "pops up") to the original life-only amount of benefit. More frequently seen in multiemployer plans.

Portability—

—Any provision for retaining pension rights and credits when changing from one employer to another. Vested rights are nonforfeitable. The retention of nonvested (contingent) rights depends upon remaining within the scope of a multiemployer plan, or its reciprocating plan under a reciprocal agreement. See also Reciprocal Agreement.

—The ability of the consumer to take health insurance from job to job. See Job Lock.

—The right of an employee to take with him or her, upon separation from the employer, the total accumulation of monies carried in his or her account.

Portfolio—

—The mix and composition of an investor's holdings among different classes of securities such as bonds, mortgages and common stocks.

—All of the products an insurance company offers.

Portfolio Mix—A combination or selection of investments, including stocks, bonds, real estate and selected limited partnership interests.

Portfolio Optimization—Starting with a universe of securities that has been valued in terms of (1) expected return, (2) variances of expected return and (3) covariance of return with every other security under consideration, the process of portfolio optimization involves selecting the portfolio that minimizes risk for a given level of risk. In practice, the computerized optimization programs can impose manifold constraints on the characteristics of the resultant portfolio. Typical constraints would be that the resultant portfolio have no more than 5% of the portfolio's value in a single stock or that the average current yield be at least 4% per annum.

Position—A market commitment. For example, one who has bought futures contracts is said to have a long position; and conversely, a seller of futures contracts is said to have a short position.

Postponed Retirement—Under some plans, it is possible for an employee to continue in employment beyond his or her normal retirement date, sometimes only with the consent of his or her employer. Most plans provide that pension payments will not begin until retirement actually occurs. Usually no benefits accrue for service after the normal retirement date.

Postretirement Adjustment—A change (usually an increase) in the amount of a retirement allowance after its commencement to reflect changes or anticipated changes in cost-of-living or living standards.

Postretirement Benefits—All forms of benefits, other than retirement income, provided by an employer to its retirees.

Power of Attorney (P/A)—An instrument authorizing another to act as one's agent or attorney in fact.

Practice Guidelines—recommended, codified procedures and techniques for the treatment of specific illnesses and medical conditions, based on the best scientific evidence and expert opinion, and designed to serve as educational support for physicians, and also as quality assurance and accountability measures for managed care plans. Also known as *practice policies, treatment protocols* and *critical pathways.*

Practitioner—One who practices medicine; may include physicians, chiropractors, dentists, podiatrists and physicians' assistants.

Pre-Authorization—See Prior Authorization.

Preadmission Certification—See Precertification.

Preadmission Testing (PAT)—A plan benefit designed to encourage patients to obtain needed diagnostic services on an ambulatory basis before a nonemergency hospital admission in order to reduce hospital length of stay.

Precedent—A previously decided court case that can serve as an authority in deciding a present controversy. In law, the term *stare decisis* refers to the practice of adhering to decided cases and settled principles, providing for the development of a consistent body of law.

Precertification—The process of obtaining certification or authorization from the health plan for hospital admissions (inpatient or outpatient) or for surgery, based on the judgment of medically appropriate care by a qualified peer. Failure to obtain precertification often results in a financial penalty to either the provider or the subscriber. Also known as *preadmission certification* or *preadmission review.*

Preemption of State Law (ERISA)—The regulatory portion of the act supersedes all state law that otherwise would be applicable to plans covered by the reporting, disclosure, fiduciary responsibility, participation and vesting, funding and plan termination insurance provisions of ERISA. However, the preemptive effect of the act does not relieve any person from state law regulating insurance, banking or securities. Nor does the act preempt any generally applicable state criminal law.

Preemptive Right—A right accorded a present shareholder, before any new shareholders are so treated, to subscribe to new shares in the company at a stipulated price on or before a fixed expiration date. Usually provided under state laws, but may be waived in the company's charter or bylaws.

Preexisting Condition—A physical and/or mental condition of an insured person that existed prior to the issuance of his or her policy. Some plans may cover these conditions after a waiting period of six months to a year, while others may permanently exclude a person with a preexisting condition from coverage.

Preferred Debt—See Senior Debt.

Preferred Provider Organization (PPO)—A group of hospitals and physicians that contract on a fee-for-service basis with employers, insurance companies or other third party administrators to provide comprehensive medical service. Providers exchange discounted services for increased volume and prompt payment. Participants' out-of-pocket costs are usually lower than under a fee-for-service plan.

Preferred Risk—A person classified as an above-average risk because the person's physical condition, health history, occupation and/or lifestyle indicate the probability of a lower-than-usual mortality rate.

Preferred Stock—Securities or shares representing an ownership interest in the business, but which have "preference" over other shares (i.e., common stock) as regards dividends, or in distribution of assets up to a certain fixed amount in the event of liquidation, or both. Preferred dividends are normally fixed, whereas common stock dividends may fluctuate depending upon company earnings. Preferred stockholders generally do not have voting rights. See also Convertible Preferred Stock; Cumulative Preferred Stock; Noncumulative Preferred Stock; Participating Preferred Stock.

Pregnancy Disability—Disability that is caused, or contributed to, by pregnancy, childbirth or related medical conditions. Under Title VII of the Civil Rights Act of 1964, employers must treat such disabilities on a parity with other, nonpregnancy-related conditions.

Pregnancy Discrimination Act of 1978 (PDA)—An amendment to Title VII of the Civil Rights Act of 1964 that requires covered employers to treat pregnancy the same as any other disability in providing employee benefits and in granting leaves of absence.

Preliminary Prospectus—The first prospectus that is distributed during the cooling-off period and that includes the essential facts about the forthcoming offering, except the underwriting spread, the final public offering price and date the shares will be delivered. Because red ink is used on its face, it is often called a *red herring.*

Premature Distributions—The Tax Reform Act of 1984 imposes a 10% tax on amounts that an individual receives from a qualified plan where he or she is, or has been, a 5% owner of the business under which the plan is established, and where he or she receives the distribution before reaching age 59½. The premature distribution tax would not be applied if the reason for the distribution was that the individual became disabled. The tax would apply only to the extent that the amounts distributed are attributable to contributions paid on behalf of the individual (other than contributions made by him or her as a 5% owner) while he or she was a 5% owner. The 10% tax is in addition to other income taxes imposed on the distribution.

Thus, Keogh plan participants who are not 5% owners do not have to pay the 10% premature distribution tax for amounts distributed to them before they reach age 59½.

Unless a participant is disabled, any distribution from an individual retirement account or annuity to an individual for whose benefit the account or annuity was established is subject to a 10% premature distribution tax if he or she has not reached age 59½. This includes a constructive distribution resulting from the disqualification of the account or annuity. Whether the individual is disabled is determined under the annuity rules.

Premium—

—The amount of money a policyholder agrees to pay an insurance company for an insurance policy or an annuity, in consideration of which the insurance company guarantees the payment of specified benefits. May be a single sum or a series of periodic payments. Synonymous with *purchase payment* or *contribution.*

—An insurance concept: premium rate is based on sex, amount and issue age, and is usually level to retirement age. Generally based on the same mortality, interest and expense assumptions used in the calculation for regular insurance contracts. Some insurance companies offer special pension series of contracts with a different set of actuarial assumptions that can be justified on the basis of special tax credit for investment income earned on pension reserves and differences in experience in pension underwriting.

—The amount by which a bond or preferred stock may sell above its par or face value. When a new issue of bonds or stocks is sold, the amount of increase over the issue price is the premium. Also refers to the charge made sometimes when a stock is borrowed to make delivery on a short sale. Also used in referring to the redemption price of a bond or preferred stock whenever it is higher than face value. (Antonym: discount)

—The price paid by the purchaser of an option and the amount received by the seller (writer).

Premium Tax—

—A state tax levied on gross premiums, usually adjusted for dividends or retroactive rate adjustments.

—(Canada) A provincial tax levied on net premiums.

Prepaid Assets—See Deferred Assets; Deferred Charges.

Prepaid Care Plan—See Prepaid Group Practice.

Prepaid Group Practice—A term used before the term *health maintenance organization* was coined to refer to multispecialty physician groups paid on a salaried or capitated basis.

Prepaid Pension Cost—Cumulative employer contributions in excess of accrued net pension cost.

Prepaid Program—A program that finances the cost of care in advance of receipt of service through a third party.

Preparticipation Service—The period of employment that an employee must complete before he or she can participate in a plan.

Prepayment—A method providing in advance for the cost of predetermined benefits for a population group, through regular periodic payments in the form of premiums, dues or contributions.

Prepayment Clause—A clause in a mortgage instrument spelling out the details under which the mortgagor is permitted to pay all or part of the unpaid loan balance before it becomes due. The amount of the prepayment fee, or penalty, if any, is usually included in this clause.

Prepayment Penalty—A fee imposed on a mortgagor for paying the mortgage off before it becomes due.

Preretirement Counseling—Program to help employees prepare financially and, sometimes, emotionally for retirement.

Preretirement Death Benefits—These are the payments payable on the death of a participant prior to attaining retirement age. If the program is based upon investments only, then customarily the full value of the investment accounts. If the plan uses life insurance, then usually this would constitute the payment. A combination of both investments and life insurance is permissible; however, in no event may the total sum delivered to the beneficiary exceed 100 times the projected monthly pension benefit, unless the former participant was in the last years of his or her service period. In such an instance, the death benefit may equal the cash value of a retirement income contract, issued under similar circumstances.

Preretirement Surviving Spouse Benefit—A benefit providing that, if the participant dies while actively employed, the spouse will receive 50% of the pension calculated as though the employee had retired the day death occurred. This benefit is required under REA at time of vesting.

Prescription Drug Formulary—A listings of prescription medications that will be covered by a plan or insurance contract that often fosters substitution of generic or therapeutic equivalents on a cost-effective basis.

Prescription Drug Plan—Usually a provision under medical coverage plans whereby the beneficiary can obtain prescription drugs without incurring potentially large out-of-pocket expense. Different types of prescription drug plans are available. The most popular are discount plan, closed panel drug plan, service-delivered plan, mail-order plan and maintenance drug option with major medical plan.

Present Value—See Actuarial Present Value.

Preservice Review—See Prospective Review.

Presumptive Method—A method of calculating and allocating withdrawal liability that generally requires an employer entering or continuing in a multiemployer plan after September 25, 1980, who subsequently withdraws, to fund a share of the increase in the plan's unfunded vested benefits during the period of the employer's required contributions to the plan.

Pretreatment Estimate—See Prior Authorization.

Prevailing Fee—A fee that falls within the range of fees most frequently charged by providers in a given locality for a particular medical service or procedure.

Prevailing Wage Rate—The amount paid by other employers in the labor market for similar work.

Preventive Care—Comprehensive care emphasizing priorities for prevention, early detection and early treatment of conditions, generally including routine physical examinations, immunization and well person care.

Price—The market value of anything being offered for sale.

Price/Earnings (P/E) Ratio—A stock's market price divided by its current or estimated future earnings. A measure of the attractiveness of a particular security vs. all other securities as determined by the investing public.

Price Index—A relative measure of the general price level over time. It is obtained by computing the ratio of the prices of a collection of goods and services during one period with the prices of the same goods and services during a selected base period.

Price Limits—The maximum price advance or decline from the previous day's settlement price permitted for a contract in one trading session by the regulations of the exchange.

Price Range—A combination of the highest price and the lowest price reached by a certain security, or the general market, during any specific day, week or year under discussion.

Price-to-Book Ratio—The current market price of a stock divided by the previous year's book value per share.

$$P/B = \frac{\text{Market Price of a Common Stock}}{\text{Book Value per Share}}$$

Primary Beneficiary—Individual designated to receive benefits under the insurance policy or trust account.

Primary Care—Basic or general health care as opposed to specialist or subspecialist care. Primary care providers often oversee the total care of patients, referring the patient to other professionals as appropriate. Physicians whose practices are predominantly primary care include general or family practitioners, internists and pediatricians. Primary care also may be provided by nurse practitioners, physicians' assistants or other midlevel practitioners.

Primary Care Case Management—See Gatekeeper.

Primary Care Network (PCN)—A group of primary care physicians who have formed a network to share the risk of providing services to enrollees in a prepaid plan.

Primary Care Physician (PCP)—The physician in a managed care plan who is responsible for coordinating all care for an individual patient, from providing direct care services to referring the patient to specialists and hospital care.

Primary Insurance Amount (PIA)—A figure used to compute how much Social Security a person is to receive upon reaching Social Security retirement age. It is based on the individual's wages, compensation, self-employment income and deemed military wage credits for years after 1950.

Primary Offering—A corporation's offering of stock to the public. Proceeds of the offering go directly to the corporation. See also New Issue.

Primary Payer—The insurance carrier that has first responsibility under coordination of benefits.

Prime Rate—The minimum rate on bank loans set by commercial banks and granted only to top business borrowers. It is affected by overall business conditions, the availability of reserves and the general level of money rates; it may vary geographically. Lending rates are also greatly influenced by the size of the loan; the largest loans naturally command the lowest rates.

Principal—
—One of the main parties in a real estate transaction; the purchaser or the seller.
—In agency law, the party to a contract who authorizes an agent to act on its behalf.
—In finances, an amount loaned, the sum that earns interest.
—The basic amount of money as distinguished from interest. The capital sum; the amount upon which interest is paid.

Principal Diagnosis—The condition established, after study, to be chiefly responsible for causing the patient to be admitted to the hospital for care.

Principal Sum—
—A lump-sum payment made upon the insured person's accidental death and, sometimes, dismemberment or loss of sight. Sometimes referred to as *capital sum.*
—The value payable to the participant upon maturity of an endowment contract.

Prior Authorization—A cost-control procedure that requires the service or medication to be approved in advance by the doctor and/or the insurer. Without prior authorization, the health plan or insurer will not pay for the test, drug or services.

Prior Service Benefit—See Past Service Benefit.

Prior Service Cost—The cost of retroactive benefits granted in a plan amendment or under a new plan. See also Unrecognized Prior Service Cost.

Priorities (Plan Termination) (Canada)—A set of rules, in an employment pension plan or legislation, under which the assets of a plan that is discontinued are allocated among members and beneficiaries to provide as far as possible for all accrued benefits.

Private Pension Plans—Pension plans established by private agencies, including commercial, industrial, labor and service organizations; nonprofit organizations; and nonprofit religious, educational and charitable institutions. Includes both single employer and multiemployer plans. Basically, all nongovernmental plans.

Private Placement—Usually associated with debt instruments where marketability is not required, but not always the case. The private placement of a loan with an institutional investor, such as a pension fund or insurance company, precludes the borrower from any SEC registration requirements, eliminates problems connected with changing market interest rates, and provides the investor with a higher interest rate and often a tailor-made maturity that might be difficult for the investor to obtain in a public offering. Also known as *direct placement.*

Privatization—Occurs when services formerly performed by public employees are contracted to private sector firms.

Pro Rata Agreement—See Reciprocal Agreement.

Probationary Period—A specified number of days after the date of the issuance of the policy during which coverage is not afforded for sickness. The purpose of the period is to eliminate sickness actually contracted before the policy went into force.

Productivity—The relationship between output, or the quantity of goods and services produced, and inputs, or the amounts of labor, material and capital needed to produce the goods and services. Usually measured in terms of output per worker, per hour. It is affected by technology level, changes in plant and equipment and quality of the labor force.

Profit—Money remaining after all costs of operating a business are paid.

Profit and Loss Statement—A detailed summary of the income and expenses of a business over a period of time (usually quarterly, semiannually or annually) showing the net income or loss incurred. Also known as *income account* or *income statement.*

Profit-Sharing Plan—Plan established and maintained by an employer to provide for the participation in its profits by its employees or their beneficiaries. The plan must provide a definite predetermined formula for allocating the contributions made to the plan among the participants and for distributing the fund accumulated under the plan after a fixed number of years, the attainment of a stated age, or upon the prior occurrence of some event such as layoff, illness, disability, retirement, death or severance of employment. Deferred profit-sharing plans are subject to the participation, vesting, reporting and disclosure, and fiduciary rules of ERISA. They are excluded from the funding and plan termination provisions of the act.

- Current profit-sharing plan (cash). Profits paid directly to employees in cash, check or stock as soon as profits are determined.
- Deferred profit-sharing plan. A defined contribution plan; a qualified program of retirement benefits wherein the employer provides retirement benefits subject to a written agreement and based on the limitations described in the IRC. The employees' benefits at retirement are based strictly upon the sum total of the contributions made and the investment result thereon.

See also Employees Profit Sharing Plan (Canada).

Profit-Sharing Retirement Plan—A program in which the employee's retirement benefit is based on the employer's contributions to a fund and on the earnings of the fund. The employer's contributions are based on a formula related to profits. See also Deferred Profit-Sharing Plan.

Profit Taking—The act of selling stock, convertible securities and/or bonds that have appreciated in value to translate a paper profit into a realized gain. Often used to explain the reason for a market decline after a noticeable runup in prices.

Progressive Tax—A tax in which the tax rates increase as taxable income increases.

Prohibited Group—Employees who are officers, shareholders or highly compensated. A qualified pension plan may not discriminate in favor of this group of employees.

Prohibited Transaction—

—With certain exceptions, a trustee or other plan fiduciary may not engage in any financial transaction with the employer or individuals in control of the employer (referred to as *parties in interest* under the regulatory provisions and as *disqualified persons* under the tax provisions) if he or she knows or should have known that such transaction is prohibited by ERISA. This includes the selling or leasing of property, the lending of money, the furnishing of goods, services or facilities, or the transfer of any assets to or for the use of a party in interest (or disqualified person). In addition, plans other than eligible individual account plans may not invest more than 10% of plan assets in the employer's securities and/or real property. A plan may not hold or acquire an employer security or employer real property that is not a "qualifying employer security" or "qualifying employer real property." See also Disqualified Person; Party in Interest.

—In regard to an IRA, any action that results in a constructive distribution from an IRA. According to the IRS, such actions are borrowing money from an IRA, selling property to an IRA or receiving unreasonable compensation for managing an IRA. The effect is a loss of favorable tax treatment.

Prohibited Transaction Exemption (PTE)—A statutory or administrative exemption that permits transactions between plans and parties in interest to occur that would otherwise be prohibited. In granting exemptions from the prohibited transaction rules, the DOL requires the exemption to be administratively feasible; in the interests of the plan, its participants and beneficiaries; and protective of the rights of the plan's participants and beneficiaries.

Projected Benefit Cost Method—See Actuarial Cost Method.

Projected Benefit Liability—The estimated amount required as of a specified date to fulfill a pension plan's future obligation to its participants. More specifically, the actuarial present value as of a specified date of a series of future annual retirement payments computed based upon assumptions relative to interest (rate of return), mortality, probability of staying to retirement and the amount of the retirement benefit. The projected benefit liability is also referred to as the *actuarial present value of future benefits* or, sometimes, as the *actuarial liability.*

Projected Benefit Obligation (PBO)—The present value of accrued benefits for a defined benefit plan, assuming no future service but anticipating salary increases; a required disclosure under FAS 87. See also Accumulated Benefit Obligation.

Projected Benefits—Those pension plan benefit amounts that are expected to be paid at various times under a particular set of actuarial assumptions, taking into account such items as the effect of advancement in age and past and anticipated future compensation and service credits. That portion of an individual's projected benefit allocated to service to date, determined in accordance with the terms of a pension plan and based on future compensation as projected to retirement, is called the *credited projected benefit.*

Projection Actuarial Cost Method—A method under which the excess of the actuarial present value of the sum of projected benefit payments for a specified period plus a funding objective as of the end of the period, over the actuarial value of assets, is allocated on a level basis over the earnings or service of the group during the specified period, including the earnings or service for any future entrants assumed. The allocation is performed for the group as a whole, not as a sum of individual allocations. The portion of this actuarial present value allocated to a valuation year is called the *annual cost allocation.*

Proration—The adjustment of benefits paid because of a mistake in the amount of the premiums paid or the existence of other insurance covering the same accident or disability.

Prospective Future Service Benefit—That portion of a participant's retirement benefit that relates to his or her period of credited service to be rendered after a specified current date.

Prospective Pricing—Setting a specific, total all-inclusive price for a service prior to the delivery of the service, often on a DRG basis (usually established by the plan or payer and not by the provider, but may be the result of negotiation).

Prospective Review—Requires the granting of authorization for payment *before* medical care is provided.

Prospectus—A legal document setting forth the complete history and current status of a security issue, which must be made available to all interested purchasers in advance of a public offering under the Securities Act of 1933.

Protocols—See Practice Guidelines.

Prototype Plan—A standardized plan, approved and qualified as to its concept by Internal Revenue Service, that is made available by insurance companies, banks and mutual funds for the use of employers. See also Master Plan; Pattern Plan.

Provident Fund (International Benefits)—A saving plan in which accumulations of employee and employer contributions are generally paid out in a lump sum when a vested employee ceases active employment.

Provider—Individual or organization whose primary source of income is derived from the provision, administration or financing of health services, or from research or teaching in the health field.

Provincial Government Plan—See Medicare (Canada).

Proxy—A written authorization given by a shareholder to someone else to vote his or her shares at a stockholders annual or special meeting called to elect directors or for some other corporate purpose.

Proxy Statement—Required SEC filing for a publicly traded company that notifies shareholders of the company's annual (or any special) meeting, transmits information about matters that will be voted upon by shareholders at the meeting (including election of directors), and encloses a ballot for voting.

Prudent Man Rule—

—A common law standard applicable to the investment of trust funds. Briefly stated:

> All that can be required of a trustee in the investment of trust funds is that he conduct himself faithfully and exercise sound discretion. He is to observe how men of prudence, discretion and intelligence manage their own affairs, not in regard to speculation, but in regard to the permanent disposition of their funds, considering the probable income as well as the probable safety of the capital to be invested.

[IF *Trustees Handbook*]

—According to ERISA, a fiduciary must act "with the care, skill, prudence, and diligence under the circumstances then prevailing that a prudent man acting in a like capacity and familiar with such matters would use in the conduct of an enterprise of a like character and with like aims." (Section 404(a)(1).)

—An investment standard adapted by the majority of states that allows a fiduciary to invest in only those securities which would be acquired by prudent men of discretion and intelligence who are seeking a reasonable return and preservation of their capital. Some states have a legal list published by the superintendent of banking to which savings banks, trust funds and similar institutions must adhere. See also Fiduciary.

PS 58 Costs—Refers to the law that determines annual cost of current life insurance protection provided by a retirement plan that is includable in the participant's taxable income.

Public Employee Retirement System (PERS)—An organization providing a formal program of retirement benefits for employees of states, provinces or their political subdivisions.

Public Offering—The sale of stocks and bonds, which have been registered with government agencies, to the public.

Public Sector Plan (Canada)—An employment pension plan offered by an employer in the public sector, covering civil servants, teachers, municipal employees, etc.

Punitive Damages; Exemplary Damages—Damages awarded by a court over and above compensatory damages because of the wanton, reckless, malicious or oppressive character of the acts committed by the wrongful party. Intended to punish or "make an example of" the wrongdoer.

Purchaser—Program sponsor, often an employer or union, that contracts with a benefits organization to provide benefits to an enrolled population.

Purchasing Power—The goods and services that can be purchased with a given amount of money. Inflation is reflected in loss of purchasing power of currency. For example, if it takes $2 to pay for goods and services that formerly cost $1, the purchasing power of the dollar has been cut in half.

Put Option—A security that gives the owner the right to sell a particular stock at a certain price within a designated period of time. See also Puts and Calls—Options.

Puts and Calls—Options—Options, better known as *puts and calls,* give one the right to buy or sell a stated amount of stock at the stated price within a specified period of time, regardless of the market price of the stock. A *call* is an option contract to buy (from the writer of the call) shares of stock at a stated price, expiring on the stated date. A *put* is an option contract to sell shares of stock at a stated price, expiring on a stated date. Options may now be traded on the Chicago Board Options Exchange (CBOE), thereby providing standardization of securities option contracts and trading practices.

Pyramiding—
- —In stock and commodity market terminology, the practice of using unrealized paper profits to make additional purchases on margin.
- —As related to financial statements, the practice of creating a highly leveraged capital structure by which only a relatively small amount of stock in the parent company controls a large number of subsidiary or related companies. Sometimes associated with conglomerates.

Q

Qualification Period (Canada)—The period of time between the beginning of a disability and the start of a policy's benefits. Called a *waiting period in* the United States.

Qualification Requirement—The rules and regulations, issued in order to determine whether a proposed pension or profit-sharing plan will be fully deductible for tax purposes.

Qualified Beneficiary—
- —An active employee, former employee and his or her spouse and dependents who are eligible for continuation coverage under COBRA because of their status on the day before a qualifying event.
- —An individual covered by a group health plan, or a dependent of such an individual, as of the day before a qualifying event takes place.

Qualified Benefits—Nontaxable benefits that can be included in a cafeteria plan: group term life insurance, accident and health insurance, dependent care assistance and cash or deferred arrangements.

Qualified Cash or Deferred Arrangement—See 401(k) Plan.

Qualified Cost—The limit on an employer's tax deduction for contribution to a welfare benefit fund. It equals the fund's qualified direct cost and permitted additions to a qualified asset account, minus the fund's after-tax income for the taxable year.

Qualified Disability Benefit—A disability benefit provided by a plan that does not exceed the benefit that would be provided if the participant separated from service at normal retirement age.

Qualified Domestic Relations Order (QDRO)—A domestic relations order is a judgment, decree or order (including an approval of property settlement agreement) that (1) relates to the provision of child support, alimony payments or marital property rights to a spouse, former spouse, child or other dependent of a participant and (2) is made pursuant to a state domestic relations law (including a community property law). A domestic relations order is a qualified domestic relations order if it creates or recognizes the existence of an alternate payee's right, or assigns to an alternate payee the right, to receive all or a portion of the benefits payable to a participant under a plan, specifies required information and does not alter the amount or form of plan benefits. An alternate payee is a spouse, former spouse, child or other dependent of a participant who is recognized by a domestic relations order as having a right to receive all, or a portion of, the benefits under a plan with respect to the participant. See also Assignment of Benefits.

Qualified Employee—An employee who works more than 30 hours per week or 120 hours per month. Qualified employees usually receive benefits, including health insurance, while temporary, seasonal or part-time employees do not.

Qualified Impairment Insurance—A form of substandard or special class insurance, which restricts benefits for the insured person's particular condition.

Qualified Joint and Survivor Annuity (QJSA)—An annuity from a pension plan that runs for the life of the participant, with a survivor annuity for the life of the spouse not less than 50% nor more than 100% of the annuity payable for their joint lives, and that is the actuarial equivalent of a single annuity for the life of the participant.

Qualified Matching Contributions (QMACs)—Matching contributions that are 100% vested at all times and that are subject to the same restrictions on distributability as elective contributions. QMACs may be treated as elective contributions for ADP testing if they are from plans with the same plan year and meet certain requirements.

Qualified Medical Child Support Order (QMCSO)—A judgment, decree or order that (1) is issued by a court of competent jurisdiction pursuant to a state domestic relations law or community property law; (2) creates or recognizes the right of an alternate recipient to receive benefits under his or her parent's employer's group health plan; and (3) includes certain information relating to the participant and alternate recipient.

Qualified Medicare Beneficiary (QMB)—A person whose income falls below 100% of federal poverty guidelines, for whom the state must pay the Medicare Part B premiums, deductibles and copayments.

Qualified Nonelective Contributions (QNECs)—Nonelective contributions that are 100% vested at all times and that are subject to the same restrictions on distributability as elective contributions. QNECs may be treated as elective contributions for ADP testing or as matching contributions for ACP testing if they are from plans with the same plan year and meet certain requirements.

Qualified Plan—A plan that the Internal Revenue Service approves as meeting the requirements of Section 401(a) of the 1954 Internal Revenue Code. Such plans receive tax advantages.

Qualified Preretirement Survivor Annuity (QPSA)—If a pension plan participant dies before starting pension benefits, the surviving spouse receives this type of annuity. Amount of QPSA depends on type of plan and age of participant at death. See Automatic Survivor Coverage.

Qualified Professional Asset Manager (QPAM)—A bank, savings and loan, insurance company or registered investment adviser satisfying certain equity capital, net worth or total assets of managed funds requirements.

Qualified Retirement Annuity—A tax deductible investment product typically purchased through insurance companies using employer contributions; used in lieu of a company pension plan.

Qualified Total Distribution—One or more distributions that (1) constitute lump-sum distributions; (2) are made within one taxable year to the employee because of termination of the plan or, in the case of a profit-sharing or stock bonus plan, complete discontinuance of plan contributions; or (3) constitute a distribution of accumulated deductible contributions.

Qualified Voluntary Employee Contribution (QVEC)—Instead of establishing an IRA to receive deductible contributions, an individual (including a self-employed person) is allowed to contribute to *a qualified employer plan* or a *qualified government plan* for taxable years beginning after 1981. For purposes of qualified voluntary employee contributions, a *qualified employer plan* is defined as (1) a tax-exempt trust that forms a part of a pension, profit-sharing or stock bonus plan under Code Section 401 (a), (2) a qualified annuity plan under Code Section 403(a), (3) a tax-sheltered annuity plan for charitable or educational employees under Code Section 403(b), (4) a qualified bond purchase plan under Code Section 405(a) or (5) a simplified employee plan pension (SEP).

Contributions will qualify as voluntary employee contributions only if (1) the contributions are not mandatory, (2) deductible employee contributions are accepted under the plan and (3) the participant does not designate the contributions as nondeductible.

Qualifying Event—An occurrence entitling a person to elect continuation coverage under COBRA, such as termination of employment (or a reduction in hours), death of a covered employee, divorce or legal separation, a covered employee's eligibility for Medicare, a dependent child's loss of dependent status, or loss of coverage due to the employees filing of a bankruptcy proceeding.

Quality Assurance—A specific process within health plans that examines the services the patient has received to see that they were of high standard, and reviews and fixes problems in patient care or other parts of the health care system.

Quality Review Committee—A committee established by a professional organization or institution to assess and/or assure quality. Unlike peer review committees, it can function on its own initiative on a broad range of topics.

Quarters of Coverage (QC)—Measurement of an individual's insured status under Social Security.

Quebec Pension Plan—See Canada Pension Plan/Quebec Pension Plan (CPP/QPP) (Canada).

Quick Assets—Those assets consisting of cash or the equivalent and receivables due within one year (i.e., current assets) minus inventories.

Quick Assets Ratio—See Acid Test Ratio.

Quitclaim—A deed that releases a right or interest in real property but does not include any covenants of warranty. The grantor transfers only that which he or she has.

Quotation—Often shortened to "quote." The highest bid to buy and the lowest offer to sell a security in a given market at a given time.

R

Rabbi Trust—So named because one of the first was created for a rabbi. Under this nonqualified arrangement, the employer sets aside money specifically for payment of excess pensions or deferred pay. Employer takes no tax deduction, and the beneficiaries pay no tax on contributions to the trusts until they start receiving their money. Although funds are subject to employer's creditors, they are unaccessible to present and future management.

Radiation Therapy—Use of ionizing radiation in the treatment of cancer patients, such service being provided by a radiation therapist or a physician qualified in therapeutic radiology.

Railroad Retirement System—The railroad retirement system was mandated by the Railroad Retirement Act of 1937 to be a retirement system for railroad employees.

Random Walk Hypothesis—A theory that denies that either fundamental analysis or technical analysis can forecast prices because security price movements are random.

Range—The difference between the highest and lowest prices recorded during a given trading session, week, month, year and so on.

Rate—

—(Insurance) The cost of one unit of a specific type of insurance.

—(Investments) The ratio of interest earned to the principal during a period of time. It is generally expressed as a percentage and is one of the factors used in computing interest.

Rate of Interest—The charge made by a borrower to a lender for use of the latter's money, expressed as a percentage upon the principal and usually in terms of one year's charges—unless otherwise stated. Thus, if the interest rate is 5%, $5 is paid for the annual use of $100.

Rate of Return—The yield obtainable on a security based on its purchase price (yield to maturity) or its current market price (current income return).

Rated Policy—A policy issued to cover a person classified as a substandard risk. The policy's premium rate is higher than the rate for a standard policy or the policy is issued with special limitations or exclusions or both. Sometimes called an *extra risk policy.*

Rating—The process that determines how much a particular package of benefits will cost and what will be charged (premium) to cover those expected costs for a specific group of people. See Community Rating; Experience Rating.

Ratio Test—The requirement that the percentage of nonhighly compensated employees covered by a plan be at least 70% of highly compensated employees covered. One of the IRS minimum coverage tests.

Real Estate—The right, title or interest that a person has in real property, as distinguished from the property itself.

Real Estate Investment Trusts (REITs)—Trusts, somewhat like mutual funds, which invest in real estate loans (mortgages and trust deeds) and/or have equity interests in real estate. Ninety-five percent of its income must be paid out to shareholders if the REIT wants to qualify for tax exemption.

Real Income—

- —Money income measured in terms of purchasing power; inflation-adjusted income.
- —Commodities and services a person receives in kind, plus what can be purchased with his or her monetary income.

Real Interest Rate—The nominal interest rate minus the rate of inflation.

Real Property—Land with all its buildings and appurtenances. As opposed to personal property, which refers to movables, or *chattels.*

Real Rate of Return—The return achieved by the fund after adjusting for the change in general prices of goods and services in the economy. Greater purchasing power for a fund results from a positive real rate of return; less purchasing power results from a negative real rate of return. The production of a real rate of return, over the longer term, can assist in providing retirement benefits at levels that are competitive to the increase in the cost of living. See also Nominal Return.

Real Terms—How purchasing power is affected by inflation.

Real Wages—See Real Income.

Reasonable Accommodation—Under the ADA, this may include: (a) making existing facilities used by employees readily accessible to and usable by individuals with disabilities; and (b) job restructuring, part-time or modified work schedules, reassignment to a vacant position, acquisition or modification of equipment or devices, appropriate adjustment or modifications of examinations, training materials or policies, the provision of qualified readers or interpreters, and other similar accommodations for individuals with disabilities.

Reasonable and Customary (R&C) Charge—The prevailing charge made by physicians of similar expertise for a similar procedure in a particular geographic area. See also Usual, Customary and Reasonable Fees.

Reasonable Care—The care that prudent persons would exercise under the same circumstances.

Reasonableness of Compensation—Compensation and fringe benefits paid to an employee (or former employee) are deductible as ordinary and necessary business expenses to the extent that such payments and the cost of such benefits represent overall compensation for services rendered.

Receivership—A situation where the bankruptcy laws apply; usually arises from the inability of the company to meet its obligations as they are due. A U.S. district court appoints a receiver who operates the company under the court's direction until a more permanent disposition of the matter is agreed to by all parties at interest.

Recertification—See Continued Stay Review.

Recession—The downward phase of a normal business cycle that follows prosperity and precedes a depression. Usually, unemployment rises, business slows and the standard of living falls. It is the opposite of recovery, which follows a depression and precedes prosperity. See also Business Cycle.

Recharacterization—A mechanism that treats excess contributions as employee contributions in order to correct an ADP test that does not meet the requirements of the law. When the contribution ratios of highly compensated employees need to be reduced, the excess elective contributions are treated as after-tax employee contributions and the excess is included in the employees' gross income or distributed to them. See also Leveling.

Recidivism (Health Care)—A relapse requiring readmission to a facility or program.

Reciprocal Agreement; Reciprocity—An agreement between two or more plans, under which service with any signatory to the agreement will be recognized for purposes such as (1) satisfying minimum service requirements for plan participation; (2) fulfilling minimum service requirements for benefit entitlement; (3) preventing a break in continuous service; or (4) accumulating benefit credits. Two principal types are the *pro rata agreement,* under which each plan pays its proportionate share of pension benefits, and the *money-follows-the-man agreement,* under which employer contributions are remitted to the participant's home or terminal fund, which then pays the full retirement benefit.

Reciprocity (Medical)—The right of a member of a group health plan, temporarily away from home, to receive necessary medical care from a group health plan in the area the member is visiting.

Record Date—The date on which a shareholder must be registered in a company's stock book in order to receive a declared dividend or vote on company matters, among other things.

Recurring Clause—

—A provision in some health insurance policies that specifies a period of time during which the recurrence of a condition is considered a continuation of a prior period of disability or hospital confinement.

—(Canada) Also known as a *recurrence clause.*

Red Herring—See Preliminary Prospectus.

Redeemable Bonds—Also known as callable bonds. May be paid at the option of the issuer during a specified period prior to maturity.

Redemption Fee—See Back End Load.

Redemption Price—

—The price at which a bond may be redeemed before maturity, at the option of the issuing company. Redemption value also applies to the price the company must pay to call in certain types of preferred stock.

—The price at which a mutual fund's shares are bought back (redeemed) by the firm.

Reduction Formula (Canada)—Designed to keep group life insurance costs within reason. When a large number of older and retired workers are covered, an attempt is made, usually starting at age 65, to reduce the amount of insurance by at least 50%.

Referee—A person to whom a cause pending in a court is referred by the court. Takes testimony, hears the parties and reports thereon to the court.

Referendum—The submission of a plan of coverage under Social Security to public employees for their approval or rejection. A majority of the employees must approve the plan if coverage is to become effective. Retirees are not eligible to participate in such a referendum.

Referral—A formal request within managed care plans by the primary care doctor, to specialists, hospitals or other services, for additional care. Also an informal suggestion from one provider for the patient to see another provider. When used in a formal environment, having a qualified referral has a direct impact on who pays for the service and how much.

Referral Agency—An agency or institution to which a person is referred for continuing treatment by a primary health source, an employee assistance program, an employee benefit plan or another health institution. For employee assistance programs, this procedure may involve referring a person with a known condition to an agency or organization that may offer counseling and other treatment.

Refinancing—A situation arising in the event a company decides to retire existing securities by the issuance of new securities to save interest costs, consolidate debt or lengthen maturities, or some combination of these three goals.

Reflation—Restoration of deflated prices to a desirable level.

Refund Annuity—A form of annuity under which any excess contributions and interest over the total of annuities actually paid are refunded after the annuitant's death to a designated beneficiary of his or her estate. Two types are *cash refund annuity* (unliquidated purchase price is refunded in a lump sum at the time of the annuitant's death) and *installment refund annuity* (monthly payments are continued to the beneficiary until the full cost has been received). See also Modified Refund Annuity.

Refunding—The redemption of an obligation on or before its maturity in order to reduce the fixed interest charge, reduce the amount of fixed payment or postpone payment, due to inability to conveniently liquidate an indebtedness when it matures. During four refunding periods each year, the U.S. Treasury sells enough of a new issue to pay off the maturing issue and raise additional funds to cover new borrowing needs.

Regional Fund (International Benefits)—A mutual fund that invests in the securities of just one country, such as Japan or Germany, or of just one geographical region, such as Southeast Asia, the Pacific Rim, Latin America or Europe.

Regionalization—The concept of shared facilities and resources for maximizing health care services.

Registered Bond—A bond that is registered on the books of the issuing corporation in the owner's name and negotiable only when endorsed by the registered owner. Most bonds held by pension funds are in the nominee name of a bank or in a street name held by a broker to make them readily negotiable and to simplify the collection of interest. The opposite of bearer bond.

Registered Home Ownership Savings Plan (RHOSP) (Canada)—A trusteed arrangement registered under Section 146.2 of the Income Tax Act whereby, subject to prescribed maximums, a resident Canadian taxpayer makes tax deductible contributions to the trust for the purpose of providing an amount that is to be used by the beneficiary for the purpose of purchasing an owner-occupied home for the beneficiary or his or her spouse, neither of whom, whether separately or jointly in the year (in which application is made for the plan) or the immediately preceding year, owns or has owned any interest in an owner-occupied home.

Registered Investment Adviser—An individual or organization that has filed with the Securities and Exchange Commission in order to provide investment advice or financial planning, or both, to clients for a fee.

Registered Pension Plan (RPP) (Canada)—An employer-sponsored pension plan that has been approved by and registered with Revenue Canada.

Registered Representative—In a New York Stock Exchange member organization, a full-time employee who has met the requirements of the exchange regarding background and knowledge of the securities business. Also known as an *account executive* or *customer's broker.*

Registered Retirement Income Fund (RRIF) (Canada)—Governed by Section 146.3 of the Income Tax Act, it is an arrangement between an authorized person or corporation (the carrier) and an individual under which the carrier accepts property from an RRSP (or another RRIF) of which the individual is the annuitant and undertakes to pay to the annuitant (or his or her spouse, as the successor annuitant; or his or her estate in lump sum, in prescribed circumstances) an annual amount determined by a prescribed formula whereby the assets of the fund will have been paid or distributed in total in the year the annuitant reaches 90 years of age.

Registered Retirement Savings Plan (RRSP) (Canada)—A contractual arrangement registered under Section 146 of the Income Tax Act between an individual and an insurer, trust company or corporation authorized (as prescribed in Section 146(l)(j)) to accept payments (contributions) from an individual (the annuitant) or his or her spouse for the purpose of providing a retirement income for that individual or his or her spouse by, upon maturation of the plan, purchase of a prescribed form of annuity or transfer of the plan assets to a registered retirement income fund (RRIF). Subject to prescribed maximums, such contributions made by a resident of Canada having (Part I) earned income are deductible for income tax purposes.

Registration (Securities)—Before a public offering may be made of new securities by a company or of outstanding securities by controlling stockholders—through the mails or in interstate commerce—the securities must be registered under the Securities Act of 1933. The registration statement is filed with the SEC by the issuer. It must disclose pertinent information relating to the company's operations, securities, management and purpose of the public offering. Securities of railroads under jurisdiction of the Interstate Commerce Commission, and certain other types of securities, are exempted. On security offerings involving less than $300,000, less information is required. Before a security may be admitted to dealings on a national securities exchange, it must be registered under the Securities Exchange Act of 1934. The application for registration must be filed with the exchange and the SEC by the company issuing the securities. It must disclose pertinent information relating to the company's operation, securities and management.

Registration of Plans—

—All plans subject to the vesting requirements of ERISA must register with the IRS annually. Thus, plans that are not qualified for tax purposes, as well as those that are qualified, must register. The registration statement that the administrator of the plan is required to file is intended to inform the IRS of plan participants with vested deferred benefits who were separated from service during the plan year. The registration statement must contain the nature, amount and form of vested deferred benefits to which the separated employees were entitled. Each separated employee is entitled to a statement of his or her vested deferred benefits, and evidence that he or she has been provided with such statement must accompany the registration statement.

—A plan administrator who is required to file a registration statement is also required to inform the IRS of any changes in the status of the plan at such times as the regulations specify. Changes that must be reported are (1) change in plan name, (2) change in name or address of the administrator, (3) termination of the plan and (4) merger or consolidation of the plan with another plan or division of it into two or more plans.

Rehabilitation—

—Services and facilities patients use as part of recovering from an accident or illness.

—Restoration of a totally disabled person to a meaningful occupation.

—A provision in some long-term disability policies that provides for continuation of benefits or other financial assistance while a totally disabled insured is retraining or attempting to resume productive employment.

Reimbursement Account—An option of most flexible benefits plans in which eligible expenses are reimbursed on a nontaxable basis.

Reinstatement—The resumption of coverage under a policy that has lapsed.

Reinsurance—An added level of coverage purchased by a self-funded employer, at-risk managed care plan or another insurance company to protect against a payout of claims in excess of a designated limit, to protect themselves from major losses or catastrophic claims. See also Stop-Loss Insurance.

Relative—A spouse, ancestor, lineal descendant or spouse of a lineal descendant.

Relative Value Scale (RVS)—A method of determining benefits based on establishing unit values as norms for various medical and surgical procedures, relating the value of each procedure to others by using a conversion factor to arrive at a dollar value for benefits.

Release Clause—

—A clause found in blanket mortgages providing for the payment of a portion of the indebtedness so that a proportionate part of the property can be released.

—Any clause that releases a party from an agreement when a specified contingency arises.

Reliance—Assurance from the IRS that an employer's plan is qualified under the IRC. Standardized plans receive automatic reliance; nonstandardized plans must apply for a Determination Letter.

Relief—The thing sought by a plaintiff in a lawsuit; usually whatever it is that would make the plaintiff whole or at least compensate for the injury.

Relocation Services—Benefits offered by an employer to a current employee accepting an assignment in a new location. Examples include reimbursement for house-hunting expenses, household moving costs or interim travel expenses; or help in orienting to a new culture or learning a new language.

Remedy—The judicial means or court procedures by which legal and equitable rights are enforced.

Renal Dialysis Center—A facility that, directly or through other network facilities, furnishes the full spectrum of diagnostic, therapeutic and rehabilitative services (except renal transplantations) required for the care of ESRD dialysis patients.

Renegotiable Rate Mortgage (RRM)—Sometimes

called a rollover mortgage. Features an interest rate that is renegotiated every three to five years. The rate can rise or fall by a maximum of half a percentage point a year. The total increase or decrease during the life of the mortgage is limited to five percentage points. Increases and decreases are based on an index linked to average mortgage rates.

Renewal—Continuance of coverage under a policy beyond its original term by the insurer's acceptance of a premium for a new policy term.

Repartition (International Benefits)—Pay-as-you-go retirement system for compulsory, complementary plans in France. The annuities due to retirees in a given year are paid from the contributions of employers and employees in the same year.

Replacement Cost Accounting—Balance sheets tend to be misleading because they typically value assets at cost plus installation. To overcome this problem, assets can be valued at replacement cost. For fiscal years ending on or after December 25, 1979, the Financial Accounting Standards Board requires approximately 1,350 of the largest U.S. corporations to report supplementary information based on constant (inflation-adjusted) dollars and current (replacement) costs.

Replacement Rate—The portion of preretirement earnings under any retirement plan that are replaced by benefits following retirement.

Report Card—A generic term for performance statements pertaining to health care professionals and providers. Involves analysis of provider performance and subsequent distribution of the analysis to interested parties such as health plans, health care providers, state governments, employer purchasing groups and consumer information organizations. Provides information for the evaluation of quality and costs.

Reportable Event—An event that must be reported to the PBGC (usually within 30 days after its occurrence) unless expressly waived by the PBGC. Notice is required to allow the PBGC adequate time to protect the benefits of participants and beneficiaries. A reportable event includes (1) disqualification for tax purposes; (2) benefit decrease by amendment; (3) a decrease in participation to less than 80% of that at the start of the plan year; (4) an IRS Determination Letter indicating partial or complete plan termination; (5) failure to meet minimum funding standards; (6) inability to pay benefits when due; (7) a distribution to "a substantial owner"; (8) filing an actuarial statement with the IRS before a plan merger, consolidation, or the transfer of assets or the granting of an alternative method of ERISA compliance by the Department of Labor; or (9) any other event determined by the PBGC, including bankruptcy, insolvency, liquidation, dissolution or a change in the plan sponsor of a single employer plan with unfunded, nonforfeitable benefits and 100 or more participants.

Reportable Transaction—A transaction that (1) involves an amount in excess of 5% of the current value of a plan's assets; or (2) is part of a series of transactions with or in conjunction with a person in a plan year if the aggregate amount of the transaction exceeds 5% of the current value of the plan's assets (other than a transaction with respect to a security); or (3) is part of a series of transactions respecting one or more securities if the transactions in the plan year exceed 5% of the current value of the plan's assets; or (4) is with or in conjunction with a person respecting a security, if any other transaction with or in conjunction with such person in the plan year respecting a security is required to be reported because of a transaction noted at (1) above.

Reporting—Refers to government filing requirements by plan administrators. Reporting requirements include filing annual reports with IRS, summary plan descriptions and summary of material modifications with DOL, and annual premium reports with the PBGC; and making certain documents available for inspection by the DOL.

Repurchase Agreement—The sale of a money instrument such as a bond or CD, usually in large amounts (by a dealer or a bank to an investor), and the simultaneous repurchase of the same security at the same price. Although the trades occur simultaneously, the settlement dates (when money changes hands and interest begins) are different. The period between gives the investor a very short-term (usually one to ten days or two weeks) investment at an attractive rate of return. Repurchase agreements that allow banks to buy temporarily idle funds isolate the investor from market fluctuation because both the purchase and the results are done at a guaranteed rate that is mutually acceptable.

Request for Proposal/Request for Information (RFP/RFI)—Two types of instruments used to solicit information from vendors interested in supplying a service. Includes services for employee benefit plans such as accounting, auditing, administration, investment consulting, computer systems, health care and legal counsel. Plan trustees prepare a list of specifications based on their goals, identify appropriate guidelines, solicit bids and proposals from candidates, conduct interviews regarding candidates' qualifications, check references, discuss fees and choose the provider accordingly.

Required Distributions—

—Payments that must be made once a participant reaches age 70½; they are calculated to span his or her life expectancy.

—When a participant dies, the payments that must be made to the beneficiary.

Reserve—A sum set aside by an insurance company to assure the fulfillment of commitments for future claims.

Reserve Requirements—The ratio of funds to deposits that banks and other institutions have to keep in their vaults. This ratio varies with the size of the bank's deposits. The Federal Reserve stipulates what these ratios must be.

Reserves—Represent claims against, or deductions from, assets in the balance sheet and are established to reduce or revalue assets to identify the existence of liabilities and to earmark a part of surplus for some future use.

Resident Alien—See Nonresident Alien.

Residential Care Facility—A facility that provides custodial care to persons who—because of their physical, mental or emotional condition—are not able to live independently.

Residential Treatment Center (RTC)—A term generally used for residential centers used to provide mental health treatment.

Residual Disability Benefits—A provision in an insurance policy that provides benefits in proportion to a reduction of earnings as a result of disability, as opposed to the inability to work full time.

Resource-Based Relative Value Scale (RBRVS)—
A classification system developed by the Health Care Financing Administration to pay providers for Medicare services based on the time, training, skill and other factors required to deliver various services. Used initially by Medicare, but has influenced other sectors to more properly assess the skill and resource relationships to specific CPT codes, thereby dictating reimbursement levels.

Respite Care—Temporary care provided in a patient's home to provide the primary caregiver with time off from the demands of taking care of a family member; short-term child care to allow a parent to get relief, or prevent child abuse.

Restraint of Trade—Monopolies, combinations and contracts that impede free competition.

Restricted Stock Plan—An executive is given stock or allowed to buy it at a discount. He or she may not sell or transfer it until a certain period of time has elapsed, usually four or five years. The executive receives the dividends, but if he or she leaves the organization before the end of the restriction period, the stock usually is forfeited.

Restructuring—Describes a variety of activities, including writeoffs, debt-for-equity swaps and reorganizations. The common denominator is dramatic change within the corporation. Although there may be long-term benefits, the objective is usually short term. In many situations, the goal has been to ward off would-be suitors.

Retail Store Dentistry—Refers to dental services offered within a retail, department or drugstore operation. Typically, space is leased from the store by a separate administrative group that, in turn, subleases to a dentist or dental group providing the actual dental services. The dental operation generally maintains the same hours of operation as the store and appointments often are not necessary. Considered to be a type of practice, not a dental benefits plan model.

Retained Earnings—Profits added to a company's capital after dividends and taxes are paid.

Retention—

—The portion of the premium retained by an insurer to cover the cost of risk, expense charges, profit or a contribution to surplus.

—Net retention plus any amounts of other reinsurance permitted under the reinsurance contract.

Retired Life Fund—See Annuity Purchase Fund.

Retired Lives Reserve Insurance (RLR)—Tax-favored application of group term life insurance by which an employer may provide employees with substantial postretirement insurance through several funding mechanisms.

Retiree Medical Account—A separate account that is contained in a pension or annuity plan, providing health benefits subordinate to the plan's retirement benefits.

Retiree Medical Plans—Generally, group-sponsored medical plans that are integrated with Medicare and are not scheduled or Medicare supplement policies.

Retirees—The group of plan participants that includes retired employees, their beneficiaries and covered dependents.

Retirement Allowance—A series of payments, usually for life, payable monthly or at other specified intervals. The term is used to describe the entire benefit payable, including both the annuity derived from the participant's accumulated contributions and the pension financed by the employer's contributions.

Retirement Allowance (Canada)—An amount paid by an employer to an employee (or former employee) upon retirement from office or service in recognition of long service or in respect of loss of office or employment.

Retirement Annuity—An insurance term describing a contract where there is no element of pure insurance. The death benefit would be the larger of the reserve or the premium paid, without interest.

Retirement Benefits—See Pension.

Retirement Bonus Plan—See Life Cycle Pension Plan.

Retirement Compensation Arrangement (Canada)—A funded supplementary pension arrangement that provides retirement benefits, but is not a registered pension plan.

Retirement, Compulsory—See Compulsory Retirement.

Retirement, Deferred—See Deferred Retirement.

Retirement, Early—See Early Retirement.

Retirement Equity Act of 1984 (REA)—
- —A federal law that amended ERISA with the purpose of providing greater pension equity for women workers and surviving spouses.
- —REA liberalizes ERISA participation, vesting and break-in-service requirements. The law requires these and other changes to be clearly communicated to employees.

Retirement Expense; Retirement Reserve—A reserve established by a company to anticipate and provide for the orderly retirement of obsolete equipment. A charge in the income account made in most, though not all, cases to reflect retirement of equipment within the next few years, and as such is usually less than the depreciation charges. On the balance sheet, a valuation reserve representing accrued retirement expense to date.

Retirement Income (Canada)—Income from pensions and other sources to which a retired person is entitled. May include both private and public pension payments, income from personal savings, government income supplements and imputed income.

Retirement, Normal Age—See Normal Retirement Age.

Retirement Plan—
- —An overall plan intended to provide for all aspects of one's retirement, including medical care, travel, residence and budgeting.
- —Any financial plan specifically designed to provide funds to cover expenses in one's retirement years.
- —(Legal) A plan maintained by an employer or employee organization (such as a union) or both that is designed to provide employees with retirement income and that allows employees to defer receipt of income until the end of their employment or even later.

Retroactive Benefits—Benefits granted in a plan amendment (or initiation) that are attributed by the pension benefit formula to employee services rendered in periods prior to the amendment. The cost of the retroactive benefits is referred to as *prior service cost.*

Retroactive Rate Reduction—See Experience Refund.

Retroactive Review—Traditional form of utilization review. The patient's chart is reviewed after the fact to determine whether the treatment provided was medically necessary and appropriate.

Retrogressive Tax—See Locked In.

Retrospective Premium—Arrangement by which a policyholder agrees to pay an additional premium at the end of the contract year if claims and retention exceed paid premium.

Retrospective Rating—An insurance plan for which the premium is not determined until the completion of the coverage period, and is then based upon the plan's actual experience for that period, subject to a stated minimum and maximum, and providing for recovery of expense and administrative factors.

Retrospective Reimbursement—The most common method of payment to health facilities, when payment is made after the services are rendered on the basis of costs incurred by the facility.

Retrospective Utilization Review—See Retroactive Review.

Return—The amount of money received annually from an investment, usually expressed as a percentage.

Return on Equity (ROE)—Return to stockholders measured by relating profits to equity of stockholders.

Return on Shareholders' Equity—See Return on Equity.

Return-to-Work Program—An employer-sponsored program of rehabilitation, job modification and monitoring to get disabled employees back to work as soon as possible.

Revalued Earnings (International Benefits)—Earnings that are adjusted, up or down, based on an index. Such indexes are provided by the government and use is mandated.

Revenue Anticipation Note—An obligation issued by a state or political subdivision to be redeemed by anticipated revenue when received.

Revenue Bonds—Bonds payable out of revenue from the operation of public facilities, or a special source of revenue, and not out of general tax collections. See also Municipal Bonds; Special Assessment Bonds; Tax-Exempt Securities.

Revenue Procedure—Issued by the IRS, it is somewhat similar to a Revenue Ruling but deals with procedural matters or details the requirements to be followed in connection with various dealings with the IRS. Revenue procedures also set forth (at times) guidelines that the IRS follows in handling certain tax matters.

Revenue Ruling—Issued by the IRS, these rulings express the views of the IRS about the tax results that apply to a specific problem.

Reverse Annuity Mortgage—A mortgage instrument that allows an elderly person to live off the equity in a fully paid-for house. Such a homeowner would enter into a reverse annuity mortgage agreement with a financial institution such as a bank, which would guarantee a lifelong fixed monthly income in return for gradually giving up ownership of the house. Such arrangements are also permitted between relatives, for example, between adult children and their parents.

Reverse Stock Split—Reducing the number of outstanding shares of corporate stock by exchanging one new share of stock for two or more old shares.

Reversion of Employer Contributions—A qualified plan (or trust) is prohibited from diverting corpus or income for purposes other than the exclusive benefit of employees. However, this prohibition does not preclude the return of a contribution made by an employer if the contribution was made, for example, by reason of a mistake of fact or conditioned on the qualification of the plan or the deductibility of the contribution.

Reversionary Annuity—A deferred annuity payable during the lifetime of a beneficiary only if the beneficiary survives a specified retiree.

Rider—A document that amends the policy or certificate. It may increase or decrease benefits, waive the condition of coverage, or in any other way amend the original contract. See also Endorsement.

Right of Direct Payment—A type of mandated benefit that requires a plan to pay for services not prescribed by a licensed physician (such as the services of a midwife).

Right-to-Work Laws—State laws that ban any form of compulsory union membership.

Rights of Participants—A participant or beneficiary cannot be discharged, fined, suspended, expelled or disciplined, or discriminated against for exercising any right under the regulatory provisions of ERISA or for giving information or testimony in an inquiry or proceeding relating to ERISA. Likewise, the interference with a participant's attaining of any right under the regulatory provisions of ERISA is prohibited. This provision is enforceable by investigation and civil suit.

Risk—
—Any chance of loss.
—An uninsured individual or item.

Risk Appraisal—See Underwriting.

Risk Aversion—The attitude of an investor who is not willing to accept increasing amounts of uncertainty about future investment returns without commensurate increases in the level of return anticipated. Another manifestation of this attitude is the investor who prefers less risk for the same rate of return expectation.

Risk Benefits (International Benefits)—Those benefits relating to the life and health of an employee, i.e., life insurance and so on. In many countries, a pension plan may also encompass the risk benefits—lump-sum benefit, widow's or orphan's income and so forth.

Risk Classification—The process by which a company decides how its premium rates for life insurance should differ according to the risk characteristics of individuals insured (e.g., age, occupation, sex, state of health) and then applies the resulting rules to individual applications. See also Underwriting.

Risk Factors—Conditions that influence a person's health and are capable of provoking ill health, including inherited or biological, environmental and behavioral risk factors.

Risk-Free Asset—Typically a noncallable, default-free bond such as a short-term government security. Although such an asset is not risk free in an inflation sense, it is (under the rationale that the government can always print money) risk free in a dollar sense.

Risk-Free Return—A theoretical return that is earned with perfect certainty; it is without risk. We approximate the risk-free return with 91-day Treasury bill yields.

Risk (Impaired or Substandard)—An insurance applicant whose physical condition does not meet the physical standards for normal health.

Risk Load—A factor that is multiplied into the premium rate to offset some adverse parameter in the group.

Risk Management—The use of insurance and other techniques that minimize an organization's exposure to loss or injury.

Risk Pool—The population of individuals (or groups) across which costs for insured expenses are spread through premiums or other mechanisms.

Risk-Reward Spectrum—A construct used to illustrate that (in a rational marketplace) higher and higher anticipated rewards are always accompanied by incremental increases in risk (measured as the deviations between expected and actual results). The left end of the spectrum represents the lowest risk investment—typically short-term government obligations. Moving to the right on the spectrum—through a continuum of common stock investments—each incremental increase in expected return is accompanied by an incremental increase in risk.

Risk Sharing—A method by which premiums and costs of medical protection are shared by plan sponsors and participants.

Rollover—The reinvestment in a qualified plan, IRA or Keogh plan of money or property received in a nonrequired distribution from another qualified plan that meets certain requirements. If the reinvestment is made within 60 days of the distribution, federal income tax on the distribution is deferred until the benefits involved are finally distributed from the recipient plan. See also Unemployment Compensation Amendments of 1992.

Rollover Mortgage—See Renegotiable Rate Mortgage.

Round Lot—A unit of trading or multiple thereof usually thought of as 100 shares of stock listed on the NYSE and 100,000 par value of bonds, particularly where institutions are concerned.

Rule of 72—A convenient technique for either mental or pencil and paper estimation of compound interest rates, derived from the fact that a 7.2%

return per year is the interest rate that will double the value of an investment in ten years. Hence, "years to double" an investment with a given annual rate of return can be estimated by dividing the rate of return into 72.

S

Safe Harbor Rules—Regulations that describe certain acts or behaviors which will not be illegal under a specific law, even though they might otherwise be illegal. Typically this refers to federal regulations that specify conduct exempt from the fraud and abuse laws.

Salaried Administrator—Person employed full time by the trustees of a multiemployer fund to provide administrative services.

Salary Continuation Plan—A benefit option designed to provide some form of protection during disability. See also Sick Leave and Workers' Compensation.

Salary Deferral SEP—See Elective Deferral Arrangement.

Salary Progression—Relates to the estimated rates at which compensation levels will increase in future periods. This assumption generally includes factors of inflation, the participant's share of productivity gains and merit and seniority increases.

Salary Reduction Plan—The employer and the employees covered by the plan enter into individual, separate contracts in which each employee agrees to take a reduction in salary (either as a stated dollar amount or as a percentage of compensation). Then, under a separate pension plan (usually a money purchase plan), the employer contributes an amount, equal to the amount of the employee's salary reduction, to a tax-exempt trust for the benefit of the employee. See also Cash or Deferred Arrangement.

Salary Reduction Simplified Employee Pension Plan (SARSEP)—See Elective Deferral Arrangement.

Sallie Mae (SLMA)—Securities issued by the Student Loan Marketing Association.

Savings Account—An account in a commercial bank, a savings and loan association or a savings bank, usually in the form of a passbook or certificate. Passbook accounts usually may be opened, added to or withdrawn in any amount. Interest is paid from the date of deposit to the date of withdrawal and is credited to the account either quarterly or semiannually. Certificate accounts generally earn a higher interest rate than passbook accounts if certain requirements are met as to minimum balances and length of time funds remain on deposit. Savings accounts in commercial banks, savings and loan associations and savings banks are insured by agencies of the federal government up to $100,000 per account, depending on the form. Trust accounts, such as pension funds, may have amounts in excess of $100,000 insured.

Savings and Loan Association—A financial institution that is state or federally chartered and privately owned by the depositors or stockholders. Its prime functions are to furnish first mortgage loans on improved real estate and to provide government-insured, interest-bearing savings accounts.

Savings Incentive Match Plan for Employees (SIMPLE)—See Pension Simplification Act.

Savings Plan—See Thrift Plan.

SBJPA—See Small Business Job Protection Act of 1996.

Schedule—A list of coverages or amounts concerning things or persons insured.

Scheduled Plan—Health plan that provides specific allowances for each type of medical care and treatment. See also Table of Allowances.

Scheme (International Benefits)—Frequently used interchangeably with *plan.*

S Corporation—A small business corporation in which the shareholders elect to be taxed like a partnership with profits and losses passing directly through to the shareholders. Income is not taxed at the corporate level. To be eligible, a corporation must meet certain requirements as to kind and number of shareholders, classes of stock and sources of income.

Screening—The initial process of separating from a group those who do not conform to predetermined quality guidelines and thus require additional investigation.

Second Country National—An employee from another country working in the country in which the company is based.

Second Injury Funds—Funds that reimburse employers for the difference between the total compensation benefits and the partial compensation benefits that would have been paid to a disabled employee, had he or she not been disabled previously while working for another employer.

Second Stage Accounting (International Benefits)—The consolidation of the various national experience reports in a multinational pool.

Second Surgical Opinion Program (SSOP)—This cost-management strategy encourages or requires participants to obtain the opinion of another doctor after a physician has recommended that a non-emergency or elective surgery be performed. Programs may be voluntary or mandatory in that reimbursement is reduced or denied if the participant does not obtain the second opinion. Plans usually require that such opinions be obtained from board-certified specialists with no personal or financial interest in the outcome.

Secondary Care—Care provided by a general short-term hospital, nursing home, emergency care facility or the more highly specialized physician consultant services.

Secondary Distribution; Secondary Offering—A redistribution of the block of stock some time after it has been sold by the issuing company, with the sale taking place at a fixed price related to the current market, off the New York Stock Exchange by a securities firm or syndicate. In most cases, a large block coming from a mutual fund or estate is involved.

Secondary Mortgage Market—The process of loan originators selling their mortgages in bulk with continually fluctuating interest rates.

Secondary Payer—The insurance carrier that is second in responsibility under coordination of benefits. Often mentioned in the context of Medicare's efforts to recoup payments made as primary payer when other primary, duplicate coverage exists.

Secretary—The term *secretary* when used in connection with an employee welfare benefit plan or an employee pension plan refers to the secretary of labor.

Section 89—A section of the Internal Revenue Code that set out certain written minimum requirements for welfare benefit plans and established highly specific nondiscrimination requirements. Section 89 was repealed in 1989 restoring the applicability of the nondiscrimination rules of IRC 105(h).

Section 125 Plan—A plan in compliance with Section 125 of the IRC, which protects an employee from *constructive receipt* of the cash he or she has as a choice of benefits under a cafeteria plan. This means that employee contributions to a Section 125 plan may be made with pretax dollars. Also called Flexible Benefit Plan. See also Cafeteria Plan; Constructive Receipt; Flexible Benefit Plan/Flexible Compensation.

Section 218 Agreements—Voluntary agreements between the state and the commissioner of Social Security that allows the states, if they so desire, to provide Social Security coverage for the services of state and local government employees.

Section 401(k)—Section of the IRC that allows profit-sharing and stock bonus plans to offer cash or deferred arrangements (CODAs) to participants. State and local governments are not eligible to maintain CODAs under 401(k) unless such a plan was adopted before May 6, 1986.

Section 401(k) Plan—A plan under which employees can elect to defer income by making pretax contributions. The plan also may allow for employer matching contributions. A Section 401(k) plan is a defined contribution plan.

Section 403(b)—Extends tax deferral to public school employees and those of other tax-exempt organizations for annuity purchases. A 403(b) tax-sheltered annuity is a retirement plan available to these employees. Benefits may be provided through employer contribution or through employee salary reduction.

Section 404(c)—Section of the IRS Code that applies to 401(k) investment possibilities. See also 401(k) Plan.

Section 414(h) Pickup—If employers pick up contributions for their employees under IRC Section 414(h), the contributions are not considered wages for federal income tax withholding purposes.

Section 415 Limits—IRC Section 415 limits the contribution and/or benefit amount that retirement plans can provide to individual participants on a tax-deductible basis.

Section 423 Plan—See Stock Purchase Plan.

Section 457—Section of the IRC that allows employees of state and local governments to defer a portion of their income in a deferred compensation plan that is not taxable until a distribution is made.

Section 501(c)(9)—See Voluntary Employees' Beneficiary Association.

Sector Funds—Mutual funds that confine their investments to one economic or industrial sector (e.g., utilities or technology).

Sector Rotator—A common stock manager whose style of management emphasizes industries expected to outperform the market.

Sector Weighting—Measures a manager's ability to allocate assets across market sectors.

Secular Trend—A long-term trend either up or down in the price or level of a commodity, price structure, inflation rate and so on that is not influenced by seasonal variations or distortions. The maxim is that a trend in force tends to perpetuate itself.

Secular Trust—So named to distinguish it from a rabbi trust. An irrevocable trust established for the exclusive purpose of holding assets to pay employees' nonqualified retirement and/or deferred compensation benefits. It has a design similar to that of a rabbi trust, but the assets contained within the trust are not subject to the claims of the company's general creditors in bankruptcy.

Securities Acts—Federal laws enforced by the Securities and Exchange Commission to protect investors; they include the Investment Advisers Act, Investment Company Act, Securities Act of 1933, Securities Exchange Act of 1934, Trust Indenture Act and Public Utilities Holding Company Act.

Securities and Exchange Commission (SEC)—

—An organization created by the Securities Exchange Act of 1934. The SEC is an independent bipartisan, quasi-judicial agency of the United States government. The laws administered by the commission relate in general to the field of securities and finance and seek to provide protection for investors and the public in their securities transactions.

—The SEC is charged with enforcing the Securities Acts.

Securities Lending—A practice whereby owners of securities either directly or indirectly lend their securities to primarily brokerage firms for a fee, and against which either cash, securities or a letter of credit is pledged to protect the tender.

Security—Any note, stock, Treasury stock, bond, debenture, evidence of indebtedness, certificate of interest or participation in any profit-sharing agreement, collateral trust certificate, preorganization certificate or subscription, transferable share, investment contract, voting trust certificate, certificate of deposit for security, fractional undivided interest in oil, gas or other mineral rights or, in general, any interest or instrument commonly known as a security, or any certificate of interest or participation in, temporary or interim certificate for, receipt for, guarantee of, or warrant or right to subscribe to or purchase any of the foregoing.

Segregated Fund (Canada)—Assets of a pension plan held by an insurance company for investment management only. Funds are segregated from assets of the insurance company, and principal and interest are not guaranteed.

Selection Against the Plan—See Adverse Selection.

Self-Administered Plan—

—(Directly Invested or Trusteed) A plan funded through a fiduciary, generally a bank, but sometimes a group of individuals, that directly invests the funds accumulated. Retirement payments are made from the fund as they fall due. This term is used to designate a plan that is not funded through an insurance company.

—(Health Care) A plan administered by the employer or welfare fund without recourse to an intermediate insurance carrier. Some benefits may be insured or subcontracted while others are self-funded.

Self-Care—An approach or philosophy that sees the patient as the primary health care provider. Includes a variety of health education strategies that allow the patient to become skilled in self-diagnosis and treatment for 70-90% of symptoms.

Self-Care Dialysis Facility—A unit where chronic maintenance dialysis is performed by a trained patient, with appropriate professional supervision and assistance.

Self-Dealing—Under ERISA, certain activities are

prohibited for fiduciaries, including using plan assets for personal profit, taking bribes or kickbacks from someone who deals with the plan, or acting on behalf of a party whose interests are adverse to those of the plan.

Self-Directed Brokerage Account (SDBA)—An option under a 401(k) plan that allows contributors to invest in various additional mutual funds or stocks to provide greater investment flexibility. The administrator is usually a large financial institution, which charges a commission for transactions just as a broker would.

Self-Directed Investment—Any plan in which plan participants control the investment of their accounts.

Self-Employed Retirement Plan—See Keogh Plan.

Self-Funding—See Self-Insurance.

Self-Insurance (Self-Funding)—A fully noninsured or self-insured plan is one in which no insurance company or service plan collects premiums and assumes risk. In a sense, the employer is acting as an insurance company—paying claims with the money ordinarily earmarked for premiums. Regardless of the specific self-funding technique a firm chooses, it will need to either buy its administrative services (ASO) outside the company or develop them in-house. Hence, self-funded arrangements are referenced as ASO or self-administered.

There are two standard self-funding techniques that companies interested in this approach usually evaluate for appropriateness to their own situation: 501(c)(9) trust and disbursed self-funded plan. See also Disbursed Self-Funded Plan; 501(c)(9) Trust.

Self-Pay Option—Under some health care plans, the opportunity offered to laid-off workers, or those with insufficient hours worked, to maintain eligibility for health benefits through the individual's payment of a premium, thus avoiding lapses in coverage. The self-pay premium frequently does not cover the costs of carrying such individuals, but represents a partial subsidy by the plan.

Self-Referral—The process whereby a patient seeks care directly from a specialist without seeking advice or authorization from the primary care physician.

Senior Citizen Policies—These contracts insure individuals over age 65. They frequently supplement Medicare coverage.

Senior Debt—Debt that may be secured or unsecured and is at the topmost of the various tiers or levels of debt.

Senior Issue—An issue of a bond or a preferred stock that occupies a top position when it comes to a claim for principal, interest or dividends.

Sensitivity—The degree to which a portfolio's fluctuations are more or less volatile than market fluctuations. See also Beta; Systematic Risk.

Separate Account—A fund established by a life insurance company. The fund is maintained separately from the insurance company's general assets and is generally used for investing pension assets in common stocks.

Separate Line of Business (SLOB)—The separate line of business exception permits electing businesses that are part of a controlled group to ignore affiliates when testing retirement and dependent care plans for nondiscrimination, thereby treating each business as a stand-alone company for these purposes.

Serial Bonds—Bonds that mature in relatively small amounts at periodic stated intervals.

Serial Maturity—See Balloon Maturity.

Series EE Bond—A nonmarketable U.S. government savings bond that is issued at a discount from par.

Series HH Bond—A nonmarketable interest-bearing U.S. government savings bond that is issued at par.

Service—Employment taken into consideration under a pension plan. Years of employment before the inception of a plan constitute an employee's past service; years thereafter are classified in relation to the particular actuarial valuation being made or discussed. Years of employment (including past service) prior to the date of a particular valuation constitute prior service; years of employment following the date of the valuation constitute future service; a year of employment adjacent to the date of the valuation, or in which such date falls, constitutes current service (included in future service).

Service Area—

—The geographic area from which a particular health care program draws the majority of its users. See also Catchment Area.

—The territory within certain boundaries that an HMO designates for providing services to members. It is generally believed that a member should not have to drive longer than 30 minutes in order to gain access to the system.

Service Cost (Component of Net Periodic Pension Cost)—The actuarial present value of benefits attributed by the pension benefit formula to services rendered by employees during that period. The service cost component is a portion of the projected benefit obligation. It is not affected by the plan's funded status.

Service Credits—See Credited Service.

Service Plan—A prepayment plan that guarantees to provide covered health care services to subscribers, as opposed to indemnifying expenses.

Setback—A procedure used in adjusting a mortality table in order to take into account the fact that people are living longer. In making a setback, actuaries apply a mortality table as if the employees were younger than they actually are.

Settlement—
—(Investment) An arrangement between brokerage houses for the payment or receipt of cash or securities. It represents the final consummation of a securities transaction and is handled through the stock clearing corporation.
—(Pension) An irrevocable action that relieves the employer (or the plan) of primary responsibility for a pension benefit obligation and eliminates significant risks related to the obligation and the assets used to effect the settlement. Examples of transactions that constitute a settlement include (1) making lump-sum cash payments to plan participants in exchange for their rights to receive specified pension benefits and (2) purchasing nonparticipating annuity contracts to cover vested benefits.

Severance Pay—A lump-sum benefit payable on termination of employment either in lieu of or in addition to a pension.

Sexual Harassment—Unwelcomed sexual advances, requests for sexual favors or other verbal or physical conduct of a sexual nature, when (1) submission to such conduct is made either explicitly or implicitly a term or condition of an individual's employment or (2) submission to or rejection of such conduct by an individual is used as the basis for employment decisions affecting such individual. Violates the Civil Rights Act of 1964.

Share—One of the equal parts into which the capital stock of a corporation is divided. It represents the owner's proportion of interest in the company and is issued to the shareholder in the form of a stock certificate.

Shared Employee—When the services of an employee are shared by several professionals, corporations or partnerships, he or she may be considered a full-time employee of each employer, whereby contributions to each employer's pension plan must be based on the portion of compensation paid by each professional or corporation.

Shared Funding—See High Self-Insured Deductible.

Shareholder-Employee—In regard to a subchapter S corporation, a more-than-5% shareholder.

Shareholders' Equity—See Net Worth.

Shoe Box Effect—When an indemnity plan has a deductible, there may be beneficiaries who save up their receipts to file for reimbursement at a later time, but never actually file claims.

Short—
—(Noun) One who has sold futures contracts (or the cash commodity, depending on the market under discussion) and has not yet offset that position.
—(Verb) The action of taking a position in which one has sold futures contracts (or made a forward contract for the sale of the cash commodity) without taking the offsetting action.
—In commercial paper loan futures, the party who contracts to deliver cash and take delivery of paper.

Short Sale—Short sales are made by people who expect the market to go down. In a regular securities transaction, shares are bought first and sold later.

Short-Term Bond—A debt security with a holding period ranging less than five years to maturity.

Short-Term Disability (STD)—Often considered to be a disability lasting usually not longer than six months.

Short-Term Disability Income Insurance—A provision to pay benefits to a covered disabled person as long as he or she remains disabled up to a specified period.

Short-Term Income Protection—See Unemployment Compensation.

Short-Term Investment Fund (STIF)—A collective investment fund consisting of highly liquid and readily marketable interest-bearing securities.

Short-Time Compensation—Prorated unemployment insurance for workers whose hours are reduced through a work-sharing plan.

Sick Leave—Plans that provide employees protection against short-term disability and typically specify a maximum number of benefit days per year or per disability that an employee may take at full pay before insured short-term or long-term disability benefits are initiated.

Side Fund—See Conversion Fund.

Silver Parachute—Is a severance and benefit plan to protect nonexecutives if their firms are acquired by another firm.

SIMPLE Plans—See Pension Simplification Act.

Simplified Employee Pension Plan (SEP)—Essentially, an IRA to which an employee and his or her employer may contribute. A SEP is a simplified alternative to a profit-sharing or 401(k) plan. The employee is immediately vested in employer contributions and generally directs the investment of the money. Elective deferrals to a SEP are treated like elective deferrals to a qualified CODA. See also Elective Deferral Arrangement; Salary Deferral SEP.

Single Country Employee—See Local Country National.

Single Coverage—See Individual Insurance.

Single Employer Plan—A pension plan maintained by one employer. Also, the term may be used to describe a plan maintained by related parties such as a parent and its subsidiaries.

Single Life Annuity Plan—An employee's accrued benefit from mandatory contributions to a defined benefit plan that provides a benefit in the form of a single life annuity (without ancillary benefits) beginning at normal retirement age is the employee's accumulated contributions multiplied by a conversion factor. (Since the accrued benefit from voluntary contributions must be separately accounted for, it does not come into consideration.) Initially, the conversion factor is to be set at 10% for a normal retirement age of 65. The conversion factor for other normal retirement ages will be fixed by regulation.

An employee's accumulated contribution consists of (1) mandatory contributions; (2) interest, if any, on mandatory contributions to the end of the last year before the vesting rules are applicable; and (3) 5% compound interest on (1) and (2) after the vesting rules are applicable.

The interest rate and conversion factor mentioned above can be adjusted by the regulations.

Single Payer System—A centralized method of financing health care delivery through public funds, with the government acting as the only payer for health care services.

Single Premium Deferred Annuity (SPDA)—A deferred annuity purchased with one investment or premium.

Single Premium Funding Method—A method of funding whereby the cost of providing an insurance or pension benefit is paid in one lump sum. When the single premium is paid at retirement age for a life annuity, it is frequently referred to as terminal funding. See also Actuarial Cost Method.

Sinking Fund—

—A fixed annual sum of money that must be allocated by a corporation to retire a portion of a bond or preferred stock issue prior to maturity, on terms as specified in the indenture of charter. The activity may be accomplished either directly by the corporation through a broker or by its agent or trustee, by call, by open market purchases or by inviting tenders.

—A separate accumulation of cash or investments (including earnings thereon) in accordance with the terms of a debt or stock security, increased periodically by contributions, generally of cash, from the security's issuer, for the purpose of assuring timely redemption.

Situs—Place or situation. The place where a thing is located. The situs of personal property is the domicile of the owner. The situs of land is the state or county where it is located.

Skill-Based Pay—A system for individual wage differentiation, based on the number of specified skills or tasks mastered by the job incumbent. Pay level is not dependent on whether any of the skills are utilized. Also called pay for knowledge.

Skilled Care—Around-the-clock nursing and rehabilitative care that can only be provided by, or under the supervision of, skilled medical personnel.

Skilled Nursing Facility (SNF)—A care setting for patients who no longer require hospital care, but need 24-hour nursing care and other defined health care services.

Slander—An oral utterance that tends to injure the reputation of another. See also Libel.

Sliding Fee Scale—A fee schedule under which the fee charged the patient for services varies with the patient's ability to pay.

Small Business Job Protection Act of 1996 (SBJPA)—Federal legislation that raises the minimum wage 90 cents by September 1, 1997; contains significant changes to encourage small businesses to offer retirement plans; and offers ways for all employers to reduce nondiscrimination burdens and ease the administration of qualified plans. The law allows tax-exempt organizations to offer 401(k) plans, requires multiemployer plans to use the same vesting standards as single employer plans, and simplifies the general definition of *highly compensated employees* for contribution limits. See also Pension Simplification Act.

Social Insurance—A compulsory insurance program legislated to provide certain minimum economic protections or security for large groups of people, particularly those of low income.

Social Investing—See Socially Responsible Investments.

Social Security—

—A federal program of old age and related benefits covering most workers and their dependents. Social Security benefits are provided by OASDHI. Programs are provided under the U.S. Social Security Act of 1935, plus amendments and additions thereto.

—(Canada) Benefits arising from the Old Age Security Plan (which provides benefits for essentially all old age persons), the Canada and Quebec Pension Plans (which cover workers and their families), and other income support programs.

—(International Benefits) Used generally in reference to any government program providing economic security for portions of the public.

Social Security Benefits or Wage Base Increase Effects—ERISA prohibits reductions in private pension benefit payments to a retiree because of an increase in Social Security benefits or the wage base. In addition, ERISA prohibits a reduction of private plan benefits because of an increase in Social Security benefits or wage base where the employee was separated from the employer's service prior to retirement and has vested deferred rights to benefits under the plan.

Social Security Disability Insurance (SSDI)—Provides for subsidized payments to eligible workers who are unable to continue working.

Social Security Freeze—A long-term disability policy provision which establishes that the offset from benefits paid by Social Security will not be changed regardless of subsequent changes in the Social Security law.

Social Security Integration—See Integration With Social Security.

Social Security Retirement Age—The age at which unreduced Social Security benefits are payable. The Social Security retirement age for individuals born before 1938 is age 65; for those born 1938 through 1942, age $65\frac{2}{12}$ through $65\frac{10}{12}$; for those born 1943 through 1954, age 66; for those born 1955 through 1959, age $66\frac{2}{12}$ through $66\frac{10}{12}$; and for those born 1960 and after, age 67.

Socially Responsible Investments—Generally considered to include those investments that (1) carry a lesser rate of return and/or, (2) have a lower credit rating and quality and/or (3) have less liquidity or marketability than other forms of investment or specific investments readily available in the marketplace, but that will (1) create employment opportunities for plan participants and/or (2) have a greater social or moral quality.

Also includes "socially sensitive" investments that otherwise are equal to other investments when compared by traditional financial analysis, but have favorable noneconomic characteristics. Socially responsible investments are known as *divergent, target* and *political investments.*

See also Economically Targeted Investing.

Soft Dollars—The portion of a plan's commissions expense incurred in the buying and selling of securities that is allocated through a directed brokerage arrangement for the purpose of acquiring goods or services for the benefit of the plan. In many soft dollar arrangements, the payment scheme is effected through a brokerage affiliate of the consultant.

Software—Computer programs and systems necessary to direct the hardware of a computer system and used to extend the capabilities of computers. *Hardware* refers to the physical (hard) components of the computer and its accessories.

Sole Proprietor—The owner of 100% of an unincorporated business.

Solvency—In a pension plan, the ability of the plan to meet its present and future obligations; the adequacy of provisions for funding.

Special Assessment Bonds—Bonds made to cover the cost of improving facilities. Property owners who directly benefit from the improvements are assessed for the improvement with the assessment spread over a series of years. See also Municipal Bonds; Revenue Bonds; Tax-Exempt Securities.

Special Class Insurance—Insurance for applicants of health insurance who cannot qualify for a standard policy by reason of health.

Special Risk Insurance—Coverage for risks or hazards of a special or unusual nature.

Specialist—

—(Medical) A physician who concentrates on medical activities in a particular specialty of medicine, based on education and qualifications.

—(Investment) A member of the New York Stock Exchange, who has two functions. First, the specialist maintains an orderly market, insofar as reasonably practicable, in the stocks in which he or she is registered as a specialist. In order to maintain an orderly market, the exchange expects the specialist to buy or sell for his or her own account, to a reasonable degree, when there is a temporary disparity between supply and demand. Second, the specialist acts as a broker's broker. When a commission broker on the exchange floor receives a limit order, say, to buy at $50 a stock then selling at $60, he or she cannot wait at the post where the stock is traded to see if the price reaches the specified level. Therefore, the broker leaves the order with the specialist, who will try to execute it in the market if and when the stock declines to the specified price. At all times, the specialist must put the customers' interest above his or her own. There are about 350 specialists on the NYSE.

Speculator—One who is willing to assume a relatively large risk in the hope of gain. Compare with Investor; Trader.

Spend Down—Depleting income and assets to meet eligibility requirements for Medicaid.

Spend-Down Eligibility—A method of determining eligibility for medical assistance that originated with Medicaid. A person may not have income above a certain level to qualify for Medicaid (for example, $500 per month). However, a person with an income of $600 may "spend-down" $100 per month for health care, and qualify for assistance for monthly expenses over $100. This is similar to a deductible.

Spinoff—A divestiture in which the stock of a subsidiary is given to the parent company's stockholders.

Split Dollar Insurance—The employer and employee share in the expenses, equity and death benefits of the policy. See also Corporate Owned Life Insurance.

Split Funding—The use of two or more funding agencies for the same pension plan. In some cases, part of the contributions to the plan is paid to a life insurance company and the remainder is invested through a corporate trustee, generally in equities.

Sponsor—See Plan Sponsor.

Sponsored Dependents—See Collateral Dependents.

Spousal Consent—Elections to waive QPSA and QJSA benefits and to elect some other form of benefit or to designate some other beneficiary are not valid unless the spouse of the participant consents in writing in the election.

Spousal Individual Retirement Account (Spousal IRA)—A trust or custodial account or subaccounts created for the exclusive benefit of an individual and his or her nonworking spouse. Such account or subaccounts also may be established by purchasing individual retirement annuities from an insurance company.

Stabilization Fund (International Benefits)—A fund established under a multinational pool with a loss-carry forward feature, which is to protect the carrier against excess losses. Also called a *contingency fund.*

Staff-Model HMO—A type of closed-panel HMO in which the physicians are employees of the HMO. The providers see members in the HMO's own facilities.

Stagflation—Stagnation in the economy accompanied by a rise in prices.

Stand-Alone Plan—A 401(k) plan that only permits elective contributions by employees with no matching grants made by the employer nor additional voluntary after-tax contributions permitted by employees.

Standard & Poor's 400—An index of the 400 industrial stocks that comprise the S&P 500.

Standard & Poor's 500 Stock Price Index (S&P 500)—A well-known gauge of stock market movements computed by Standard & Poor's Corporation and determined by the price action of a carefully selected list of 400 leading industrial issues, plus 20 transportation issues, 40 utilities and 40 finance issues.

Standard Deviation—Measures the total risk of an asset or a portfolio. This risk is defined as the normal variation of returns from an expected return. Standard deviation is a measure of the dispersion of a set of numbers around a central point. If the standard deviation is small, the frequency distribution is concentrated within a narrow range of values. For many distributions, about two-thirds of the observations will fall within one standard deviation of the mean.

Standard of Living—A measure of the average cost of goods and services consumed by a person or family. Differs from cost of living in recognizing the changes in consumption that arise from increases in wages and productivity.

Standard Risk—Average risk; a person who has an average or less-than-average likelihood of loss.

Standard Termination—A voluntary pension plan termination in which plan assets are sufficient to pay all vested and nonvested employee benefits.

Standardized Plan—A qualified prototype plan written to satisfy various tax qualification requirements under the Internal Revenue Code.

State Bank—A bank that receives its charter from the government of the state where it is located. The bank may join the Federal Reserve system and the Federal Deposit Insurance Corporation provided it qualifies under the law and regulations.

State Disability Plan—A plan for accident and sickness, or disability insurance required by state legislation of those employers doing business in that particular state.

State Earnings Related Pension Scheme (SERPS) (Great Britain)—The second tier of the state pension scheme that provides an additional pension linked to one's earnings and paid at state pension age out of national insurance contributions.

Statutory Reserve—See Policy Reserve.

Step Rate—A method of calculating benefits by assigning a different value to income below and above a certain breakpoint, such as the Social Security level.

Step-Rate Method—See Unit Credit Actuarial Cost Method.

Stock—A certificate of ownership; a contract between the issuing corporation and the owner that gives the latter an interest in the management of the corporation, the right to participate in profits and, if the corporation is dissolved, a claim upon assets remaining from all debts that have been paid. Also known as *equity securities* or *equities.* See also Common Stock; Preferred Stock.

Stock Appreciation Right (SAR)—An executive can receive the difference between the stock option price and current market price of the company's stock without buying any; often used in conjunction with an incentive stock option.

Stock Bonus Plan—A plan established and maintained by an employer to provide benefits similar to those of a profit-sharing plan, except that the contributions by the employer are not necessarily dependent upon profits and the benefits are distributable in stock of the employer company. For the purpose of allocating and distributing the stock of the employer that is to be shared among employees or their beneficiaries, such a plan is subject to the same requirements as a profit-sharing plan. See also Employee Stock Ownership Plan; Profit-Sharing Plan.

Stock Certificate—An engraved piece of paper representing legal evidence of ownership of a stipulated number of shares of stock in a corporation.

Stock Dividend—A dividend payable in shares of stock and generally disbursed in lieu of cash by corporations wanting to conserve capital for expansion or other purposes.

Stock Option—The right to buy company stock at a certain price within a particular period of time.

Stock Purchase Plan—

—(Nonqualified) A plan that allows senior management or other key personnel to purchase employer stock. Certain restrictions apply: (1) the stockholder must be employed for a particular length of time, (2) the employer has the right to buy back the stock and (3) stockholders cannot sell the stock for a specific time period.

—(Qualified) A program under which employees buy shares in the employer's stock. The employer contributes a certain amount for each unit of employee contribution. Also, stock may be offered at a fixed price (usually below market) and paid for in full by the employees. Benefits are distributed in the form of employer stock.

Stock Purchase Warrant—See Warrant.

Stock Split—A proportionate increase in the number of stock shares outstanding, usually intended to effect a decrease in the market value of the stock.

Stock Swap—Allowing an executive to deliver already-owned stock, instead of paying cash, to exercise a stock option.

Stock Yield—The rate of return on a stock based upon its market value as of a particular date and the dividend currently being paid by the company.

Stockholder—The owner of one or more shares of corporate stock who is entitled to (1) a proportionate share of the issuing company's undivided assets; (2) dividends when declared by the directors; (3) the right of proportionate voting power; and, frequently, (4) the opportunity to subscribe to additional stock before public offerings are made.

Stockholder of Record—A stockholder whose name is registered on the books of the issuing corporation, often stated as of a given date.

Stockholders' Equity—The residual claims that stockholders have against a company's assets. Calculated by subtracting total liabilities from total assets.

Stop-Loss Insurance—Contract established between a self-insured group and an insurance carrier providing carrier coverage if claims exceed a specified dollar amount over a set period of time. May apply to an entire plan or a single component. Also called *excess loss insurance*. See also Reinsurance.

Stop-Loss Provision—A health insurance policy provision. A stop-loss provision is determined in two ways: either after a certain amount of benefits are paid from the plan or after a certain amount of out-of-pocket expenses are paid by the individual or family unit. When the dollar amount specified is reached, the coinsurance factor is raised to 100%.

When there is a stop-loss provision in the plan (besides the separate maximums and coinsurance levels on outpatient mental and nervous disorders), outpatient mental and nervous charges usually do not apply toward the dollar figure used to calculate when the stop-loss begins; after the stop-loss does begin, it does not apply to these charges.

Straddle—Either a long or short position in a call and a put on the same stock with the same expiration date and the same exercise price.

Straight Bonds—As opposed to income or convertible bonds. Bonds conforming to the standard description (i.e., unquestioned right to repayment of principal at a specified future date; unquestioned right to fixed interest payments on stated dates; and no right to additional interest, interest in assets or profits, or voice in management).

Straight Life Insurance—Whole life insurance on which premiums are payable for life.

Street—Another word for Wall Street and/or the New York financial district.

Striking Price—See Exercise Price.

Subordinate Mortgage—See Junior Mortgage.

Subpoena—A process issued out of a court requiring the attendance of a witness at a trial. Term is derived from the first words of the document, "Under penalty of . . ." or "Sub poena . . ."

Subrogation—The right of the employer or insurance company to recoup benefits paid to participants through legal suit, if the action causing the disability and subsequent medical expenses was the fault of another individual. Used as a cost-containment measure. Generally, the substitution of one person or entity for another in regard to a legal right, interest or obligation.

Subscriber—The employee or member who elects coverage under the plan.

Subsidiary Company—A firm that has a majority of its voting stock owned by a parent company.

Substantive Plan—According to Financial Accounting Statement 106, it is a welfare plan not just as it is written, but as it is understood by employee and employer. It includes historical practices and employer practices.

Successor Plan—A plan established after the termination of a group health plan. If an employer terminates a group health plan and does not establish a new plan, it is not required to provide COBRA continuation coverage; however, if a new group health plan is established shortly after the old plan is terminated, the employer may have to provide continuation coverage.

Sullivan Principles—A code of conduct advocated by the Rev. Leon H. Sullivan for corporations doing business in South Africa. The code dictates nonsegregation in work facilities; equal pay for equal work; fair employment practices; training programs for blacks, those of mixed race and Asians; and improved facilities in housing, schooling and other quality-of-life areas.

Summary Annual Report (SAR)—A summary report on the financial status of an employee benefit plan; must be given to participants. See also Annual Report (Employee Benefit Plans).

Summary of Material Modifications (SMM)—A summary of any material change or modification of a plan or the information contained in the summary plan description that must be furnished to each participant and beneficiary.

Summary Plan Description (SPD)—A requirement of ERISA for a written statement of a plan in an easy-to-read form, including a statement of eligibility, coverage, employee rights and appeal procedure. It is provided to participants, beneficiaries and the Department of Labor.

Superannuation—Retirement because of old age or infirmity.

Superimposed Major Medical—See Supplemental Major Medical Coverage.

Supermarket—A program offered by brokerage firms that makes funds from many different families available on a no-load, fee-only basis.

Supplemental Benefits—Benefits provided by a pension plan in addition to regular retirement benefits. Supplemental benefits vary according to the terms of a plan and include such items as the payment of benefits in the event of terminations, death, disability or early retirement. See also Ancillary Benefits; Supplemental Unemployment Benefits.

Supplemental Executive Retirement Plan (SERP)—A nonqualified pension plan that allows an employer to offer greater benefits to its highly paid employees. See also Top-Hat Plan.

Supplemental Liability—See Actuarial Accrued Liability.

Supplemental Major Medical Coverage—This coverage is designed to insure expenses not covered by a basic plan. Covered persons are first reimbursed for their medical expenses under the employer's basic plan, usually with no deductible or copayment applied, to the extent that the basic plan covers the expenses. Expenses may not be covered by the basic plan, however, because they are not the types covered by the basic plan or because they exceed the limits of the basic plan. If these expenses are covered under the major medical plan, they can be reimbursed under the supplemental major medical plan, usually after the satisfaction of a corridor type deductible. After the covered expenses exceed the deductible, the major medical plan takes over and typically pays a percentage, such as 80%, of the covered expenses in excess of the deductible amount. There frequently is a stop-loss limit on the amount of covered expenses that are subject to a coinsurance provision, after which the covered expenses are reimbursed in full.

Supplemental Security Income (SSI)—A state-supplemented federal income support program for the aged, blind and disabled who fall below specified income and resource thresholds.

Supplemental Unemployment Benefits (SUB)—Amounts provided under a labor contract as additions or supplements to the unemployment compensation provided by law. See also Unemployment Compensation.

Supplementary Medical Insurance (SMI)—Also known as Part B, it is a voluntary insurance program that provides insurance benefits for physician and other medical services in accordance with the provisions of Title XVIII of the Social Security Act for aged and disabled individuals who elect to enroll under the program.

Surgicenter—A freestanding operating facility where outpatient surgery is performed. An intermediate level of surgical care is provided for procedures that are too complex to be done in a physician's office but do not require patient hospitalization.

Surplus—

—That part of the accumulated profits of a corporation that has not been capitalized.

—The balance of income in a trust that, at the end of the fiscal year, may be paid to the beneficiary.

Surrender Charge—A charge for the cancellation of an insurance or annuity policy.

Surrender Value—Generally, the net proceeds, after applicable charges, available from the termination or cancellation of an insurance or deferred annuity contract.

Surviving Spouse Benefit—Payments to the spouse of a deceased participant. See also Automatic Survivor Coverage.

Survivor Annuity—See Joint and Survivor Annuity.

Suspension—Some contributory plans that do not permit employees to withdraw from the plan while continuing in employment do permit them, on application, to suspend contributions temporarily. The term also refers to a temporary interruption of employer contributions that may sometimes be permitted by an insurance company and/or the secretary of the treasury without terminating the plan.

Syndicate—A group of investment banking firms that bands together to underwrite (i.e., distribute to the public) a new security issue or that engages in a secondary distribution of an already outstanding security.

Systematic Risk—Tendency of the asset price to move along with the market index. The measure of systematic risk is widely known as beta. If beta is 1.0, the asset price tends to fall in the same proportion that the market falls, other things being equal, and to rise by the same proportion that the market rises. If beta is 1.5, the asset price tends to fall (or rise) proportionally by 1.5 times as much as the market falls (or rises).

T

Table of Allowances—A list of covered health care services that assigns to each service a sum that represents the total obligation of the plan with respect to payment for such service, but that does not necessarily represent the provider's full fee for that service. Sometimes called a fee schedule. See also Scheduled Plan.

Taft-Hartley Act (Labor-Management Relations Act of 1947)—An amendment to the National Labor Relations Act of 1935 based on the theory of equalizing the bargaining power of management with that of labor. Principal provisions: (1) specification of unfair labor practices by labor, (2) granting individual workers the right to prosecute for unfair labor practices by union or company officials, (3) anti-Communist provisions, (4) restriction of the closed shop, (5) prohibition of secondary boycott. See also Multiemployer Plan.

Tangible Assets—Physical property, including land, buildings, machinery and equipment, timber and other growing products, mineral resources, merchandise and others.

Target Benefit Plan—Contributions are based upon an actuarial valuation designed to provide a target benefit to each participant upon retirement. The plan does not guarantee that such benefit will be paid; its only obligation is to pay whatever benefit can be provided by the amount in the participant's account. A hybrid of a *money purchase plan* and a *defined benefit plan.* See also Cash Balance Plan.

Tariff Rates (International Benefits)—Rates established by regulatory authorities for use by all insurers within the country.

Tax Anticipation Bills (TABs)—See Treasury Bills.

Tax Assistance (Canada)—Federal, provincial or territorial government incentives to taxpayers, usually in the form of tax deductions or tax credits.

Tax Deferral—Tax treatment granted to qualified retirement plans where taxes are not imposed when benefits are accrued (under a defined benefit plan) or contributions are made (under a defined contribution plan), but instead are imposed when benefits are paid to participants in cash.

Tax-Deferred Annuity—Offered by savings and loans, brokers and others, it offers high interest rates when the account is opened, but future interest rates are not guaranteed. Tax is deferred on the account until money is withdrawn.

Tax Equity and Fiscal Responsibility Act of 1982 (TEFRA)—Lowered limits on contributions and benefits for corporate plans; certain loans from plan to be treated as distributions; reduced estate tax exclusion for retirement plan death benefits to maximum of $100,000; repealed special Keogh plan and subchapter S restrictions; added "top-heavy" plan requirements; stopped employers and health plans from forcing employees ages 65 to 69 to use Medicare rather than group health plan.

Tax-Exempt Securities—Certain obligations issued by state and local governments, the interest of which is exempt from federal income tax. See also Municipal Bonds; Revenue Bonds; Special Assessment Bonds.

Tax-Qualified Plan—See Qualified Plan.

Tax Reduction (International Benefits)—The corporate taxation policy that, depending upon the foreign country involved, (1) permits expatriates to gain from the differences in income taxes in their home countries and the foreign country to which they are assigned or (2) adjusts the compensation of expatriates so they experience no loss in income as a result of the net effect of income taxes, both foreign and their home country.

Tax Reform Act of 1984—Among major changes made: delayed until 1988 cost-of-living increases in contributions and benefits; repealed the estate tax exclusion for death benefits from a pension plan or an IRA; allowed partial distributions from a pension plan to be rolled over to an IRA; applied restrictive distribution rules to 5% owners only. It attempted to redefine net earned income from self-employment. Top-heavy plan rules were modified. Deductions were extended to stock held under an ESOP. Welfare benefit rules were modified.

Tax Reform Act of 1986—Dictated extensive changes in the law governing the qualifications of pension and profit-sharing plans and the tax treatment of employers and employees. Imposed the comprehensive nondiscrimination rules of IRC Section 89.

Tax Shelter—
- —An investment that provides tax savings by creating losses to offset taxable income.
- —An investment upon which taxes are deferred.

Tax-Sheltered Annuity (TSA)—This describes special regulation under IRC Sections 501(c)(3) and 403(b) wherein employees of certain institutions may reduce their income by permitting the employer to pay part of their earned income into a deferred annuity.

Taxable Wage Base (TWB)—With respect to any year, the maximum amount of earnings that may be considered wages for such year under Code Section 3121(a)(1); i.e., Social Security wage base.

Taxable Year—The 12-month period used by an employer to report income for income tax purposes. The employer's taxable year does not have to coincide with the year used by the plan to keep its records.

Teacher's Annuity—See 403(b) Plan.

Technical Analysis—An approach to analysis of futures markets and future trends of commodity prices that examines the technical factors of market activity. Technical analysts normally examine patterns of price change, rates of change and changes in volume of trading and open interest, often by charting, in hopes of being able to predict and profit from future trends.

Technical and Miscellaneous Revenue Act of 1988 (TAMRA)—Revised Section 89 nondiscrimination rules and amended the penalties for noncompliance with COBRA. Provided technical definitions and rules concerning required distributions, excess distributions, IRA rollovers, and vesting schedules for all pension and profit-sharing plans. Increased excise tax on excess pension assets upon termination of qualified plans.

Telecommuting—An arrangement whereby an employee performs full- or part-time work at home, usually with a computer, while maintaining communication with the office via a modem.

Telemedicine—A technology that allows medical services to be conducted over a geographic distance. It involves application of interactive audiovisual technology in actual patient care, as well as education of physicians and other health care personnel. Can be especially useful in home monitoring of patients.

Temporary Disability Insurance (TDI)—Income protection for disabilities resulting in individuals not being able to perform their jobs for up to 24 months after illness or injury.

Ten-Year Averaging—A special tax calculation that can minimize ordinary income tax liability and that is applicable only to certain lump-sum distributions made from qualified retirement plans.

Tender Offer—An offer to buy securities for cash, other securities or both.

Term Certain—See Annuity Certain.

Term Insurance—Life insurance payable to a beneficiary only when an insured dies within a specified period. There are no permanent policy benefits such as cash or loan value. Premiums are age based.

Term Mortgage—A mortgage having a stipulated duration, usually under five years, in which only interest is paid. At the expiration of the term, the entire principal amount becomes due.

Terminal Illness (TI) Benefit—An accelerated death benefit provided by some individual life insurance policies under which the insurer pays a portion of the policy's death benefit to an insured who suffers from a terminal illness and has a life expectancy of 12 months or less.

Termination—Describes the final phase of an interrupted pension program. If the plan has enough assets to meet all its obligations, it is called a *standard termination.* In the case of a *distress termination,* the PBGC acts as trustee and uses its insurance funds as necessary to guarantee pension payments. Strict regulations govern all payout periods. Essentially all participants must vest 100%. However, the assets will have to be distributed according to the present formula. No money may return to the employer, except in the case of an actuarial error. It is also possible to discontinue contributions, but keep the trust in force, in order to preserve the tax-sheltered status of future payouts. See also Distress Termination; Standard Termination.

Termination Benefits—See Severance Pay.

Termination Date—See Expiration Date.

Termination Indemnities (International Benefits)—Obligation by law for payments on separation based on age, service or reason for termination.

Termination Insurance—See Plan Termination Insurance.

Termination Rate (Canada)—Rate of termination of employment for reasons other than death or retirement.

Tertiary Care—Specialized health care, needed by relatively few people, such as select rehabilitation services, highly technical medical procedures, burn centers and so on.

Therapeutic Substitution—The practice of substituting one drug for another when both are thought to produce the same therapeutic effects.

Third Country Nationals (TCNs) (International Benefits)—Citizens of one country who are employed by a company headquartered in a second country to work in a third country.

Third Party Administrator (TPA)—The party to an employee benefit plan that may collect premiums, pay claims and/or provide administrative services. Usually an out-of-house professional firm providing administrative services for employee benefit plans. (Synonyms: administrative agent, contract administrator)

Third Party Payer—The insurer that pays for the services provided to a patient.

Thirteenth Check—An annual supplemental retirement allowance arising from earnings on the investments of a system in excess of those determined as needed for other purposes.

30 and Out—A retirement option that permits retirement after 30 years' credited service, regardless of age.

Three-Legged Stool—Theory that a combination of an individual's savings, Social Security and a private pension will provide secure retirement income.

3% Rule—The employee's accrued benefit must be at least equal to 3% of the projected normal retirement benefit for each year of participation, to a maximum of 100% after 33⅓ years of participation. See also Accrued Benefit.

Thrift Plan—A defined contribution plan to which employees make contributions, usually as a percentage of salary. Incentive matching or partially matching contributions are also made on behalf of the participating employees by the employer.

Tight Money—A condition existing when interest rates are high and credit is stringent.

Timing—The art of deciding upon the exact moment to buy before an advance gets underway, or to sell before a decline. Timing is perhaps the most difficult of all market factors to achieve correctly. The wrong timing of a purchase or sale is a major factor responsible for loss in the stock market.

Tin Parachute—A play on the term *golden parachute,* it assures that rank and file workers receive cash payment, if the company changes hands against the will of the board of directors. Helps discourage hostile takeovers.

Title—The legal right to ownership of property, real or personal.

Title XVIII—The section of the Social Security Act that describes the Medicare program's coverage for eligible persons (i.e., the aged, the blind and the disabled).

Title Insurance—A policy of insurance that indemnifies the owner of real estate for any loss sustained by reason of defects in the title that was passed to him or her.

Title XIX—The section of the Social Security Act that describes the Medicaid program's coverage for eligible persons who may be medically indigent.

Title VII of the Civil Rights Act of 1964—A federal law, covering employers with 15 or more employees who are engaged in interstate commerce, that prohibits discrimination on the basis of national origin, race, color, religion and sex; also covered are employment agencies and unions.

Tolerable Loss Ratio (TLR)—The loss ratio the insurer can fund without losing money on the group.

Top-Down Investment Manager—Common stock manager who develops the portfolio with a primary emphasis on the economy and industries, as opposed to one who places his or her selection emphasis on recognizing favorable characteristics of individual companies.

Top-Hat Plan—An unfunded deferred compensation plan or welfare plan that is maintained to provide deferred compensation for a select group of management or highly compensated employees.

Top-Heavy Plan—A qualified plan in which the share of benefits allocable to key employees is more than 60%. The plan may be subject to special accelerated vesting provisions and minimum contribution rates. See also 5% Owner; Key Employee.

Tort—Any wrongful act or omission that causes damage to the person, property or reputation of another. Commonly spoken of as a private wrong, as opposed to a public wrong, which is called a crime.

Total Compensation—Value of direct pay plus benefit package.

Total Disability—An illness or injury that prevents an insured person from continuously performing every duty pertaining to his or her occupation or from engaging in any other type of work for remuneration. (This definition varies among insurance policies and benefit plans.) See also Disability.

Total Quality Management (TQM)—A comprehensive management process designed to control quality and improve all aspects of an organization's activities using statistical techniques, employee teamwork, joint problem solving and open communication on a continuous basis.

Total Return—The aggregate increase in the value of the portfolio resulting from the net appreciation (or depreciation) of the principal of the fund, plus or minus the net income (or loss) experienced by the fund during the period.

Trade Date—The date on which a transaction occurred.

Trader—A person who actively buys and sells securities for his or her own account using very short time horizons for the most part.

Trading Floor—See Floor.

Trading Limit—The maximum number of contracts, as determined by an exchange and/or the Commodity Futures Trading Commission, that one may trade in a given trading day.

Trading Post—One of 23 trading locations on the floor of the New York Stock Exchange at which stocks assigned to that location are bought and sold. About 75 stocks are traded at each post.

Transactions—All the activity of a portfolio: purchases and sales of securities, contributions to the fund and disbursements out of the fund, transfers, income receipts from dividends or bond interest, and payment of any administrative expenses.

Transfer Payment (International Benefits)—A payment from one pension scheme to another when a member/employee has changed jobs. The individual thus receives some credit in the new scheme for rights accrued in the old.

Trauma—A severe, life-threatening injury that requires emergency care and possibly extensive life-saving measures.

Treasury Bills—The safest and most liquid investment next to cash, Treasury bills are short-term direct obligations of the U.S. government and are usually issued with maturities of three months, six months or one year. Bills are only offered in bearer form and therefore cannot be registered in any legal name. They are issued in amounts of $10,000 and up, in multiples of $5,000, and there is a subscription charge on auction purchases by the purchasing broker or bank. Bills do not bear a stated interest rate. The interest is calculated by taking the difference between the discount price, date of purchase, and the face amount (par) collected at maturity. The yield is figured on a 360-day basis, vs. 365 days for interest-bearing securities, using the actual number of days remaining in the life of the issue. A conversion table is used to make this calculation. In addition to the three-month, six-month and one-year bills, the Treasury also offers *tax anticipation bills* called *TABs*, when it has special need for cash usually due to seasonal demands. These bills mature generally a week after the corporate income tax dates and are acceptable at par on the tax date.

Treasury Bonds—These very liquid government-guaranteed issues have maturities from five to 30 years, are limited by statute to a 4¼% coupon interest rate except for $10 billion, which may be issued without regard to any interest rate ceiling; are available in coupon or registered form; are issued either for cash or in an exchange for "rights" offering; pay interest semiannually; and are available on the market at a dollar price plus accrued interest in amounts from $500 up to round lots of $100,000 or more.

Treasury Notes—These readily marketable obligations of the U.S. Treasury are issued at par in coupon form, enjoy an active trading market in volume, have maturities of one to seven years and pay interest semiannually; the outstanding notes are noncallable and, of course, are guaranteed as to principal and interest payments by the government. There being no statutory limit on the amount of interest the Treasury can pay on notes, these issues are fully competitive with other money market instruments.

Treasury Regulations—Regulations promulgated by the U.S. Department of the Treasury. IRS is a part of the Treasury Department, and regulations interpreting the Internal Revenue Code are technically Treasury regulations.

Treasury Stock—Common stock that has been issued and reacquired (purchased) by the corporation from the public at the current market price.

Trend—A persistent and pervasive change in direction over a period of time of commodities, prices, earnings and so on.

Triage—The sorting and classification of patients in accordance with the nature or degree of injury or illness.

Triple Option Plan—Administered by one insurance carrier, it is a health insurance plan offered by employers that includes an HMO, a PPO and traditional indemnity insurance with utilization reviews and joint underwriting.

Trust—A legal entity that is created when a person or organization transfers assets to a trustee for the benefit of designated persons.

Trust Agreement—

—An agreement that spells out the methods of receipt, investment and disbursement of funds under a retirement plan. It contains provisions for investment powers of trustees; irrevocability and nondiversion of trust assets; payment of legal, trustee and other fees relative to the plan; exculpatory clauses pertaining to the liability of trustees; periodic reports to the employer or union by the trustees; records and accounts to be maintained by the trustees; conditions for removal, resignation or replacement of trustees; benefit payments under the plan; and the rights and duties of the trustees in case of amendment or termination of the plan. The plan agreement is often separate from the trust. See also Plan and Plan Document.

—(Canada) Also called a *trust deed.*

Trust Fund—A fund whose assets are managed by a trustee or a board of trustees for the benefit of another party or parties. Restrictions as to what the trustee may invest the assets of the trust fund in are usually found in the trust instrument and in applicable state and federal laws. In the case of ERISA-controlled employee benefit plan trust funds, there are specific requirements that should be referred to.

Trustee—

—A person, bank or trust company that has responsibility over financial aspects (receipt, disbursement and investment of pension funds). Where this responsibility is not exercised by a bank or trust company, it is usually exercised by a board of trustees in which the individual trustee has but one vote.

—A person, bank or trust company designated in trust agreement as having responsibility for holding and investing plan contributions (and possibly having responsibility over other financial aspects of the plan).

—One who acts in a capacity of trust as a fiduciary and to whom property has been conveyed for the benefit of another party. Under the terms of ERISA, a *fiduciary* is "one who occupies a position of confidence or trust and who exercises any power of control, management or disposition with respect to monies or other property of an employee benefit fund or who has authority or responsibility to do so."

Trusteed Pension Plan—

—A pension plan in which the corporation's contributions to the plan are placed in a trust for investment and reinvestment, as distinguished from a plan in which the benefits are secured by life insurance.

—A negotiated employee benefit plan established under the Taft-Hartley Act and governed by a board of trustees composed of equal numbers selected by the employers, or management, and individuals selected by the union. All trustees of a trusteed plan are charged with the fiduciary responsibility of discharging their duties with respect to the plan "solely in the interests of participants and beneficiaries." See also Trust Fund.

Turnover, Turnover Rate—

—The rate at which securities within a portfolio are exchanged for other securities.

—Termination of employment for a reason other than death or retirement.

—In general labor terms, the number of persons hired to replace those leaving or dropped, within a stated period of time; also, the ratio of this number to the average workforce maintained. In pension plans, the ratio of those leaving or dropped to the total number of plan participants at any age or length of service.

12(b)—A type of mutual fund in which the fund's operators are permitted to cover marketing expenses by using the fund's assets.

24-Hour Coverage—A combination of workers' compensation benefits and regular medical insurance coverage. A single plan would cover both medical and disability benefits for any injury, job related or not.

Two-Tier Pay Plan—A dual pay structure that attempts to control labor costs by grandfathering the current structure for existing employees, but starting new employees under a second, lower level pay structure.

U

Ultrasound—A technique that uses high-frequency sound waves to provide structural information on many parts of the human anatomy that cannot be obtained by traditional X-ray and radioisotopic methods. It permits visualization of both surface and internal structures of many body organs.

Often used for fetal monitoring.

Unbundling—

—Charging separately for services that normally are covered under one procedure code.

—Under Part B of Medicare, billing for nonphysician services provided to hospital inpatients by a source other than the hospital.

—If an employer offers a core coverage plan and a plan that combines core and noncore coverage, qualified beneficiaries under COBRA usually must be allowed to choose core-only continuation coverage—even if they were covered under the plan providing core and noncore coverage. When the cost of the core-only plan is at least 95% of the cost of the core and noncore coverage plan, however, this rule does not apply.

Unconditional Vesting—That form of vesting in a contributory plan under which entitlement to a vested benefit is not conditional upon the nonwithdrawal of the participant's contributions.

Underdistribution—See Excess Accumulation.

Underfunded Benefit Plan—An employee benefit plan in which the company's past contributions are insufficient to cover current and future liabilities.

Underinsured—People who do not have enough insurance coverage to meet their current or anticipated needs.

Undertreatment—Failure to recommend at the proper time one or more of those services that, consistent with diagnosis and treatment planning, are necessary and appropriate. See also Overtreatment.

Underwriter—

—(Insurance) Can mean (1) the company that receives the premiums and accepts responsibility for fulfilling the policy contract, (2) the company employee who decides whether or not the company should assume a particular risk or (3) the agent who sells the policy.

—(Investments) With respect to a mutual fund, the entity responsible for marketing the shares of the fund. See also Investment Banker.

Underwriting—

—(Insurance) The process of identifying and classifying the potential degree of risk represented by a proposed insured.

—(Investments) The procedure by which investment bankers channel investment capital from investors to corporations and municipalities.

Unemployed Person—Described by the government as a civilian who, during a given week, had no employment but was available for work and sought a job during the prior four weeks or was waiting to be called back to work or to a new position within 30 days.

Unemployment Compensation—Payments made under state-administered programs to workers who are unemployed and meet the requirements of the law involved to qualify for such payments. The requirements usually are (1) that the worker not be unemployed voluntarily; (2) that the worker has worked in employment that is "covered" by the law; (3) that the worker be willing and able to take employment offered him or her; and (4) that an initial period (the waiting period) of unemployment elapse before compensation is due. Programs are entirely employer financed except in four states that require small employee contributions. See also Supplemental Unemployment Benefits.

Unemployment Compensation Amendments of 1992—The law contains three directives for plan administrators of qualified plans and payers of Section 403(b) annuities: (1) provide a direct rollover option from qualified plans or Section 403(b) annuities, (2) withhold 20% federal income tax on eligible rollover distributions (ERDs) not directly rolled over into an eligible retirement plan and (3) give written notice to recipients before ERDs are made.

Unfunded—Means the plan is not insured or trusteed. The benefits are paid solely from the employer's current assets.

Unfunded Accrued Pension Cost—Cumulative net pension cost accrued in excess of the employer's contributions.

Unfunded Accumulated Benefit Obligation—The excess of the accumulated benefit obligation over plan assets.

Unfunded Actuarial Accrued Liability—The excess of the actuarial accrued liability over the actuarial value of assets. This value may be negative, in which case it may be expressed as a negative unfunded actuarial accrued liability; the excess of the actuarial value of assets over the actuarial accrued liability; or the funding excess.

Unfunded Deferred Compensation Agreement—A contract between employer and employee to pay certain sums of money at any later date, usually upon retirement, without payment by the employer into any funding agency.

Unfunded Frozen Actuarial Accrued Liability—The portion of the frozen actuarial accrued liability remaining after the addition of interest and the deduction of amortization payments.

Unfunded Past Service Cost—See Unfunded Actuarial Accrued Liability.

Unfunded Plan—A plan funded by the employer out of current income. See Pay As You Go.

Unfunded Projected Benefit Obligation—The excess of the projected benefit obligation over plan assets.

Uniform Provisions—Statutory policy provisions that specify the rights and obligations of the insured and company.

Unilateral Plan—A pension plan that does not result from collective bargaining. See, in contrast, Collectively Bargained Plan.

Union-Sponsored Plan—A program of health benefits developed by a union. The union may operate the program directly, or may contract for the benefits. Funds to finance the benefits are usually paid out of a welfare fund, which receives its income from (1) employer contributions, (2) employer and union member contributions or (3) union members alone.

Unit Benefit Method of Funding—A method of funding whereby the amount contributed by or on behalf of an employee at a given age is sufficient to purchase a unit of benefit at the normal retirement age. The required contribution increases with advancing age.

Unit Benefit Plan—A type of pension plan providing retirement benefits expressed as a definite amount or percentage for each year of service with the employer. The plan may define the benefit as a small unit of annuity for each year of membership in the plan, usually a percentage of the employee's earnings, such as 1%. The total of these units is the amount the employee will receive each year upon retirement. Sometimes referred to as a *multi-purchase* type of plan. If a unit of annuity is purchased each year to fund the ultimate benefit, this also may be called a *unit purchase* type of plan.

Unit Credit Actuarial Cost Method—

—A method of computing pension benefits based on certain units, such as percentage of salary and years of service.

—An acceptable actuarial cost method under which the plan's normal cost for a year is the present value of the benefit credited to all participants for service in that year and the accrued liability is the present value at the plan's inception of the units of benefits credited to participants for service before the plan's inception. This method is also known as the *accrued benefit cost method.*

—See also Actuarial Cost Method.

Unit Investment Trust—An investment company that has its own portfolio of securities in which it invests. It sells interest in this portfolio in terms of redeemable securities. They include two types: fixed (no portfolio changes are made) and nonfixed (portfolio changes are permissible). Unit investment trusts are organized under a trust indenture, not a corporate charter.

Universal Life Insurance—Flexible premium life insurance policy under which the policyholder may change the death benefit from time to time (with satisfactory evidence of insurability for increases) and vary the amount or timing of premium payments. Premiums (less expense charges) are credited to a policy account from which mortality charges are deducted and to which interest is credited at rates that may change from time to time.

Unlisted Securities—Securities not listed on a stock exchange.

Unrealized Profits—Paper profits that have not yet been made actual.

Unrecognized Prior Service Cost—That portion of prior service cost that has not been recognized as a part of net periodic pension cost.

Unrelated Business Income (UBI)—Income to trust that is taxable if it is derived from any unrelated trade or business in which the trust is engaged. Dividends, interest, annuities, royalties, rents from real property and gains from the sale or exchange of capital assets are not considered unrelated business income. Rental from "business lease" (lease of real property for a term of more than five years if there is indebtedness incurred to the trust to acquire or improve the property) is considered unrelated business income.

Unsecured Bond—A bond that is not backed by any pledge of assets that the debt will be paid. The debtor pledges its credit standing, secured by full faith. Government bonds and most corporate debentures are in this category.

Upcoding—A deceptive practice of health care providers in which service codes are reported at their highest service value for payment, although the procedures actually performed were less complex.

Uptick—Designates a transaction made at a price higher than the preceding transaction. Also called a *plus tick.* A stock may be sold short only on an uptick or on a "zero-plus" tick (a term used for a transaction at the same price as the preceding trade, but higher than the preceding different price). Conversely, *downtick* or *minus tick* designates a transaction made at a price lower than the preceding trade. A *zero-minus tick* is a transaction made at the same price as the preceding sale but lower than the preceding different price. A plus sign or a minus sign is displayed throughout the day next to the last price of each company's stock traded at each trading post on the floor of the New York Stock Exchange.

Urgent Care Center—An ambulatory care facility that provides extended or 24-hour service to treat minor conditions such as cuts, bruises and suture removal; less costly than emergency room treatment. Also called *emergicenter* or *urgicenter.*

Use-It-or-Lose-It Rule—A rule forbidding cafeteria plans to let participants defer receipt and taxation of compensation from year to year by carrying over unused pretax contributions or plan benefits.

Usual, Customary and Reasonable (UCR) Fees—*Usual* is the fee usually charged for a given service by a provider; *customary* is a fee in the range of usual fees charged by similar providers in area; *reasonable* is a fee that, according to the review committee, meets the lesser of the two criteria or is justified in the circumstances.

Usury—An illegal rate of interest.

Utilization—
—Proper and efficient use of hospital facilities, labor force, services and equipment.
—The extent to which a given group uses specified services in a specific period. Usually expressed as the number of services used per year per 100 or per 1,000 persons eligible for the services, but utilization rates may be expressed in other types of ratios, e.g., per eligible person covered. Utilization rates are established to help in comprehensive health planning, budget review and cost containment.

Utilization Management (UM)—A generic term for the preadmission certification, concurrent review and retrospective review techniques to evaluate health care on the basis of appropriateness, necessity and quality.

Utilization Review (UR)—A cost-control mechanism for reviewing the appropriateness and the quality of care provided to patients. UR may be before (prospective), at the same time (concurrent) or after (retroactive) the services are rendered.

Utilization Review Organization (URO)—Independent review organizations, insurance companies or in-house programs providing utilization review services.

V

Vacation Trading—A feature of flexible benefit plans that permits participants to trade excess time off for other benefits, including cash.

Valdez Principles—See CERES Principles.

Valid—Sufficient in law; effective.

Valuation—A determination of the value, as of a given date, of an investment or investment portfolio (asset valuation). See also Actuarial Valuation.

Valuation Assets—See Actuarial Value of Assets.

Valuation Reserves—Reserves established to anticipate a decreased value of an asset (i.e., depreciation or depletion reserves).

Value Added—A term, more precisely called *value added by manufacture,* used in economics to describe the value that is added to a product by industry.

Value Manager—A manager who invests in companies believed to be undervalued on an absolute basis, or relative to the market and/or historical basis. Value stocks or portfolios tend to have lower-than-average per share growth, low debt and be of higher quality. Value portfolios have a lower-than-average portfolio turnover (purchases and sales).

Variability—Measures, the fluctuations in rates of return. These measurements are used frequently as proxies for risk management.

Variable Annuity—

—Annuity expressed in terms of benefit units instead of fixed dollar amounts.

—Annuity in which the amount of each periodic payment fluctuates according to some variable factor. Under an equity annuity plan, payments vary according to the value of a specific portfolio of common stocks and similar investments. Under a cost-of-living plan, benefits are adjusted to reflect variations in a specific index, such as the Consumer Price Index of the Bureau of Labor Statistics. An insured variable annuity is one under which the benefit varies according to the investment results of an insurance company's separate account (usually invested primarily in common stocks) in which funds have been set aside to provide the annuity.

Variable Benefit Plan—

—A pension plan in which the retirement benefits otherwise specified are varied from time to time to provide a measure of protection to the purchasing power of the benefits. In a *cost-of-living plan,* the benefits are adjusted to reflect variations in a specific index, such as the Consumer Price Index of the United States Bureau of Labor Statistics. In an *equity annuity plan,* the periodic benefit (or, more frequently, one-half of the benefit) is dependent on the investment experience of a specific portfolio containing equity securities.

—A pension plan that describes the monthly pension to be received in units, rather than in dollars. The value of each unit is being determined, based upon the investment portfolio of the plan, at the time of either retirement or payment of actual benefits.

Variable Life Insurance—Life insurance under which the premiums are level but the benefits are not. Above a guaranteed minimum, benefits relate to the value of assets behind the contract at the time benefits are paid.

Variable Rate Mortgage—The interest rate and the buyer's monthly payment fluctuate, depending on interest rates in the economy. When rates decline, homeowners benefit. When rates go up, however, the monthly payment will go up or the amount or length of the mortgage might be increased. See also Fixed Rate Mortgage.

Variable Universal Life—A form of life insurance (also called *Universal Life II* or *flexible life*) offering a guaranteed death benefit that combines the flexible premium features of universal life with the investment component of variable life.

Variance—A measure of variability based on squared deviations of individual observations from the mean value of the distribution. Its square root is the standard deviation. See also Standard Deviation.

Venture Capital—Capital subject to more than a normal degree of risk, usually associated with a new business or venture. Also called *risk capital.*

Vest; Vesting—

—An employee's right to receive a present or future pension benefit vests when it is no longer contingent upon remaining in the service of the employer. Employee contributions are always fully vested; however, interest upon such contributions may not be vested or may be paid at a specified rate, depending upon plan provisions. A vested benefit may be paid as a lump sum or, frequently, is paid as a deferred annuity upon retirement. See also Vesting Schedules.

—(Canada) Usually requires contributions as a result of membership in the plan to be locked in for a specified period of time.

Vested Benefit Obligation—The actuarial present value of vested benefits.

Vested Benefits—Accrued benefits of a participant that have become nonforfeitable under the vesting schedule adopted by the plan.

Vested Liabilities—The plan's liability for the nonforfeitable immediate and deferred benefits due at retirement age for participants and their beneficiaries; the present value of vested benefits ultimately owed to separated and current plan participants.

Vesting Schedules—Under the Tax Reform Act of 1986, there are two minimum schedules: 100% vesting after five years of service and graduated vesting beginning after three years, with 100% vesting after seven years.

Ten-year cliff, 5-15 year rule, rule of 45 and class year vesting are no longer permitted. If a plan has immediate 100% vesting, the eligibility period may be two years of service.

Viatical Settlement—A provision of the Health Insurance Portability and Accountability Act of 1996, this form of living benefit allows severely ill patients tax-free access to the face value of their life insurance policies to help them meet medical and other necessary expenses. A qualified individual can sell his or her policy to a viatical settlement company or other such investor that pays out a percentage of the policy's face value to the policyholder, assumes responsibility for future premium payments and becomes the policy's beneficiary.

Vision Care Coverage or Plan—A separate plan covering medical treatment relating to eye conditions. Ophthalmologists, optometrists or opticians can render care. Most plans limit an eye examination to not more than once in a 12-month period, and new lenses and frames may be provided every 24 months.

Vocational Provisions—The specific stipulations written into a workers' compensation law regarding the employer's duties specific to providing vocational rehabilitation.

Voice Response Technology—A form of communication using a touch-tone phone, in which recorded voice messages lead users through a list of options and prompt a response made by pressing a button on the telephone keypad. Responses are then fed into a computer. Voice response technology, also called *interactive voice response (IVR),* is used by financial institutions, health care plans, etc. See also Interactive Benefits Communication.

Volatility—That part of total variability due to sensitivity to changes in the market. It is systematic and unavoidable risk. It is measured by the beta coefficient. Efficient portfolios have no additional risk, and volatility is the only source of variability in rates of return.

Volume—The aggregate number of shares of stock traded during a given period.

Voluntary Compliance Resolution Program—The IRS allows plan sponsors to identify and correct operational defects in their plans and to obtain a compliance statement indicating how the defects will be fixed. The program allows defects to be corrected without negative tax consequences to workers and without significant financial penalties being imposed on employers. Failure to remedy defects results in plan disqualification.

Voluntary Contribution—The amount of money the employee pays into the plan. Not required for employee participation; voluntary contributions do not affect the level of employer contributions. See also Contributory Plan.

Voluntary Death Payments—Payments made to a surviving spouse or other beneficiary of a deceased employee. If made pursuant to a contract with the employer, they will be considered taxable to the recipient as ordinary income.

Voluntary (Employee-Pay-All) Benefits—Specific benefits that the employer administers and the employees pay for. Commonly used for benefits that employees want but which the employer views as nonessential to the business.

Voluntary Employees' Beneficiary Association (VEBA)—Usually covered by IRC Section 501(c)(9), it serves as the base of an employer-sponsored employee benefit plan. It is a tax-exempt fund that pays death, health, accident or other benefits to members, their dependents and/or beneficiaries.

Voting Right—A right enjoyed by a stockholder to participate in the affairs of the company to the extent he or she deems necessary or desirable. In the case of the passing of a preferred dividend, preferred holders may, if the default exceeds a specified time period, have the right to vote their shares to protect their interests. This right may be delegated to another party.

W

Wage Loss Insurance—See Disability Income Insurance.

Wagner Act—See National Labor Relations Act of 1935.

Waiting Period—

—The duration of time between the beginning of an insured person's disability and the start of the policy's benefits. Called a *qualification period* in Canada.

—The period between employment or enrollment in a program and the date when an insured person becomes eligible for benefits.

—See also Participation Requirements.

Waive—To waive at law is to intentionally give up a known right. It may be done expressly through words, or through conduct involving acts that are inconsistent with the claiming of a known right.

Waived Funding Deficiency—If an employer is not able to satisfy the minimum funding standard without substantial business hardship and if the application of the standard would be adverse to the interests of plan participants in the aggregate, the IRS may waive part or all of the minimum funding standard for the plan year. The amount waived must be amortized in no more than 15 equal annual payments. The term *waived funding deficiency* means the part of the minimum funding standard determined without regard to previously waived amounts and not satisfied by employer contributions.

Waiver—

—An agreement attached to a policy that exempts from coverage certain disabilities or injuries normally covered by the policy. Also known as *exclusion endorsement.*

—A supplementary life insurance policy benefit under which the insurer gives up its right to collect renewal premiums if the policy owner dies or becomes disabled. Also known as *waiver of premium.*

—In health care, a common usage is exemption of a state from participating in the Medicare program under the prospective payment system (PPS) when the state has presented an alternate method of payment that the government has accepted.

Warehousing—The process of borrowing funds on a short-term basis and using mortgage loans as collateral.

Warrant—A certificate giving the holder the right to purchase shares of stock at a stipulated price within a specified time span or, in some cases, forever. They are often attached to other securities (e.g., bonds) as an added purchase inducement and may be traded separately after issuance.

Warranty Deed—A deed conveying real property containing the usual covenants of warranty of title.

Wasting Trust—A plan under which participants no longer accrue benefits but that will remain in existence as long as necessary to pay already accrued benefits.

Wealth—Accumulated funds and the material resources they represent. If the funds lose purchasing power through inflation, wealth is reduced.

Weekly Indemnity Insurance—See Disability Income Insurance.

Weighting—The specification of the relative importance of each of a group of items that is combined.

Welfare Fund—When employer and/or employee contributions for health are placed in a fund that is administered by a board, usually with equal representation from labor and management. (Synonym: health and welfare fund)

Welfare Plan—A plan that provides medical, surgical or hospital care or benefits in case of sickness, accident, disability, death or unemployment. These plans may also include such other benefits as vacation, prepaid legal or scholarship plans.

Wellness (Health Promotion) Programs—A broad range of employer- or union-sponsored facilities and activities designed to promote safety and good health among employees. The purpose is to increase worker morale and reduce the costs of accidents and ill health such as absenteeism, lower productivity and health care costs. May include physical fitness programs, smoking cessation, health risk appraisals, diet information and weight loss, stress management and high blood pressure screening.

White Knight—A company, friendly to management, that rescues another firm that is faced with a hostile bid.

Whole Life Insurance—Insurance payable to a beneficiary at the death of the insured, whenever that occurs. Premiums may be payable for a specified number of years (limited payment life) or for life (straight life). The premiums may remain level or decrease (by accumulating cash in the initial years of the policy).

Window Plan—An early retirement program providing an employee with an incentive to terminate employment within a specified time.

Withdrawal Liability (Multiemployer Plans)—

—The liability of a contributing employer to a qualified multiemployer defined benefit plan to make contributions necessary to fund benefits of employees before it can cease contributions to the plan.

—The Multiemployer Pension Plan Amendments Act of 1980 (MPPAA) imposes liabilities on contributing employers upon a complete or partial withdrawal of the employer from the plan, rather than on plan termination as is the case for multiple and single employer plans.

—MPPAA removed multiemployer plans from the termination insurance system that governs single and multiple employer plans and substituted a system that imposes liability for certain unfunded vested benefits when an employer partially or totally withdraws from a multiemployer plan.

Withdrawal of Employee Contributions—Whenever a participant whose benefit attributable to employer contributions is less than 50% vested withdraws all or any part of his mandatory contributions, ERISA permits a forfeiture of the benefit attributable to employer contributions. If the benefit attributable to employer contributions is 50% or more vested, no forfeiture is permitted.

If an employee withdraws his or her mandatory contributions, the employee must be permitted to repay the amount he or she received with interest at 5% initially. (The interest rate may be adjusted.)

Withdrawal of Vested Benefits—The right of an employee to withdraw monies credited to him or her in the employer's program. Not permissible under pension plans but often available in profit-sharing plans. Special regulations apply. Typically, the IRS does not allow accumulations to be distributed in less than two years. Thus, after a contribution has been credited to an employee's account for three years, he or she can withdraw an amount equal to the first year's contributions and the investment income credited that year only. The withdrawn amount is taxable as ordinary income in the year received.

Work Sharing—The practice of spreading a firm's available work hours among its employees during a cutback; used as an alternative to layoffs.

Work Teams—Groups of multiskilled employees responsible for a business product or service.

Workers' Compensation—Every state has a system of providing for the cost of medical care and weekly payments to employees who suffer job-related illnesses or injuries and to dependents of those killed in industry. Absolute liability is imposed on the employer, which is required to pay benefits prescribed by law. See also 24-Hour Coverage.

Working Capital—Found by subtracting current liabilities from current assets.

Working Control—Used in referring to corporate ownership of another company's securities. Where the amount owned is of sufficient size (but under 50%) to assure effective control inasmuch as all the other holders are quite scattered.

Working Papers—The body of information prepared by an independent CPA used to support his or her conclusions in an audit. They are the property of the CPA and not part of the permanent records of the audited company. Working papers are privileged and private information, available to third parties only with proper consent.

Works Council (International Benefits)—Elected representatives of employees, excluding management. Generally mandatory if a minimum employment figure is reached; however, a works council does not have to be established until the employees ask for one. Works councils are particularly strong in Western Europe in countries such as Germany.

World Wide Web (WWW)—An application to run on the Internet that makes its vast amount of information available to the masses. Users now access the Web using front end software called Web *browsers* such as Netscape and Mosaic that are relatively simple to use.

Wraparound Mortgage—Buyers who do not have enough cash to assume a loan and compensate the seller sufficiently for the equity can sometimes get a lender to combine the seller's old mortgage with additional new financing needed to satisfy the seller. Often the wraparound carries a lower rate than conventional mortgages.

Wraparound Plan—A major medical plan and a basic surgical/regular medical plan are wrapped around a basic hospital plan and cover all charges other than those provided for by the basic hospital plan. Commonly used for Medicare.

Y

Yankee Certificate of Deposit—A certificate evidencing a time deposit issued by the U.S. branch of a foreign bank.

Year of Service—ERISA defines a *year of service* in

terms of 1,000 compensable hours during a consecutive 12-month period.

For the purpose of the participation rules, an individual has one year of service if he or she works for 1,000 hours during the initial 12-month period after he or she is employed. Assuming that he or she has reached age 21 (and that the plan is not one that requires a three-year waiting period), the employee who has met the above requirement must be permitted to participate in the plan on the earlier of (a) the beginning of the first plan year after the anniversary date of his or her employment or (b) six months from the anniversary date of his or her employment. If an employee fails to work 1,000 hours during the initial 12 months of his or her employment, he or she must begin meeting the 1,000-hour requirement in the next 12-month period.

For purposes of determining where an individual stands on the vesting schedule, a *year of service* is a calendar year, plan year or other consecutive 12-month period designated in the plan during which the employee worked 1,000 hours.

Special rules govern the maritime industry and certain seasonal industries.

Years Certain Annuity—See Annuity Certain.

Year's Maximum Pensionable Earnings (YMPE) (Canada)—The maximum amount of annual earnings, prior to reduction of the amount of the year's basic exemption, upon which benefits and contributions for purposes of the Canada Pension Plan and the Quebec Pension Plan are based. The YMPE has been subject to yearly adjustments and is targeted, at some future point, to equal the average wage of industrial workers in Canada.

Yield—The return of an investment expressed as a percentage of cost or market. There are various ways to calculate *yield* depending upon whether you are dealing with a bond or stock. *Straight yield* on either a bond or stock is found by dividing the price into the expected dollar amount to be received from interest or dividends. A stock selling at $40 and paying a $2 dividend yields 5% ($2 divided by $40), and a bond with an 8% coupon selling at $1,000 yields 8% (i.e., $80 divided by $1,000). Where a bond is purchased at a premium or discount, the yield will vary depending upon whether the bond is held to its first call date or to maturity. *Amortized yield* allows for an actual gain or loss of principal to be realized at maturity.

Yield to Call—The rate of return on an investment that accounts for the cash difference between a bond's acquisition cost and its proceeds calculated to the earliest date that the bonds can be called in by the issuing corporation.

Yield to Maturity—The yield, or return, provided by a bond to its maturity date; determined by a mathematical process, usually requiring the use of a "basis book." For example, a 5% bond pays $5 a year interest on each $100 par value. To figure its current yield, divide $5 by $95—the market price of the bond—and you get 5.26%. Assume that the same bond is due to mature in five years. On the maturity date, the issuer is pledged to pay $100 for the bond that can be bought now for $95. In other words, the bond is selling at a discount of 5% below par value. To figure *yield to maturity,* a simple and approximate method is to divide 5% by the five years to maturity, which equals 1% pro rata yearly. Add that 1% to the 5.26% current yield, and the yield to maturity is roughly 6.26%.

Z

Zero Balance Reimbursement Account (ZEBRA)—A type of flexible spending arrangement under which amounts are allocated to the account only when an expense is incurred. The employee is then reimbursed by the employer by subtracting the amount of the covered expenses from his or her taxable income at the end of the year. Such arrangements are specifically forbidden in cafeteria plans.

Zero-Base Budget —A financial plan in which all expenditures must be justified.

Zero-Coupon Bond —A bond which is unique in that no interest payments are made to the holder by the issuer. The difference between the purchase price and the redemption value represents the imputed interest paid. A zero-coupon bond is a fixed income security sold at a steep discount from the value at maturity. An attractive feature is that reinvestment rate risk is avoided by the holder. The holder locks in a certain internal rate of return, provided the issuer is financially able to repay the face value of the bond when it matures.

Zero Premium —The practice, in some Medicare marketplaces, of not charging any added monthly premium to what is already paid for Part B coverage, as opposed to the practice of an HMO getting a monthly premium in addition to what is paid to the federal government by the patient.

EMPLOYEE BENEFITS: ACRONYMS AND ABBREVIATIONS

The employee benefits field encompasses many subjects: accounting, actuarial practice, business, government regulations, health care, human resources, insurance, investments, law, real estate and so forth. Each has a wealth of *acronyms* (words formed from the initial letters of the major words in compound terms) and other abbreviations. Therefore, the International Foundation has published this new edition of its acronyms and abbreviations dictionary. Use this dictionary as a guide rather than as an authority since no such list can ever be complete. Send suggested additions to the glossary editor at the Foundation since an updated version of this dictionary will appear periodically.

Notes on Arrangement

Entries are alphabetized as if they were single words. Ampersands, commas, slashes and spaces are ignored in alphabetization. Letters combined with numbers appear *before* letters combined with letters.

If an entry has more than one definition, those definitions appear in alphabetical order within the entry.

AAA (1) American Academy of Actuaries
(2) American Accounting Association
(3) American Arbitration Association
(4) Area Agency on Aging

AABD Aid to the Aged, Blind and Disabled

AAC (1) Actual Acquisition Cost
(2) Affirmative Action Clause

AALL American Association for Labor Legislation

AAP Affirmative Action Program

AAPCC Adjusted Average Per Capita Cost

AAPPO American Association of Preferred Provider Organizations

AARP American Association of Retired Persons

ABA (1) American Bankers Association
(2) American Bar Association

ABO Accumulated Benefit Obligation

ABP Average Benefit Percentage

ACA (1) American Chiropractic Association
(2) American Compensation Association

ACC Ambulatory Care Center

ACE (1) Additional Compensable Elements
(2) Average Current Earnings (Social Security)

ACH Automated Clearinghouse

ACLU American Civil Liberties Union

ACP (1) Actual Contribution Percentage
(2) Average Contribution Percentage

ACR (1) Actual Contribution Ratio
(2) Adjusted Community Rating

ACRS Accelerated Cost Recovery System

ACV Actual Cash Value

ACVVB Actuarially Computed Value of Vested Benefit

ADA	(1) American Dental Association (2) Americans with Disabilities Act of 1990
ADB	Accidental Death Benefit
AD&D	Accidental Death and Dismemberment
ADEA	Age Discrimination in Employment Act of 1967
ADEC	Accumulated Deductible Employee Contributions
ADL	Activities of Daily Living
ADP	Actual Deferral Percentage
ADR	(1) Actual Deferral Ratio (2) Adverse Drug Reaction (3) Alternate Dispute Resolution (4) American Depository Receipt (5) Asset Depreciation Range (6) Average Deferral Ratio
ADS	Alternative Delivery System
AEC	Additional Extended Coverage
AEE	Additional Expediting Expense
AEP	Appropriateness Evaluation Protocol
AFL-CIO	American Federation of Labor-Congress of Industrial Organizations
AFR	Applicable Federal Rate
AFSCME	American Federation of State, County and Municipal Employees
AGI	Adjusted Gross Income
A&H	Accident and Health
AHA	American Hospital Association
AHC	Alternative Health Care
AHCPR	Agency for Health Care Policy and Research
AHP	(1) Accountable Health Partnership (2) Accountable Health Plan (3) Approved Health Plan
A&I	Accident and Indemnity
AI	Artificial Intelligence
AIA	American Insurance Association
AICPA	American Institute of Certified Public Accountants
AIDS	Acquired Immune Deficiency Syndrome
AIMA	As Interest May Appear
AIME	Average Indexed Monthly Earnings (Social Security)
AIR	Assumed Investment Return
AKA	Also Known As
ALE	Additional Living Expense
ALI-ABA	American Law Institute-American Bar Association
ALOS	Average Length of Stay
ALR	(1) Acceptable Loss Ratio (2) Actual Loss Ratio
ALV	Annual Leave Value (cars)
AMA	(1) Against Medical Advice (2) American Management Association (3) American Medical Association
AMCS	Automated Medical Coding System
AMEX	American Stock Exchange
AML	Adjustable Mortgage Loan
AMW	Average Monthly Wage (Social Security)
ANA	American Nurses' Association
AO	At Occupation
AP	Annualized Premium
APA	American Psychiatric Association
APB	Accounting Principles Board
APBM	Accumulated Plan Benefit Method
APG	Ambulatory Patient Group
APHA	American Public Health Association
APIP	Additional Personal Injury Protection
APL	Automatic Premium Loan
APO	Accounting Principles Opinion
APPWP	Association of Private Pension and Welfare Plans
APS	Attending Physician's Statement
APTD	Aid to the Permanently and Totally Disabled

APV	(1) Actuarial Present Value (2) Administrative Point of View
AQL	Acceptable Quality Level
AR	Accounts Receivable
ARC	AIDS-Related Complex
ARM	Adjustable Rate Mortgage
ARPS	Adjustable Rate Preferred Stocks
ART	Annually Renewable Term
A&S	Accident and Sickness
ASA	Associate, Society of Actuaries
ASC	(1) Administrative Services Contract (2) Ambulatory Surgical Center
ASO	Administrative Services Only
ASPA	American Society for Personnel Administration (former name for SHRM)
ASTD	American Society for Training and Development
ASTM	American Society for Testing and Materials
AV	Audiovisual
AWP	(1) Any Willing Provider (2) Average Wholesale Price

BA	Bankers Acceptance
BAI	Bank Administration Institute
BAN	Bond Anticipation Note
BAT	Bureau of Apprenticeship and Training
BBB	(1) Bankers' Blanket Bond (2) Better Business Bureau
BBC	Balance Billing Caps
BBSU	Bid Bond Service Undertaking
BC/BS	Blue Cross/Blue Shield
BFOQ	Bona Fide Occupational Qualification
BI	Bodily Injury
BIC	Bank Investment Contract
BII	Business Interruption Insurance
BLS	Bureau of Labor Statistics
BNA	Bureau of National Affairs
BOP	Business Owners Policy
BPB	Blanket Position Bond

CA	(1) Chartered Accountant (2) Current Assets
CAC	Consumers' Association of Canada
CAD	Computer-Aided Design
CAI	Computer-Assisted Instruction
CalPERS	California Public Employees' Retirement System
CAM	Computer-Aided Manufacturing
CAPM	Capital Asset Pricing Model
CAPP	Cash Account Pension Plan
CAPSA	Canadian Association of Pension Supervisory Authorities
CAS	Casualty Actuarial Society
CASB	Cost Accounting Standards Board
CAT	Computerized Axial Tomography Scanner (health diagnostic device)
CB	Cumulative Bulletin (IRS)
CBA	Collective Bargaining Agreement
CBO	Congressional Budget Office
CBOE	Chicago Board Options Exchange
CCC	Care, Custody and Control
CCM	Certified Case Manager
CCP	Certified Compensation Professional
CCRC	Continuing Care Retirement Community
CCU	Coronary Care Unit
CCUS	Chamber of Commerce of the United States
CD	Certificate of Deposit or Time Deposit
CDC	(1) Centers for Disease Control (2) Community Development Corporation
CD-ROM	Compact Disc Read Only Memory

CDT	(1) Commissioners Disability Table (2) Current Dental Terminology
CEA	Council of Economic Advisers
CEB	Council on Employee Benefits
CEBS	Certified Employee Benefit Specialist
CED	Committee for Economic Development
CEO	Chief Executive Officer
CERES	Coalition for Environmentally Responsible Economies
CESOP	(Tax) Credit ESOP
CFA	Chartered Financial Analyst
CFO	Chief Financial Officer
CFP	Certified Financial Planner
CFR	Code of Federal Regulations
CFTC	Commodity Futures Trading Commission
CHAMPUS	Civilian Health and Medical Program of the Uniformed Services
CHESOP	Charity ESOP
ChFC	Chartered Financial Consultant
CHP	Comprehensive Health Planning
CHPA	Community Health Purchasing Alliance
CIC	Certified Insurance Counselor
CIG	Community Investment Grant
CIID	Chemically Induced Immune Disregulation
CIO	Congress of Industrial Organizations
CLU	Chartered Life Underwriter
CLUW	Coalition of Labor Union Women (AFL-CIO)
CME	Chicago Mercantile Exchange
CMI	Case Mix Index
CMO	Collateralized Mortgage Obligation
CMP	Competitive Medical Plan
CMV	Current Market Value
COB	(1) Continuation of Benefits (2) Coordination of Benefits
COBRA	Consolidated Omnibus Budget Reconciliation Act of 1985
CODA	Cash or Deferred Arrangement
C of C	Chamber of Commerce
COLA	(1) Cost-of-Living Adjustment (2) Cost-of-Living Allowance
COLI	Corporate-Owned Life Insurance
CON	Certificate of Need
COO	Chief Operating Officer
COPE	Committee on Political Education (AFL-CIO)
CORF	Comprehensive Outpatient Rehabilitation Facility
CPA	Certified Public Accountant
CPC	Certified Pension Consultant
CPCU	Chartered Property and Casualty Underwriter
CPI	Consumer Price Index
CPI-M	Medical Care Component of the Consumer Price Index or Consumer Price Index for All Medical Goods and Services
CPP	Canada Pension Plan
CPP/QPP	Canada Pension Plan/Quebec Pension Plan
CPR	(1) Cardiopulmonary Resuscitation (2) Customary, Prevailing and Reasonable
CPT	Current Procedural Terminology
CPU	Central Processing Unit
CQI	Continuous Quality Improvement
CRT	Cathode Ray Tube
CSO	Claims Services Only
CSR	(1) Civil Service Retirement (System) (2) Continued Stay Review
CTD	Cumulative Trauma Disorder (see also RSI)
CTF	Common Trust Fund

DA	Deposit Administration (Contract)
DAW	Dispense As Written
D&B	Dun & Bradstreet
d/b/a	Doing Business As
DBO	Death Benefit Only
DC	Doctor of Chiropractic
DCAP	Dependent Care Assistance Plan
DCI	Duplicate Coverage Inquiry
DCP	Dental Capitation Plan
DDB	(1) Deemed Death Benefit (2) Defined Dollar Benefit
DDD	(Comprehensive) Dishonesty, Disappearance and Destruction (Policy)
D/E	Data Entry
DEC	Deductible Employee Contribution
DEFRA	Deficit Reduction Act of 1984
DGA	Deferred Group Annuity Contract
DHHS	Department of Health and Human Services
DI	(1) Disability Income (2) Disability Insurance (3) Double Indemnity
DJIA	Dow Jones Industrial Average
DK	Don't Know (the Trade)
DLP	Date of Last Payment
DLV	Daily Leave Value (cars)
DME	Durable Medical Equipment
DNC	Direct Notice of Cancellation
DNR	(1) Department of Natural Resources (2) Do Not Renew
DO	Doctor of Osteopathy
DOB	Date of Birth
DOL	Department of Labor
DOT	(1) Department of Transportation (2) Designated Ordered Turnaround (System) (3) *Dictionary of Occupational Titles*
DPP	(1) Deferred Payment Plan (2) Deferred Premium Payment
DPSP	Deferred Profit Sharing Plan (Canada)
DR	(1) Daily Report (2) Debit Balance
DRG	Diagnosis-Related Group (also Diagnostic Related Group)
DRP	Dividend Reinvestment Plan
DRR	Drug Regimen Review
DSM	(1) Diagnostic and Statistical Manual of Mental Disorders (2) Disease State Management
DSP	Decessit Sine Prole (Died Without Issue)
D&T	Diagnostic and Treatment Center
DTC	Depository Trust Company
DUE	Drug Use Evaluation
DUM	Drug Utilization Management
DUR	Drug Utilization Review
DVP	Delivery Versus Payment
DXL	Diagnostic X-Rays and Laboratory

EA	Enrolled Actuary
EAFE	Europe, Australia, Far East Stock Market Index
EAP	Employee Assistance Program
EAPA	Employee Assistance Professionals Association
EAPI	Equivalent Annual Percent Increase
EBDITE	Earnings Before Depreciation, Interest, Taxes and Any ESOP Contribution
EBIT	Earnings Before Interest and Taxes
EBITE	Earnings Before Interest, Taxes and Any ESOP Contribution
EBRI	Employee Benefit Research Institute
EBS	Employee Benefits Security
EBT	Educational Benefit Trust

EC	(1) European Community (formerly EEC) (2) Extended Coverage
ECE	Extended Cover Endorsement
ECF	Extended Care Facility
ECI	Employment Cost Index
ED	Exposure Draft
EDA	Economic Development Administration
EDI	Electronic Data Interchange
EDP	Electronic Data Processing
EEC	European Economic Community (former name for EC)
EEG	Electroencephalogram
EEO	Equal Employment Opportunity
EEOC	Equal Employment Opportunity Commission
EFTS	Electronic Funds Transfer System
EIN	Employer Identification Number
EITC	Earned Income Tax Credit
EKG	Electrocardiogram
EL	Employers' Liability
ELOS	Estimated Length of Stay
EME	Extended Medical Expense (Canada)
EMS	Emergency Medical Service
EMU	European Monetary Union
E&O	Errors and Omissions (Insurance)
EOB	Explanation of Benefits
EOE	Equal Opportunity Employer
EP	Earned Premium
EPA	(1) Environmental Protection Agency (2) Equal Pay Act
EPL	Equity Participation Loan
EPEO	Employee Plans and Exempt Organizations (Division of IRS)
EPO	Exclusive Provider Organization
EPS	Earnings Per Share
EPSDT	Early and Periodic Screening, Diagnosis and Treatment
EPSP	Employees Profit Sharing Plan (Canada)
ER	(1) Emergency Room (2) Employee Relations
ERA	(1) Equal Rights Amendment (2) Expense Reimbursement Allowance
ERD	Eligible Rollover Distributions
ERISA	Employee Retirement Income Security Act of 1974
ERP	Employee Referral Program
ERTA	Economic Recovery Tax Act of 1981
ESA	Employee Spending Account
ESOP	Employee Stock Ownership Plan
ESOT	Employee Stock Ownership Trust
ESRD	End Stage Renal Disease
ETI	Economically Targeted Investing
ETR	Easy Growth Treasury Receipt
EVA	Economic Value Added
EWL	Employer Withdrawal Liability

FAP	Five-Year Average Pay
FAQ	Frequently Asked Questions
FAS	Financial Accounting Standard
FASB	Financial Accounting Standards Board
FAX	Facsimile
FDA	Food and Drug Administration
FDIC	Federal Deposit Insurance Corporation
FFS	Fee for Service
FHA	Federal Housing Administration
FHLB	Federal Home Loan Bank
FHLBB	Federal Home Loan Bank Board
FHLMC	Federal Home Loan Mortgage Corporation (Freddie Mac)
FI	Fiscal Intermediary
FICA	Federal Insurance Contributions Act (Social Security and Medicare)
FIFO	First In, First Out

FLMI	Fellow, Life Management Institute
FLSA	Fair Labor Standards Act
FMB	Family Maximum Benefit
FMLA	Family and Medical Leave Act of 1993
FMV	Fair Market Value
FNMA	Federal National Mortgage Association (Fannie Mae)
FOMC	Federal Open Market Committee
FP	Faithful Performance
FR	(1) Federal Register (2) Financial Responsibility
FS	Financial Statement
FSA	(1) Federal Security Agency (2) Fellow, Society of Actuaries (3) Flexible Spending Account (4) Flexible Spending Arrangement (5) Funding Standard Account
FSLIC	Federal Savings and Loan Insurance Corporation
FSPA	Fellow, Society of Pension Actuaries
FTC	Federal Trade Commission
FUTA	Federal Unemployment Tax Act
FY	Fiscal Year
GA	General Agent
GAAP	Generally Accepted Accounting Principles
GAAS	Generally Accepted Auditing Standards
GAINS	Guaranteed Annual Income System (Canada)
GAO	General Accounting Office
GASB	Governmental Accounting Standards Board
GATT	General Agreement on Tariffs and Trade
GAW	Guaranteed Annual Wage
GDP	Gross Domestic Product
GEM	Growing Equity Mortgage
GIC	(1) Guaranteed Investment Certificate (Canada) (2) Guaranteed Investment Contract
GIS	Guaranteed Income Supplement (Canada)
GMR	Group Medical Report
GNMA	Government National Mortgage Association (Ginnie Mae)
GNP	Gross National Product
GO	General Obligation (Bond)
GPCI	Geographic Practice Cost Index
GPM	Graduated Payment Mortgage
GPO	(1) Government Printing Office (2) Guaranteed Purchase Option
GPP	Group Practice Prepayment (Plan)
GSOP	General Stock Ownership Plan
GST	Goods and Services Tax (Canada)
GTC	Good-Till-Canceled Order
GULP	Group Universal Life Plan
HA	Health Alliance
HCE	Highly Compensated Employee
HCFA	Health Care Financing Administration
HCO	Health Care Organization
HCPCS	Common Procedural Coding System
HEDIS	Health Plan Employer Data and Information Set
HEW	(Department of) Health, Education, and Welfare (now split into HHS and DOE)
HHA	Home Health Agency
HHS	(Department of) Health and Human Services
HI	Hospital Insurance
HIPAA	Health Insurance Portability and Accountability Act
HIPC	Health Insurance Purchasing Corporation
HIV	Human Immunodeficiency Virus
HMO	Health Maintenance Organization

HO	Homeowners (Policy)
HP/DP	Health Promotion/Disease Prevention
HPPC	Health Plan Purchasing Cooperative
HR	Human Resources
HRA	Health Risk Appraisal
HRD	Human Resources Development
HRIS	Human Resource Information System
HSID	High Self-Insured Deductible
HSM	Hospital-Surgical-Medical (Benefits)
HSOP	Health Stock Ownership Plan
HSP	Health Systems Plan
HTML	HyperText Markup Language
HUD	(Department of) Housing and Urban Development
IAAC	Income Averaging Annuity Contract (Canada)
IAG	International Auditing Guidelines
IASC	International Accounting Standards Committee
IB	Interpretive Bulletin
IBA	International Bar Association
IBNR	Incurred but Not Reported (Claims)
ICC	Interstate Commerce Commission
ICD-9-CM	International Classification of Diseases-9th Edition-Clinical Modification
ICF	Intermediate Care Facility
ICM	Individual Case Management
ICU	Intensive Care Unit
IFEBP	International Foundation of Employee Benefit Plans
IHCA	Individual Health Care Account
IHMDS	Integrated Health Management Delivery System
ILP	Independent Living Program
ILWU-PMA	International Longshoremen's and Warehousemen's Union-Pacific Maritime Association
IME	Independent Medical Examination
IMF	International Monetary Fund
I/O	Input/Output
IO	Investment-Only (Contract)
IOM	Institute of Medicine
IOU	Written Acknowledgment of a Debt
IP	Integrated Provider
IPA	(1) Independent Practice Association (2) Individual Practice Association
IPG	(Group) Immediate Participation Guarantee (Pension Plan)
IPO	Initial Public Offering
IQA	International Quality Award
IRA	Individual Retirement Account
IRB	Internal Revenue Bulletin
IRC	Internal Revenue Code
IRR	Internal Rate of Return
IRS	Internal Revenue Service
ISCEBS	International Society of Certified Employee Benefit Specialists
ISO	(1) Incentive Stock Option (2) Insurance Services Office
ISOP	Investment Stock Option Plan
ISSI	Intensity of Service, Severity of Illness Criteria (InterQual)
ITC	Investment Tax Credit
IUC	Incurred but Unreported Claims
IVR	Interactive Voice Response (System)
IYM	Investment Year Method
JCAHO	Joint Commission on Accreditation of Healthcare Organizations
JHG	Jackson Hole Group
JIT	Just-In-Time (System)
JOBS	Job Opportunities and Basic Skills Training
J&S	Joint and Survivor (Annuity)

KBS	Knowledge-Based System
KLN	Key Local National
KSA	Knowledge, Skills and Abilities
KSOP	401(k) Employee Stock Option Plan
L	Long-Term Funds (Money Supply)
LAN	Local Area Network
LBO	Leveraged Buyout
LCD	Living Cost Differential (International Benefits)
LCI	Lifestyle Cost Index
LCN	Local Country National
LDBM	Level Dollar Benefit Method
LDCM	Level Dollar Cost Method
LEAT	Least Expensive Alternative Treatment
LEPAAT	Least Expensive Professionally Acceptable Alternative Treatment
LESOP	Leveraged Employee Stock Ownership Plan
LIBOR	London InterBank Offered Rate (of Interest)
LIFO	Last In, First Out
LLC	Limited Liability Company
LMRA	Labor-Management Relations Act of 1947 (Taft-Hartley Act)
LMRDA	Labor-Management Reporting and Disclosure Act
LOS	Length of Stay
LPBM	Level Percentage Benefit Method
LPCM	Level Percentage Cost Method
LSIF	Labour-Sponsored Investment Fund (Canada)
LSVC	Labour-Sponsored Venture Capital Corporation (Canada)
LTC	Long-Term Care
LTD	Long-Term Disability
M_{1B},M_2,M_3	Money Supply
M&A	Mergers and Acquisitions
MAAC	Maximum Allowable Actual Charge
MAC	Maximum Allowable Cost (List)
MADD	Mothers Against Drunk Drivers
MBB	Mortgage-Backed Bond
MCCA	Medicare Catastrophic Coverage Act of 1988
MCM	Medical Case Management
MDB	Multilateral Development Bank
MDC	Major Diagnostic Category
MDIB	Minimum Distribution Incidental Benefit
Medigap	Medical Supplement Insurance
Medsupp	Medicare Supplement Insurance
MERP	Medical Expense Reimbursement Plan
MET	Multiple Employer Trust
MEWA	Multiple Employer Welfare Arrangement
MFB	Maximum Family Benefit (Social Security)
MGIC	Mortgage Guaranty Insurance Corporation
MH/CD	Mental Health/Chemical Dependency
MI	Medically Indigent
MIA	Medically Indigent Adult
MID	Mortgage Interest Differential
MIS	Management Information System
MIT	Modern Investment Theory
MLE	Maximum Loss Expectancy
MLR	(1) Medical Loss Ratio (2) Multiple Location Risk
MOB	Maintenance of Benefits
MOE	Maintenance of Effort
MP	(1) Medical Payment (2) Minimum Premium (3) Monthly Premium
MPL	Maximum Possible Loss
MPP	Minimum Premium Plan

MPPAA	Multiemployer Pension Plan Amendments Act of 1980
MPT	Modern Portfolio Theory
MRI	Magnetic Resonance Imaging (formerly NMR)
MSA	(1) Medical Savings Account (2) Medical Spending Account (3) Multi-Source Assessment
MSDS	Material Safety Data Sheets
MSP	Medicare Secondary Payer
MSPA	Member, Society of Pension Actuaries

NA	Not Applicable
NAAP	Net Annual Average Premium (Canada)
NAFTA	North American Free Trade Agreement
NAIC	National Association of Insurance Commissioners
NASDAQ	National Association of Securities Dealers Automatic Quotation System
NAV	Net Asset Value
NCHPD	National Council on Health Planning and Development
NCI	(1) National Cancer Institute (2) No Common Interest
NCQA	National Committee on Quality Assurance
NHCE	Nonhighly Compensated Employee
NHI	National Health Insurance
NIH	National Institutes of Health
NIMH	National Institute of Mental Health
NIOSH	National Institute for Occupational Safety and Health
NIT	New Investment Technology
NLN	National League of Nursing
NLRA	National Labor Relations Act
NLRB	National Labor Relations Board
NMB	National Mediation Board
NMR	Nuclear Magnetic Resonance Scanner (former name for MRI)
NNP	Net National Product
NOI	Net Operating Income
NOL	(1) Net Operating Loss (2) Not Officially Lapsed
Non-Par	*Non-Par*ticipating (policies on which dividends are not paid)
NOW	Negotiable Order of Withdrawal Account
NPC	No Previous Carrier
NPEA	National Preretirement Education Association
NQA	(1) National Quality Award (2) Net Quick Assets
NRA	Normal Retirement Age
NRD	Normal Retirement Date
NSF	Not Sufficient Funds
NTO	Not Taken Out
NW	Net Worth
NYFE	New York Futures Exchange
NYSE	New York Stock Exchange

OA	(1) Office Automation (2) Open Access
OAA	Old Age Assistance
OAS	Old Age Security (Canada)
OASDHI	Old-Age, Survivors, Disability, and Health Insurance
OASDI	Old-Age, Survivors, and Disability Insurance
OASI	Old-Age and Survivors Insurance
OBRA	Omnibus Budget Reconciliation Act
OCA	Outstanding Claims Account
OCC	Options Clearance Corporation
OCL	Outstanding Claims Liability
OCONUS	Outside the Continental United States
OD	(1) Occupational Disease (2) Organizational Development

OECD	Organization for Economic Cooperation and Development
OEM	Original Equipment Manufacturer
OEO	Office of Economic Opportunity
OH	Outpatient, Hospital
OID	Original Issue Discount
OJT	On-the-Job Training
OMB	Office of Management and Budget
OOA	Out of Area
OOP	Out-of-Pocket Maximum
OR	(1) Operating Room (2) Operations Research
OSHA	(1) Occupational Safety and Health Act (2) Occupational Safety and Health Administration
OT	Occupational Therapy
OTC	Over the Counter
OWBPA	Older Workers Benefit Protection Act

PA	(1) Pension Adjustment (Canada) (2) Performance Appraisal (3) Physician's Assistant
P/A	Power of Attorney
PAP	Pension Administration Plan
PAR	Pension Adjustment Reversal (Canada)
PARSAP	Performance-Accelerated Restricted-Stock Award Plan
PAT	Preadmission Testing
PAYSOP	Payroll-Based Stock Ownership Plan
P/B	Price-To-Book (Ratio)
PBGC	Pension Benefit Guaranty Corporation
PBM	Pharmacy Benefits Management/Manager
PBO	Projected Benefit Obligation
PC	(1) Participation Certificate (Mortgage) (2) Personal Computer (3) Professional Corporation
P/C	Property and Casualty (Premium)
PCN	Primary Care Network
PCP	Primary Care Physician
PD	Property or Physical Damage
PDA	Pregnancy Discrimination Act of 1978
PDC	Physician-Developed Criteria
P/E	Price/Earnings (Ratio)
PEC	Preexisting Condition
PEPPRA	Public Employee Pension Plan Reporting and Accountability Act
PERS	Public Employee Retirement System
PFK	Pay for Knowledge and Skills Plan
PGP	Prepaid Group Practice
PHO	Physician-Hospital Organization
PHS	Public Health Service
PI	Personal Injury
P&I	Protection and Indemnity
PIA	Primary Insurance Amount (Social Security)
PIE	Payroll (Audit) Indexing and Expiration
PIN	Personal Identification Number
PIP	Personal Injury Protection
PL	(1) Public Law (2) Public Liability
PLAD	Price Level-Adjusted Deposit
PLAM	Price Level-Adjusted Mortgage
PLI	Professional Liability Insurance
PMPM	Per Member Per Month
POP	Premium Only Plan
POS	Point of Service
PPA	(1) Pension Protection Act of 1987 (2) Preferred Provider Arrangement
PPD	Permanent Partial Disability
PPO	Preferred Provider Organization
PPP	Personal Property Policy
PPS	(1) Policy Processing Sheet (2) Prospective Payment System

PR	Pro Rata
PRD	Pro Rata Distribution
PRI	Program-Related Investment (Social Investing)
PRO	Peer Review Organization
PSBR	Public Sector Borrowing Rate
PSC	Personal Service Corporation
PSN	Provider Services Network
PSP	Performance Share Plan
PT	(1) Physical Therapy (2) Prohibited Transaction
PTCE	Prohibited Transaction Class Exemption
PTCM	Plan Termination Cost Method
PTD	Permanent and Total Disability
PTE	Prohibited Transaction Exemption
PTO	Paid Time Off
PWA	Person With AIDS
PWBA	Pension and Welfare Benefits Administration
QA	Quality Assurance
QBU	Qualified Business Unit
QC	(1) Quality Control (2) Quarters of Coverage (Social Security)
QDEC	Qualified Deductible Employee Contribution
QDRO	Qualified Domestic Relations Order
QERP	Qualifying Employer Real Property
QJSA	Qualified Joint and Survivor Annuity
QMAC	Qualified Matching Contributions
QMB	Qualified Medicare Beneficiary
QMCSO	Qualified Medical Child Support Order
QNEC	Qualified Nonelective Contribution
QPAM	Qualified Professional Asset Manager
QPP	Quebec Pension Plan (Canada)
QPSA	Qualified Preretirement Survivor Annuity
QSLOB	Qualified Separate Line of Business
QTD	Qualified Total Distribution
QVEC	Qualified Voluntary Employee Contribution
RAF	Risk Adjustment Factor
RBRVS	Resource-Based Relative Value Scale
R&C	Reasonable and Customary
R&D	Research and Development
REA	Retirement Equity Act of 1984
REIT	Real Estate Investment Trust
REOC	Real Estate Operating Company
RESP	Registered Education Savings Plan (Canada)
RFI	Request for Information
RFP	(1) Registered Financial Planner (2) Request for Proposal
RHCF	Resident Health Care Facility
RHOSP	Registered Home Ownership Savings Plan
RI	Risk Improvement
RIF	Reduction in Force
RIPA	Retirement Income Policy Act of 1985
RLR	Retired Lives Reserve
ROC	Return of Capital (Tax-Advantaged Utility Stock)
ROE	Return on Equity
ROEA	Return on Employed Assets
ROEBI	Return on Employee Benefits Investment
ROI	Return on Investment
RONA	Return on Net Assets
ROS	Return on Sales
ROSA	Return on Selected Assets
ROSE	Return on Shareholders' Equity
RP	Return Premium
RPA	Registered Pension Account (Canada)

RPP	Registered Pension Plan
RR	Railroad Retirement (Program or System)
RRB	(1) Railroad Retirement Board (2) Retirement-Replacement Betterment Accounting (Method)
RRIF	Registered Retirement Income Fund (Canada)
RRM	Renegotiable Rate Mortgage
RRSP	Registered Retirement Savings Plan (Canada)
RSI	Repetitive Stress Injury (see also CTD)
RTC	Residential Treatment Center
RTK	Right to Know
RUI	Railroad Unemployment Insurance
RVS	Relative Value Scale (benefit determination system)
R/W	Returned to Work
SAE	Supplemental Accident Expense
SAM	Shared Appreciation Mortgage
SAR	(1) Stock Appreciation Right (2) Summary Annual Report
SARSEP	Salary Reduction Simplified Employee Pension Plan
SBA	Small Business Administration
SBJPA	Small Business Job Protection Act of 1996
SDB	Survivor's Death Benefit
SDBA	Self-Directed Brokerage Account
SEC	Securities and Exchange Commission
SEM	Shared Equity Mortgage
SEP	Simplified Employee Pension (Plan)
SEPPAA	Single Employer Pension Plan Amendments Act of 1986
SERP	Supplemental Executive Retirement Plan
SERPS	State Earnings Related Pension Scheme
SFAS	Statements of Financial Accounting Standards
SHRM	Society of Human Resource Management (formerly ASPA)
SIMPLE	Savings Incentive Match Plan (for employees of small employers)
SIPC	Securities Investor Protection Corporation
SIW	Service Intensity Weight (DRG)
SLEV	Salaried Legal Expense Voucher
SLMA	Student Loan Marketing Association (Sallie Mae)
SLOB	Separate Line of Business
SMI	Supplementary Medical Insurance
SMM	Summary of Material Modifications (summary of changes in an SPD)
SMR	Supplemental Medical Report
SNF	Skilled Nursing Facility
SOP	Standard Operating Procedure
SP	Sine Prole (Died Without Issue)
S&P	Standard & Poor's
SPD	Summary Plan Description
SPDA	Single Premium Deferred Annuity
SPIRA	*Sp*ousal IRA
SR	Short Rate
SSA	(1) Social Security Act (2) Social Security Administration
SSDI	Social Security Disability Insurance
SSI	(1) Supplemental Security Income (Social Security) (2) Supplemental Security Insurance
SSOP	Second Surgical Opinion Program
SSRA	Social Security Retirement Age
STD	Short-Term Disability
STIF	Short-Term investment Fund
SUB	Supplemental Unemployment Benefit

TA	Technology Assessment
TAB	Tax Anticipation Bill
TAMRA	Technical and Miscellaneous Revenue Act of 1988
TCN	Third Country National
TD	Time Deposit (or Certificate of Deposit)
TDA	Tax-Deferred Annuity
TDB	Temporary Disability Benefits
TDD	Telecommunications Device for the Deaf
TDI	Temporary Disability Insurance (System)
TEFRA	Tax Equity and Fiscal Responsibility Act
TEO	Tax-Exempt Organization
TI	Terminal Illness
TIA	Trend Impact Analysis
TIGR	Treasury Investment Growth Receipt
TIN	Taxpayer Identification Number
TJTC	Targeted Jobs Tax Credit
TLR	Tolerable Loss Ratio
TMJ	Temporomandibular Joint Syndrome
TPA	Third Party Administrator
TQM	Total Quality Management
TRA	Tax Reform Acts 1984, 1986
TRASOP	Tax Reduction Act of 1975 (Employee) Stock Ownership Plan
TRESOP	Tax Reduction (Act) ESOP
TSA	Tax-Sheltered Annuity
TWB	Taxable Wage Base

UAW	United Auto Workers
UBTI	Unrelated Business Taxable Income
UC	Unemployment Compensation
U&C	Usual and Customary
UCC	Uniform Commercial Code
UCCC	Uniform Consumer Credit Code
UCD	Unemployment Compensation Disability
UCI	Unemployment Compensation Insurance
UCR	Usual, Customary and Reasonable
UI	Unemployment Insurance (System)
UM	Utilization Management
UP	Unearned Premium
UP-1984	Unisex Pension Table, 1984
UQCPRO	Utilization and Quality Control Peer Review Organization (full TEFRA title for PRO)
UR	Utilization Review
URO	Utilization Review Organization
U.S.C.	United States Code
USERRA	Uniformed Services Employment and Reemployment Rights Act of 1994
USL&H	United States Longshoremen and Harborworkers Act
USWA	United Steelworkers of America
UTU	United Transportation Union
UVB	Unfunded Vested Benefits
UVL	Unfunded Vested Liability

VA	Veterans Administration
VAT	Value-Added Tax
VCR	Variable Coupon Rate (Notes)
VDT	Video or Visual Display Terminal
VEBA	Voluntary Employees' Beneficiary Association
VNA	Visiting Nurse Association
VRM	Variable Rate Mortgage

W-2	Wage and Tax Statement
W/C	Waiver of Coinsurance
WC	Workers' Compensation
WC&EL	Workers' Compensation and Employers' Liability
WHEA	Women's Health Equity Act
WHO	World Health Organization

WI	When Issued (Security or Transaction)
WP	Weekly Premium
WPE	Weekly Premium Equivalent
WSJ	*Wall Street Journal*
WPM	Words Per Minute
WWW	World Wide Web
XCL	Excess Current Liabilities
XRA	Expected Retirement Age
YMPE	Year's Maximum Pensionable Earnings (Canada)
YRT	Yearly Renewable Term
YTD	Year to Date
ZBB	Zero-Base Budget
ZEBRA	Zero Balance Reimbursement Account
ZPG	Zero Population Growth